Auctions and Auctioneering

Auctions
and Auctioneering

BY RALPH CASSADY, JR.

UNIVERSITY OF CALIFORNIA PRESS

Berkeley, Los Angeles, London

University of California Press
Berkeley and Los Angeles, California

University of California Press, Ltd.
London, England

© 1967 by The Regents of the University of California
California Library Reprint Series Edition 1980
ISBN 0-520-03978-5
Library of Congress Catalog Card Number: 67-25051

Designed by Peter Keep

2 3 4 5 6 7 8 9

dedication

To the hundreds of individuals throughout the world who graciously shared their knowledge of particular auction operations with me, thus contributing immeasurably to the preparation of this book.

Preface

THIS ANALYSIS of auction selling and buying was conceived some years ago, but the project was not brought to fruition earlier because of other commitments as well as difficulties in assembling and arranging the data necessary for a definitive study of this very complex marketing mechanism. As the investigation on which the presentation is based covers many industries and trades, including antiques, cotton, fish, furs, household goods, livestock, tea, stamps, used automobiles, and wool, the gathering of data took place at various times in many countries throughout the world.

While I consulted innumerable published materials, most of the data were acquired by direct contact with those having firsthand knowledge of the auction phenomenon. Credit should be given first to Admiral Charles D. Wheelock, former director of the Institute of Marine Resources, University of California, San Diego, who provided the travel grant for a study of worldwide fisheries which first brought me into contact with auction people. I am grateful to the University Research Committee, as well as to the Division of Research of the Graduate School of Business Administration, University of California, Los Angeles, for financial assistance at later stages of the project.

Since the time of my initiation into the mysteries of auctioning, scores and even hundreds of individuals have given generously of their talents and time in connection with the project. Many of these not only interpreted the otherwise unintelligible goings-on in the auctioning of the product or products with which they were concerned, but responded to penetrating questions during long discussion sessions; some, indeed, provided specific answers to my detailed follow-up mail queries. It is impossible to name here these many individuals, but I do want to express my heartfelt appreciation of their efforts and indicate the pleasure it gives me to dedicate this volume to them.

The lengthy task of corresponding with informants, organizing materials, and analyzing findings required much cooperation and patience from various people. Thanks are due my wife, who accompanied me on most of my field trips, for doubling as a remarkably efficient secretary-stenographer. Thanks, also, should go to Miss Patricia Hay, administrative assistant of the Bureau of Business and Economic Research, who gave generously of her time to assist me in the formidable task of compiling this book in addition to handling her own volume of work. I wish to express my gratitude also to Mrs. Joan Harbaugh, Miss Andra Potter, and Miss Mary Ellen Zack, who assisted with the typing of the manuscript at various stages of preparation; to Philip Schary, research assistant, who initiated the search for bibliographical materials; and to Mrs. Ramona R. McNulty, who continued his assignment.

Acknowledgment is due my eldest son, Ralph Cassady, III, attorney-at-law, for reading critically the chapter on the legal aspects of auctioning. I also extend my appreciation to the late Louis Piacenza and his staff for the use of the very fine UCLA Law Library in the preparation of certain parts of the study. Finally, my hearty thanks to the many individuals who directly by overt suggestion or indirectly by their interest in my material encouraged me to make my findings available to the general reader as well as to those technically oriented.

Needless to say, I assume full responsibility for any and all blunders that may have slipped into the manuscript undetected.

R. C., Jr.

Contents

Illustrations

following page 204

Introduction

1 LITTLE OF a substantial nature has been written on the subject of auctions and auctioning; indeed, most of the published items are superficially descriptive or merely anecdotal. Such accounts, though interesting to read, can make few contributions to the present study, which seeks to explain in some depth the nature and role of auctioning in our economic system. My analysis is based on examination, both extensive and intensive, of the auctioning process in market distribution. Field trips to twenty-five or more countries were undertaken in pursuit of data on this phenomenon as it is practiced in scores of different commodity fields. The investigation was also intensive in that a conscious attempt was made to transcend mere surface observations and through analytical means to discover the most subtle aspects of price making by auction method.

The project germinated in 1956 when I accepted an invitation to prepare a paper for a round-table discussion on world fishery problems, held in Rome, Italy, under the sponsorship of the International Economic Association and the Food and Agriculture Organization of the United Nations.[1] The Rome meeting proved so stimulating that

1 See Ralph Cassady, Jr., "The Marketing of Fishery Products in the U.S.A.," in Ralph Turvey and Jack Wiseman, eds., *The Eco-*

in 1958 I requested sabbatical leave from the University of California and, with the support of Admiral Charles D. Wheelock and the Institute of Marine Resources of the university's campus at San Diego, spent six months studying the marketing and distribution of fishery products in various parts of the world. This latter experience aroused a deep interest in the auctioning procedure, the method typically employed in the fishing industry for the transference of title to goods at the primary distribution level.

This book is designed not only to analyze an important phase of marketing economics, but also to enlighten the general reader about this fascinating method of selling and price making. The dual task of satisfying the scholar and technician while making the discussion intelligible to those without economics training or previous acquaintanceship with the auctioning process is basically difficult, as is any attempt to probe uncharted areas. The highly technical subject matter requires some understanding of the nature of demand and competition, as well as of other economic tools, and of complex trade practices in the actual marketing process. The latter range all the way from the functions of auctioneers, including bid calling and the interpretation of certain types of auctioneer's chants, to the operation of buyer rings and the *modus operandi* of mock auctions.

The sound factual foundation necessary for an intelligent discussion of auctioning had to be constructed piecemeal from far-flung sources of varying degrees of reliability. Then came the problems of synthesizing the data, of classifying the results, and, just as important, of analyzing key issues and extending the findings by the application of theoretical analysis. Because of the dearth of written records, the fact-finding was based on observation of the behavior of those engaged in auctioning and questioning such individuals.

Although the interrogation process, often carried out in considerable depth, was indispensable for tapping the memories of those who possessed needed information, some reliance was placed on direct observation. In fact, I personally observed auctions of fish and other commodities and properties in almost every corner of the globe. Yet the method of observation by itself is extremely limited in its effectiveness. It is almost impossible to understand what is

nomics of Fisheries (Rome: Food and Agriculture Organization of the United Nations, 1957), pp. 180–205.

actually taking place simply by watching an auction and listening to the auctioneer. The speed of the transactions (some are concluded in five seconds, or even less!), the secret nature of certain types of bidding, the unintelligible jargon sometimes used—all may prove bewildering to the uninitiated observer. Moreover, the esoteric and unstandardized procedures characterizing a complex trading operation also hinder comprehension, to say nothing of the difficulties raised by language barriers.

The method of investigation used in this study was largely a combination of direct observation and unstructured interrogation of informed practitioners. Hypotheses are also employed throughout the study to discover precisely the way a mechanism operates or why a certain phenomenon exists and to focus investigative attention on relevant issues.

The formulation of penetrating questions is the key to successful investigations. Good questions provide a logical structure for the project, and this structure in turn aids the investigator in the presentation of his findings. In this study, the preliminary observation of certain auctions was followed by the interrogation of participants as well as of direct observers, in an attempt to interpret the initial observations. As knowledge of auction operations increased, key questions came to mind, and possible explanations, based on apparent conflicts with observed behavior, overheard comments of participants, hypothetical possibilities, sheer imagination, and so forth, began to evolve. Also, with the accretion of knowledge, the observation technique became more effective; one now understood the phenomenon being observed.

In an investigation of this kind secondary interrogation is even more important than primary interrogation. Interrogation in depth on certain aspects of a particular subject—for example, buyer rings or the *modus operandi* of the Dutch auction system—was usually conducted by correspondence. That is, I would often lay the groundwork at the time of the visit, and after returning from the field trip would write letters requesting further information on, or clarification of, the more subtle aspects of the auctioning process as practiced in particular areas.

The initial bibliographical research was not very rewarding, but as time went on articles in trade journals or business magazines and reports of government agencies were found to be of limited usefulness. They were more valuable in suggesting different facets of the subject than in providing usable data. The method of studying such materials I have designated as indirect observation.[2]

Because so little of the available written material was of an analytical nature, and because direct observation of a highly technical operation requires supplementary questioning to be effective, interrogation became my most important source of information. Interrogation is not a simple process, though the layman might think of it as merely asking questions of someone who knows all the answers. But interrogation in scientific investigations is much more than an unsophisticated question-and-answer procedure. Since no one informant is omniscient, the investigator must determine what questions to ask of each person and, indeed, must seek out the scores or even hundreds of knowledgeable people who are needed to provide accurate information on the subject of inquiry. Often the persons possessing such knowledge are far apart from one another and from the investigator, and always they have the final say as to whether they will cooperate in the investigation. The language barrier further complicates the process, for an interpreter must be found who knows both languages involved and who is sufficiently informed on the subject to accurately communicate questions and answers between investigator and respondents.

I was extremely fortunate in being able to establish good rapport with those who possessed the information sought. Most informants gave me full cooperation, taking great pains to reveal the information in their possession. The following factors contribute to helpful relations between a researcher and his informants:

1. Cooperation of individuals and organizations that have close contact with key informants, even though they may not be able to supply information directly.

2. Firsthand contact with knowledgeable individuals in order to obtain personal involvement of the informants and thus full cooperation.

3. Enthusiastic interest in the subject on the part of the investigator, which tends to have a contagious effect on the respondents.

4. Theoretical knowledge of actual procedures and behavior

2 See Ralph Cassady, Jr., "Market Measurement in a Free Society," *California Management Review*, II (Winter, 1960), 57-66.

patterns, which provides a structural basis for questioning those who possess technical knowledge.

5. Substantially enhanced technical understanding on the part of the investigator as the study progresses so as to permit more and more subtle interrogation and sharper direct observation.

One of my problems was to develop a way to check preliminary findings for authenticity and accuracy. Beyond adopting the ultra-critical attitude of "believing nothing he hears and only half of what he sees," an investigator must check his findings against independent sources and by the application of logic—that is, does a certain explanation or interpretation seem reasonable? If a tentative finding appears illogical, it should be carefully rechecked. Even a finding that appears logical cannot be accepted until the investigator is satisfied, after confirmation of the data, that he is dealing with fact and not fiction.

A word of caution is in order at this point. Because a study like this one is a mosaic made up of findings from various geographical areas and commodity fields, generalizations do not necessarily apply to all locations or even to all trades. Statements that are correct from a general point of view may be inapplicable to a particular operation, such as that of an individual auctioneer in a certain locality specializing in the sale of a specific type of merchandise.

The framework for such a study is the responsibility of the investigator, not of his informants. Here the experienced researcher is able to make a special contribution; the process of determining the format of a presentation for which there is no precedential basis is extremely challenging. One must attempt this process early in the investigation, for without some idea of direction and of the data needed, it is wasteful of effort to seek information.

This volume, it is hoped, will provide a penetrating analysis of auctioning on a rather wide front. The study of auctions has been the most stimulating one I have ever undertaken, partly because the investigation led me to many exotic parts of the globe. Who could forget, for example, riding up the Bosporus toward the Black Sea in a fishing vessel to inspect a fishery laboratory; visiting a Chinese cooperative and being the guest of honor at tea in the New Territories of the British crown colony of Hong Kong; watching the frenzied but quasi-organized bidding of would-be buyers in an Australian wool auction; observing the "upside-down" auctioning

of fish in Tel Aviv and Haifa; watching the purchasing activities of
several hundred screaming female fishmongers at the Lisbon auction market; viewing the fascinating "string selling" in the auctioning of furs in Leningrad; eating fish from the Sea of Galilee while
seated on the shore of that historic body of water; observing
"whispered" bidding in such far-flung places as Singapore and
Venice; watching a "handshake" auction in a Pakistanian go-down
in the midst of a herd of dozing camels; being present at the
auctioning of an early Van Gogh in Amsterdam; observing the sale
of flowers by electronic clock in Aalsmeer, Holland; listening
to the chant of the auctioneer in a North Carolina tobacco auction;
watching the landing of fish at 4 A.M. in the market on the north
beach of Manila Bay by the use of amphibious landing boats;
observing the bidding of Turkish merchants competing for fish in a
market located on the Golden Horn; and answering questions
about auctioning posed by a group of eager Japanese students at the
University of Tokyo.

But the fascination of the subject of auctioning itself is much
more than the sum of these and other similar experiences. Is it
perhaps the excitement of discovery, particularly characteristic of
the antique field? Or is it the possibility of getting a desired item at
a price far below its value? On the other hand, might it be the
nature of the game itself—trying to outdo one's competitor? Whatever the reason, there is something inherently intriguing about an
auction, and it possesses uncommon interest as a subject of study. In
the process of discussing this topic with hundreds of lay individuals
over the years—people who have had no knowledge of or association with the auction process—I have yet to find one whose eyes do
not light up when the subject is discussed in depth.

I hope that I have been able to provide fresh insights into a
complex price-making mechanism, and, further, that sounder
knowledge of this type of operation in its broad aspects will increase understanding of other marketing problems. In any event, I
have tried to convey to the reader some of the excitement of the
"auction game."

Nature and Application of Auction Selling

2 OF THE several introductory matters to be considered in an approach to the subject of auctioning, two—the nature of auctioning and the applicability of auction selling—are discussed in this chapter.

Nature of Auctioning

In analyzing auctioning, several phases of the subject must be considered in depth: what auctioning actually is, how it fits into the marketing structure, and how it is used as a price-making mechanism.

Definition of auctioning.—It is important to suggest at the outset that the popular conception of auctioning—that prices are bid upward until only one bidder remains—is not entirely correct. The term itself (the root *auctio* means increase) is misleading, for auctions are by no means always ascending price schemes. *Webster's Third New International Dictionary, Unabridged,* defines "auction" as a "public sale of property to the highest bidder (as by successive increased bids)," but this method of bidding, though quite familiar to most readers, is only one of several auctioning systems in use around the world. Various types of auctions, such as the Dutch, or upside-down, auction, and the Japanese simultaneous bidding system, do not fall into this category.

There is, furthermore, a difference between a public auction and a private sale based on auction principles. The former is a sale of property at an auction which anybody who chooses may attend and register bids. The phrase "public auction" suggests a sale to the high bidder with absolute freedom for competitive bidding.[1] The inference follows that a "private auction," though based on the competitive bidding principle, is not open to the public. Despite contrary opinion by at least one court,[2] it would appear that if an auction sale is in fact private (i.e., open only to certain individuals or classes of individuals), it is not subject to the same legal circumscriptions that apply to public sales.[3]

Basically, auctioning is a unique system of allocating scarce chattels or other property based on price making by competition of buyers for the right to purchase. In auction selling, vendors put up for sale a lot of goods, for example, and would-be buyers are invited to bid in competition with one another for the right to acquire title to the property. Obviously, buyers play an active and, indeed, dominant role in price making by auction method, while sellers ordinarily play a passive role.

Not all auctions are of the ascending-bid type; in some prices actually move down, whereas in others all would-be buyers bid simultaneously. In still others, bids may be up or down, as in the written bid or other secret bidding systems. Regardless of the type of auctioning utilized, however, the scheme focuses the forces of supply and demand, as related to a particular sale, on one time and place, and competition of rival buyers is supposed to force prices to maximum levels.

Admittedly, differences in efficiency prevail among the various types of auction schemes; some bring more pressure of buyer competition to bear on prices than do others. That is, some auction

---

1 *State* v. *Miller,* 52 Mont. 562, 160 P. 513, 515 (1916).

2 See *Territory* v. *Toyota,* 19 Haw. 651 (1909), in which selling to retail fish dealers on a highest-bid basis was found in a majority opinion to constitute a public auction within the meaning of an act that required auctioneers to have licenses and to give bond, although bids were accepted *only* from such dealers.

3 See pp. 221–224.

methods may be superior to others in forcing buyers to maximize their bids. Would-be buyers obviously bid no higher than necessitated by the competitive pressure exerted by others similarly motivated.

The auction firm in the market structure.—One of the most interesting aspects of auctioning is that those who conduct auction operations usually do not own the goods that are up for sale, but simply act for the vendor. In marketing parlance, the auctioneer is typically a broker to whom the owner consigns the goods for sale under certain mutually agreed upon conditions, though in some circumstances he may actually acquire title to the goods before offering them for sale. The relationships between the auctioneer and the vendor and between the auctioneer and the buyers who patronize the auction firm or alternative functionaries are shown in figure 1. The broken lines between auctioneers and vendors and between auctioneers and buyers indicate only physical movement of property from vendor to marketing functionary, not passage of title. The solid lines roughly paralleling the broken lines in the middle segment of the chart, short-circuiting the box representing the auction firm and passing directly from vendor-owners to buyers, represent the actual passage of title from those owning to those purchasing the property.

Auction firms occasionally, or perhaps even regularly, may acquire title to goods in order to resell them at auction rather than act simply as agents. This type of activity is indicated in figure 1 by making the edges of one auction-firm box partly broken and partly solid. The suggestion is that such firms act as merchants in some of their dealings (purchasing merchandise outright) and as agents in others (merely acting for the vendor).

In most market situations involving auctioning, alternative marketing channels are available to those who wish to use them. One of these is direct negotiation between vendor and buyer. As shown in figure 1, the buyer in this situation may be a consumer of the item being sold, or he may be a dealer who, in turn, sells to others, even to other dealers. In direct transactions between owner and buyer the vendor may seek out a dealer or private buyer and offer the item to him; conversely, the buyer may go to the owner with an offer. Such negotiations may, of course, extend over a long period of time. Solid lines are used to depict these direct transac-

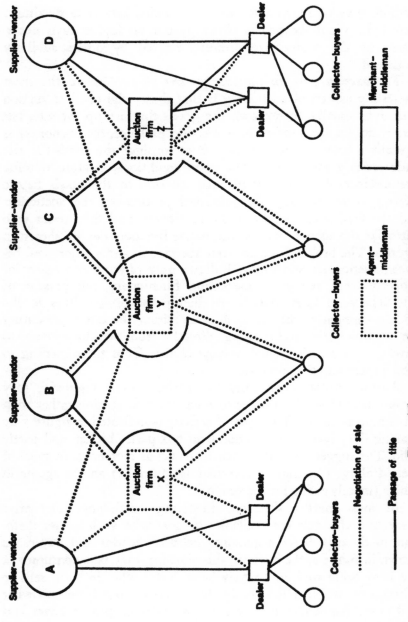

Fig. 1 The auction firm in the distribution structure.

Supplier–vendor

Collector–buyers

Merchant–middleman

Agent–middleman

······· Negotiation of sale

——— Passage of title

tions because in sales of this type, unlike auction transactions, the title actually does pass from one negotiating party to another simultaneously with the change in title.

Another possible marketing channel goes from vendor to dealer and then from dealer to collector-user. In such a transaction the dealer becomes a merchant-middleman who buys outright for purposes of resale; the solid line correctly depicts passage of title in addition to physical possession of the property (see fig. 1). Actually dealers may acquire goods for resale by purchase at auction as well as from original owners; as shown by the broken lines from vendor to auction house and from auction house to dealer, but by the solid lines from dealer to collector. In other words, the dealer in this instance acquires title from the vendor through the services of the auctioneer-agent, and then resells the goods to customer-clients.

Auctioning as a price-making mechanism.—The very complex procedure of price making involves, among other things, consideration of the type of functionary actually determining the prices and of the forces that influence the quotations ultimately established. Generally speaking, there are three basic methods of price making, and auctioning is a subtype of one of them. The basic price-making schemes are:

1. Fixed or take-it-or-leave-it pricing. In this scheme, which is likely to be the most familiar to the ultimate consumer in developed economies, such as the United States, the price maker sets a price that clients are expected either to accept or to reject without higgling. Although the seller ordinarily sets the price, the buyer—a canner, for example—may post a price at which he will purchase his raw product. Potential buyers, of course, may reject this price simply by absenting themselves. An adjustment must then be made which again puts the price on take-it-or-leave-it terms, and, as before, it is not subject to negotiation.

2. Private treaty pricing. This pricing scheme is very common in emerging countries and even in advanced societies at preretail levels. Either a price is specified which both buyer and seller know is subject to negotiation, or no price is specified and the intitial quotation is made by one of the parties, presumably at a level that will provide "maneuvering room." Then follow one or more counteroffers or compromises, often accompanied by discussion or stratagems designed to gain an advantage for one side over the

other. Adjustments are made by both buyer and seller until a price is reached on which they can agree.

3. Competitive bid pricing. There are two types of price making in this category:

a. Sealed-bid arrangements. This type of price making may be classified into two subtypes: (1) those in which vendors (building contractors, for example) compete with one another by bidding on a job at a figure each hopes will be lower than those of the others; and (2) those in which competing buyers (of timber rights, say) bid high in an attempt to purchase a certain type of property.

b. Auctioning. In this type of price making would-be buyers attempt to outbid one another, thus tending to force the selling price to, or at least toward, the level of the successful bidder's highest demand price. Usually (but not necessarily) auctioning requires an immediate decision by the auctioneer as to the successful bidder.

It is perfectly clear from the foregoing that competitive bidding arrangements are fundamentally different from the other basic pricing schemes. For example, competitive bidding, in contrast with take-it-or-leave-it pricing, is a flexible pricing scheme by means of which prices are tailor-made for each transaction. Private treaty selling and competitive bidding schemes also differ widely; the former brings the seller into contact only with buyers individually, whereas the latter pits buyer against buyer.

It is more difficult to distinguish basically between the subtypes within the competitive bidding category, for they are similar in certain respects. It should be obvious that sealed-bid schemes which are designed to find the low bidder in a building-construction operation should not be classified as auctions. The applicability of the sealed-bid device in a sale of property is much less clear-cut. Some might characterize such a sale as an auction because it is intended to find the highest price by competitive means, but others might regard it as a tender scheme, to be distinguished from an auction by the considerable interval between the time the bids are registered and the time the award is made.

One difference between sealed-bid arrangements and auctions is that in the former vendors are usually striving to sell something, whereas in the latter buyers are striving to purchase something. A more basic distinction is perhaps the amount of time permitted those who file sealed bids, time that may be used to plan strategy and to complete the necessary costing of the job to be done. Those who participate in an auction have no such advantage. Two minor points should be mentioned in this connection: (1) In contrast with the English type of auction, at least, the bidder in a sealed-bid situation is unable to adjust his bid to meet the competition of others, but the same is true of certain other auction schemes as well. (2) Ordinarily the one submitting a sealed bid in competition with others is acting more blindly than the bidder in an auction, for the latter can judge how strong is the interest in the property that is up for sale by the presence or absence of would-be buyers.

In some respects auction pricing is a distinctive, possibly even a unique, method of price making. Its basic characteristic is the focusing of supply and demand and competition on each transaction. It is true that auctioning is a buyer-set method of pricing, but the buyer who determines the price is in direct competition with other would-be buyers. Moreover, in each transaction the price is made by the successful bidder, who may be quite a different buyer in each instance; and a different price may be set in each transaction even for identical property, depending on how much the high bidder has to offer in order to acquire the desired item. In these respects auctions, though closely related to tender systems, differ from them.

It is necessary also to distinguish between exchanges and auctions. In its simplest form, an exchange is merely a place where buyers and sellers meet in order to negotiate individual deals. For example, the famous exchange in Bradford, England, is a center for trading in wool tops; another well-known exchange is the Diamond Dealers Club in New York City.[4]

An exchange, of course, may also be a place where sellers bid against one another to supply an item and buyers bid against one another to obtain an item, as in the New York stock exchange. The stock market has been designated by some as a "double" auction because the exchange process is based on competition among sellers as well as among buyers. It is perhaps better characterized as a multiple negotiation scheme in which competitive sellers and rival

4 For a very interesting account of the Diamond Dealers Club, see Daniel Lang, "A Reporter at Large: Pelikaanstraat Midtown," *New Yorker*, July 10, 1943, pp. 42, 44, 46–53.

buyers attempt through designated brokers to find a mutually satisfactory basis for effecting trades.[5] Under strong market situations, would-be purchasers of securities in competition with one another tend to bid prices up. In weak market situations, on the other hand, rival sellers may make concessions in order to find willing purchasers. As in individual negotiations, sellers and buyers who are apart and unyielding have no common meeting ground for effecting a trade, and no sale takes place. Exchanges really are not a different type of price-making arrangements: the simple exchange involves merely private negotiation between individual buyers and sellers, while the more complex exchange is based on competitive bidding by both buyers and sellers.

The Evolution of Auctioning

If it may be assumed that individual negotiation preceded auctioning in the evolution of trading arrangements, it may be that the latter developed out of the former. No one can be sure that auctioning actually did evolve from private-treaty arrangements, but that it easily could do so is demonstrable.

Let us take a hypothetical example based on an actual commercial experience. Many years ago, possibly sixty or so, fishing boats landed in a certain Pacific coast port at various wharves, and fish merchants would go down to the ships on the waterfront and individually negotiate with the skipper of a craft for all or part of the cargo. The negotiations undoubtedly were based on the alleged state of the market and the quality of fish, combined with the supply available from other sources, as well as on the relative skill of the traders. As time passed, fishing boat captains went to waterfront taverns to telephone distributor-buyers in order to get their prices. Marketers who needed fish would learn about the habits of skippers, and by going to their hangouts could negotiate with them. Thus the dealer would again be negotiating with the skipper in much the same way as when he visited the ship. The

5 See *Report of Special Study of Securities Markets of the Securities and Exchange Commission,* 88th Cong., 1st sess, H. Doc. 95, pt. 2 (Washington, 1963), pp. 40–47. See also *The Modern Auction Market: A Guide to Its Use for Institutional Investors* (New York: New York Stock Exchange, March, 1965).

public gathering place, however, differed from the ship as a trading center in two ways: (1) the would-be buyer could not necessarily expect to have the skipper to himself, as other buyers might be present; and (2) the skipper would not necessarily have the buyer to himself, as other skippers with cargoes to sell might also be present.

It is not difficult to imagine that at some point in the not-so-private private treaty trading, the germ of auctioning was born, particularly when the product was in short supply. For example, somewhere along the line it might have happened that, when a dealer was offering a skipper two cents a pound for the cargo, another dealer, overhearing the offer and particularly needing the fish for his trade, said, "Don't take it, skipper. I will give you two-and-a-half cents." The skipper would quickly recognize that he was indeed in a seller's market, and that he could enhance his returns by letting the dealers bid against one another for his goods. It would be a simple step from this type of selling to an agreement among fishermen to sell only through the auction and to decide on a more appropriate meeting place; they might also determine a regular trading time and adopt certain rules under which trading would take place—that is, the conditions of sale.

Application of Auction Selling in Market Distribution

It is difficult to analyze the applicability of auctioning to market distribution. One reason is the absence of adequate data on which to base firm statements. There is very little precise information about the relative volume handled by auction systems as compared with other sales systems. Because of the paucity of reliable data, one must depend largely on qualitative information in attempting to solve this problem.

General applicability.—Auctioning is an important method of selling in most countries, at least for certain types of commodities. In the United States, for example, auctioning is big business. According to a government survey, at least 20,000 auctioneers, and possibly as many as 35,000, were at work in the country a few years ago. At the same time, 1,872 wholesale auction houses were doing a business of about $3.4 billion a year, and 1,630 retail firms were earning $22.8 million in commissions each year. Auctioneers sell the large bulk of tobacco in the United States, nearly all the livestock moving from farm to farm, large amounts of fruits and vegetables, poultry and eggs, used cars, jewelry, at wholesale, art objects, and even buildings and building lots.[6] The use of auctioning in certain types of sales extends into most countries of the world.

Table 1, listing commodities and properties that have been sold by auction at one time or another in the United States, illustrates the wide applicability of the auction system. The list was compiled by following advertisements in metropolitan and country newspapers and by checking the guides to periodical literature. Conceptually, it is possible to classify the commodity fields in which auctioning is found in three categories: (1) those in which there is little if any auctioning (such as the sale of new automobiles); (2) those in which heavy reliance is placed on auctions (for example, the sale of fresh fish); and (3) those in which auctioning and alternative sales schemes operate side by side (as in the sale of antiques).

Although the applicability of the auction system to a marketing problem depends in part on subjective considerations by those making decisions, basically it is a matter of comparative economic efficiency. In general, if the scheme maximizes returns in relation to the effort expended by both buyers and sellers, it will be utilized. If it does not, a more efficient sales mechanism will be preferred. Changes in comparative efficiency may take place over a period of time, but, even more important, those making decisions may become aware of the potentialities of new schemes.

A careful examination of table 1 reveals that most kinds of property that come under the hammer are either raw materials that serve as a basis for processing or manufacturing, or man-made goods used previously by others. Very little of the property sold at auction consists of new manufactured goods; property commonly sold at auction includes not only rare old items but almost new second-hand items, such as late-model used cars. Moreover, such sales include small items (diamond rings) as well as gigantic properties (entire lumber mills).

As is well known, the auction process is utilized in the sale of certain types of agricultural (or natural) products or raw materials.

6 See Russell Chappell, "The Auctioneer's Big Bid," *Newsweek*, Feb. 3, 1958, pp. 78–80.

TABLE 1   17

TYPES OF PROPERTY SOLD BY AUCTION IN THE UNITED STATES

Airplanes
Alfalfa feeder ranch
Antique furniture
Antiques
Apples
Art treasures
Autographs
Automatic screw machines
Automobiles (new, used, imported, domestic, sport)
Automotive garage and equipment
Bar and license
Batch plant and mixer trucks
Bicycles
Books (old)
Building materials
Buttons
Cameras and camera shop equipment
Cargo ships
Carpets
Cattle
Cattle ranch
Chemical plant
Clothes (men, women)
Coins (old)
Comic books
Construction equipment
Contractor's supplies
Cotton (Egyptian)
Customhouse goods
Dairy cattle
Diesel parts
Dress-manufacturing plant (sewing machines, mirrors, office furniture)
Drilling equipment
Earth-moving equipment
Eggs

Electrical contractor's equipment
Electrical supplies
Electric hand tools
Electronic test equipment
Estates (private and county)
Farm equipment
Farmland
Fish
Flowers (Holland)
Foundry shop
Fruits and vegetables
Furniture (new and used)
Furs
Garage and shop
Garment-manufacturing plant
Government surplus goods
Hardware store
Heavy equipment (diesel logging truck, cat, earth-moving tractor, etc.)
High-rise office building
Hogs
Holly
Horses and mules
Household goods
Houses (for removal)
Houses (new, custom built)
Houses (other)
Jewelry
Knitting machines
Lamp parts
Laundry equipment (dryers, boilers, counters)
Liquor-store fixtures
Livestock
Logging and lumber construction machinery and equipment
Lumber

Machine shop
Marble-manufacturing plant
Market and restaurant equipment
Medical equipment supply
Metal fabricating shop (tool room and factory equipment)
Metalworking tools
Mexican groceries and staples
Milling machines
Model-home furniture
Molding plant
Motel units
Movie-studio equipment (Hal Roach Studio)
Musical instruments
Office and engineering equipment (calculator, IBM typewriter, files, etc.)
Office furniture
Offset print plant
Oil leases
Paintings, etchings
Paper pulp mill
Pears
Pipe
Plant equipment (fork lift, compressor, etc.)
Plastic extrusion and vacuum-forming plant
Plumbing stock
Police auction (unclaimed items—bikes, shotguns, rifles, typewriters, musical instruments)
Porcelain
Poultry
Precision inspection equipment
Precision lathes
Precision machinery
Precision tooling
Printing shop and equipment

Produce
Purebred stock
Real estate (unimproved commercial buildings, homes, apartments)
Recordings (first pressings)
Reproduction plant
Restaurant-bakery
Restaurant equipment
Road-building equipment
Rock-crushing equipment
Rugs
Sash-and-door company
Sawmill
Securities (long term)
Sewing machines
Sheep
Shoes (boots, oxfords)
Shopping centers
Silverware
Small appliances
Sporting equipment
Stamps
Strawberries
Structural steel
Supermarket equipment
Surgical supply company
Tape recorders
Tea
Television sets (new and used)
Tobacco
Tool and die shop
Tool rental equipment
Toys
Trailer-manufacturing plant (equipment and stock)
Trucks and trailers
Truck service station
Unclaimed baggage
Unclaimed storage

TABLE 1—*Continued* 19

Unimproved land	Violins
Upholstering shop	Woodworking machine equipment
Variety store merchandise	Woodworking plant
Vegetable ranch	Wool (Australian)
Vegetables	Wool and rags
Vending machines	Yachts

The best-known example, perhaps, is cigarette tobacco. The data in table 1 show that fruit, furs, tea, timber, vegetables, wool, and many other commodities are sold on an auction basis at the primary distribution level. Fish is commonly marketed by auction at the first-sale level in most areas of the world. One of the most common uses of auctions on the West Coast of the United States is for selling used machinery of various types (such as factory tools, earth-moving equipment, and shipbuilding facilities).

The lengthy list of properties sold by auction (see table 1) tends to exaggerate the importance of auctioning in the present-day economy, in several ways. First, it suggests that this method of selling is used exclusively in these fields. In fact, however, in many instances other systems are employed, as in the sale of surplus or outmoded machinery. Moreover, a firm that uses the auction method to liquidate its business probably does so only once. Even when the auction is the usual sales method, as for tobacco, live-stock, wool, and tea, its use is confined largely if not entirely to the primary market level, and other distribution schemes are utilized at subsequent levels. Second, many of the items listed differ only on a technical basis—the use to which the specific type of goods is put—and not in the market situation. That is, the vendors of machinery or equipment, regardless of its precise nature, face the same problem of liquidating their goods most advantageously.

Some goods sold at auction are brand-new. For example, new furniture may be traded at auction; the same is true of appliances and even automobiles. Usually, however, goods of this type are manufactured for retail sale on a take-it-or-leave-it basis, but occasionally an unforeseen commercial development requires the vendors or the creditors to bypass usual marketing channels and sell at auction in order to liquidate the stock. On the other hand, some new merchandise (for example, living room furniture) may be specifically made to sell at auction. Such goods may ostensibly have been made for sale through regular channels, and are then sold at auction purportedly because they are of second quality or must be disposed of quickly to satisfy creditors. Actually, the goods may have been designed for sale at auction to obtain benefits expected to be derived from the use of that selling device. The success of such an operation depends on its appeal to bargain hunters, many of whom confidently expect to get something for nothing.

Why are auctions so prevalent in some fields? One answer is, perhaps, that some products have no standard value. For example, the price of any catch of fish (at least of fish destined for the fresh fish market) depends on the demand and supply conditions at a specific moment of time, influenced possibly by prospective market developments. For manuscripts and antiques, too, prices must be remade for each transaction. For example, how can one discover the worth of an original copy of Lincoln's Gettysburg Address except by the auction method? [7] Only slightly less difficult is the problem of determining the value of secondhand machinery. Moreover, certain, if not all, commodities in this category possess subtle quality characteristics for which some individual buyers are willing to pay premium prices; on the contrary, vendors of goods of inferior quality may be forced to give concessions in order to sell them.

We may conclude that, on the basis of commodity fields in which auctioning is found, this selling practice is quite prevalent in present-day distribution. There are qualifications, however. Auctioning is not universally practiced in all segments of the fields in which it is used, and even in fields where it is most prevalent it is not found at all distribution levels. Furthermore, in some fields auctioning exists alongside other title-transferring schemes, such as private treaty selling.

When flexible pricing is called for, auctioning will be employed unless an alternative plan, such as individual negotiation, appears to be superior. If, in addition, producers of the goods to be sold prefer, or even demand, a buyer-competitive scheme in order to guarantee maximum returns, the auction method is an obvious choice. In this

7 "Happy Bibliophile: Cuban Collector Buys Manuscript of Lincoln's Gettysburg Address," *Life*, May 16, 1949, pp. 145–148.

way the consignor can influence the type of sales scheme utilized, especially at the primary distribution level.

It is not easy to explain the absence of auctions in some commodity areas. Perhaps in such fields a flexible pricing mechanism is not needed because the end-product price is stable, or perhaps a different pricing scheme, such as individual negotiation, serves the purpose more effectively. It is interesting to note that auctioning, so widely used for selling fish, is not employed at all in Iceland, presumably because practically all the fish caught by Icelandic fishermen is either canned or frozen, thus becoming a standard, stable-price grocery item. Also, auctioning is seldom employed in sales transactions in Mexico, a fact that is just as puzzling to me as it will be to readers. An exception, oddly enough, is the periodic *remate,* or auction, of unclaimed articles by the government pawnshop.

In some commodity fields the product is so standardized and the prices are so stable that buyers purchase their requirements by grade or brand designation without inspection. They may simply order the product directly from the source (through company salesmen, letters, teletype, and the like) because of the timesaving potential. Purchasing by auction does require more buyer time, and hence is avoided for standardized products under normal supply and demand conditions.

Differences in applicability within fields.—There is evidence that the applicability of auctioning differs within certain commodity or property areas. In the sale of antiques, auctioning and direct sale to collectors, or to dealers for resale to collectors, exist side by side. The dealer, in attempting to acquire title to the item, may argue that he knows a particular buyer who will pay a maximum price and thus provide the vendor with immediate cash. The auction representative may counter with the suggestion that the vendor, by waiting for the proper time and circumstances, may realize a better return through the bidding process. Neither method appears to have so clear-cut an advantage over the other as to prevail in all circumstances. Apart from vendor preference, differences in the property being sold affect the applicability of a particular method of sale in a field where two or more systems can be used.

The representative of a leading London produce auction firm

says that the auction method is usually employed in the sale of the more bulky commodities that arrive in England by sea, such as oranges, grapefruit, lemons, apples, pears, melons, grapes, and onions. Several thousand packages of such items can be sold at auction in one or two hours, whereas in a full day probably only a few hundred packages could be sold privately. On the other hand, soft fruits, such as plums, apricots, and peaches, which arrive daily during the season from the Continent, are sold immediately by private treaty to avoid spoilage while waiting for a semiweekly auction. High-quality produce with a limited outlet—strawberries and asparagus, for example—is also sold entirely by private treaty, usually to buyers like fine restaurants, which have standing orders and pay high prices for such merchandise. Even commodities advertised for sale at auction are often subject to prior sale by individual negotiation.

Auctioning as a sales medium is effective for certain types of real property. A British student of the subject argues that success attends the auctioning of real estate only when (1) competition for the particular type of property is currently strong, as for top-quality commercial development sites in expanding metropolitan areas; (2) competition between two or more parties for one specific parcel already exists, including perhaps the lessee as a certain bidder; (3) the sale must be consummated by a certain date, as when executors are closing an estate; (4) the value of the property is not known and the auction is used in part, at least, as a value-detecting device as well as a sales medium; and (5) vendors are in a fiduciary position and must not only ensure the best possible price but also remove any doubts from the minds of suspicious relatives or friends.[8]

The same authority lists as *not* suitable for auction (1) property with known market resistance, that is, property that has been "flogged" in the private treaty market without success, such as a worn-out terrace house with no room for a garage; (2) property with a limited appeal, sometimes designated as "freak" property suitable only for highly specialized purposes; (3) property whose owners have an exaggerated idea of its worth, and whose auctioning would undoubtedly end in an aborted sale; and (4) small suburban houses, usually attracting young and impecunious buyers

8 Geoffrey G. Rogers, "The Sale of Real Estate by Auction," *Chartered Auctioneer and Estate Agent,* XLIII (Nov., 1963), 520.

who should not be subjected to the sales pressure of an auction.[9]

A real estate broker, however, may have confidence in auctions as a sales mechanism, and may become very proficient in application of the method. I know an American broker, for example, who feels that the auction is an effective way of selling most kinds of real estate. One key to success, he believes, lies in the price the vendor is willing to accept. A reasonable reserve price means a good chance of success, if the auction is well managed, whereas an excessively high price is bound to abort an auction sale. Yet, if only one party is interested in a certain piece of property, the use of the auction method is futile.

Changes in applicability over time.—A final aspect of the applicability of auction selling concerns the changes that take place in the use of auction selling over a period of time. Modifications in auctioning arise from changes in business conditions from one period to another. When industrial activity is slowed down, a boom in a certain type of auctioning results from business failures and bankruptcy court orders. During the great depression of the thirties, many such sales were conducted in behalf of creditor institutions, and, in some rural areas, led to serious social disturbances. This court-directed type of auction might serve, in fact, as a barometer of business conditions; there are relatively few such auctions in good times and a sharply increased number in bad times.[10] Yet the use of the auction for liquidation purposes is not necessarily a depression phenomenon. It may simply be a way of turning specialized capital goods into liquid assets needed for other purposes, including the expanding of a business in a different direction.

Some types of auctions, however, thrive in good times. For example, people who are prosperous may satisfy a latent desire to possess items they would not think of buying in poor times, such as antiques, including furniture and rugs, and art treasures. Antique auctions, both in metropolitan centers and in smaller communities, tend to expand sales in good times, usually at higher prices. It is not surprising, then, that the great auction houses of the world— Sotheby's and Christie's of London and Parke-Bernet in New York—have been enjoying a peak sales volume in the middle sixties. This type of activity may be partly cyclical, but the enhanced

9 *Ibid.*, p. 521.

10 "Prosperity Index: Plant Auctions," *Business Week*, Oct. 15, 1949, p. 31.

prices of masterworks stem, in part at least, from simple supply and demand factors: more and more of the great paintings are going to museums, and often the masters are no longer here to increase the supply.

In fields where the auction is utilized exclusively, or nearly so, any advance in sales volume will increase the use of the auction. For instance, increases in population and income expand the demand for furs, and the auction, which is relied on at the primary level, automatically becomes more important. Much the same thing is true of sales of cigarette tobacco, where the auction is utilized almost entirely, although here the increase may reflect population growth rather than enhanced income.

Some new applications have developed for the auction method. Since World War II, for example, it has been adopted for the wholesaling of used cars so successfully that now the large bulk of secondhand automobiles are sold in this way.[11] In fact, used-car prices, once based on dealers' reports, are now based largely on auction quotations. A similar, though less dramatic, change has taken place in the sale of eggs and live poultry in certain areas. New uses for auctioning may be expected with the passing of the years. Various articles describe auction sales of buttons,[12] holly,[13] and even toys.[14] One of the latest applications of the auction is to the sale of long-term securities by the federal government.[15]

Although new uses for auctions are, perhaps, relatively rare, application of this selling method to the sale of real property seems to have been increasing,[16] partly because of the development of more effective techniques, and partly because of gradual elimination of prejudice against the auction method. Despite the pre-

11 See Frederic Taylor, "Auto Auctions," *Wall Street Journal*, Aug. 7, 1963, pp. 1, 11.

12 "World's First Auction Sale of Buttons," *Hobbies*, XLV (Sept., 1940), 30-31.

13 H. W. Dengler, "Holly Auction," *American Forests*, LXVIII (Dec., 1962), 4-6.

14 B. H. Leffingwell, "New York City Doll-Toy Auction," *Hobbies*, LXIV (April, 1959), 38, 40, 57.

15 "Treasury Auctions Off $250 Million in Bonds," *Los Angeles Times*, Jan. 9, 1963, Pt. III, p. 8.

16 Roger B. May, "Going, Going, Gone! More Americans Sell Real Estate at Auction," *Wall Street Journal*, Sept. 7, 1965, pp. 1, 15.

dominance of the private treaty system in this field, the auction is unquestionably superior to all other methods of selling real property, given certain favorable factors. Its use is therefore likely to increase.

All the changes in the application of selling have not, however, been gains. For example, the use of the auction in the wholesaling of fruit in the United States has declined in recent years. This development is in sharp contrast with the overwhelmingly successful use of auctions by Netherlands growers of both fruit and vegetables during approximately the same period of time. Much of the decline in the United States may be attributed, at least indirectly, to the shift from independent store to chain store operations, and the resulting buying by large purchasers directly from growers before shipment.[17] The new large-scale operations require the short-circuiting both of terminal markets (where fruit was formerly offered for sale) and of the auction system in order to assure volume retailers of needed supplies and to increase buying efficiency. Nevertheless, auctioning is still utilized in many terminal markets in the wholesaling of produce. Auctions supply the remaining independents and the fill-in needs of the chains, and serve as a channel for the sale of certain types of fruits to which they are particularly suited.

17 Alden C. Manchester, *The Changing Role of the Fruit Auctions,* Marketing Research Report no. 331 (Washington: U.S. Dept. of Agriculture, 1959), p. 6.

Historical Perspectives

3 AS YET no general study of auctioning on a historical basis has appeared. The miscellaneous material available, however, suggests that auctions have had a long and colorful history.

Auctioning in Ancient Times

According to Herodotus, auctions existed around 500 B.C. in Babylon, where once a year women of marriageable age were sold on condition that they be wed.[1] When beautiful maidens were offered, bidding among well-to-do swains was lively; but when less attractive girls were put up for sale, those seeking wives accepted them only in return for monetary compensation. In a kind of inverse auction, the plainer lasses went to impecunious, or perhaps miserly, persons who agreed to marry them in exchange for money (see fig. 2). Payment took the form of dowries, presumably derived from the premium prices obtained for the handsome maidens, and the rivals made successive reductions in bids until they reached the minimum amount they would be willing to accept in return for the acquisition of less comely mates.

1 Herodotus, *The Histories of Herodotus,* trans. Henry Cary (New York: D. Appleton and Company, 1899), p. 77.

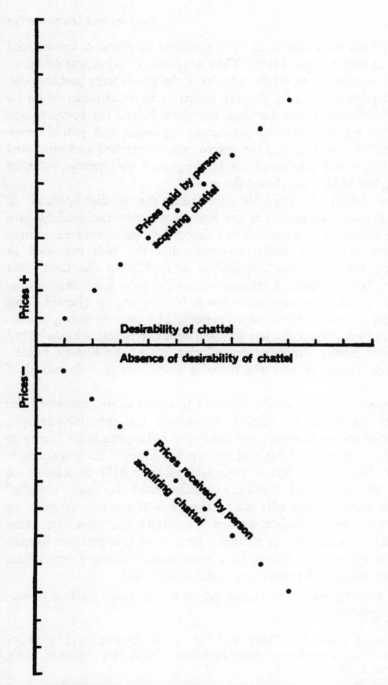

Fig. 2 Orthodox and reverse procedures in Babylonian wife auctions.

Auctions were also used by the ancient Romans in commercial trade, at least to some extent. They were held in what was called an *atrium auctionarium,* where samples of the goods were probably displayed prior to the sale. Trading activity was usually carried on by four functionaries: the *dominus,* on whose behalf the property was sold; the *argentarius,* who organized, regulated, and possibly even financed the auction sale; the *praeco,* who advertised and promoted the auction and conducted the bidding; and the *emptor,* who, as the highest bidder, purchased the goods.[2]

Few details are available concerning the *modus operandi* of these Roman auctions. It is not known whether the bidding procedure followed an ascending or a descending pattern, or an entirely different one. It is likely, however, that the bids increased in amount, for the word "auction" is derived from the Latin root *auctus,* "an increase." Attention was called to a forthcoming auction in public announcements made by the *praeco* (herald) and through a written *proscriptio* (notice). The *praeco,* acting as auctioneer, then put up the lots for sale, stimulated and acknowledged bids, and finally "knocked down" each lot to the highest bidder. Bidding reportedly took the form of a wink or a nod instead of public outcry.[3]

Apparently the Romans, when in financial straits, employed the auction also in the liquidation of property. Caligula, for example, auctioned off the furniture and ornaments belonging to his family to help him meet his debts and recoup his losses.[4] To cover a state deficit, Marcus Aurelius is even said to have held an auction of royal heirlooms and furniture which lasted for two months.[5] Roman soldiers reportedly put up their loot at auction *sub hasta,* or "under the spear." In fact, the word "subhastation," now rare, came to mean "a public sale or auction." Because of this practice, Roman business agents were said to have accompanied military expeditions in order to bid in the war booty at public auction.[6]

2 J. A. C. Thomas, "The Auction Sale in Roman Law," *Juridical Review,* Pt. I (April, 1957), p. 43.

3 *Ibid.*

4 Tenney Frank, ed., "Rome and Italy of the Empire," Vol. V of *An Economic Survey of Ancient Rome* (Baltimore: Johns Hopkins Press, 1940), pp. 39–40 n. 12.

5 *Ibid.,* p. 77.

6 *Ibid.,* p. 26 n. 47.

Perhaps the most preposterous auction in history was held in 193 A.D., when the whole Roman Empire was placed on the block by the Praetorian Guard. After having killed the preceding emperor, Pertinax, the leaders of the guard announced that they would bestow the crown upon the Roman who offered the largest donation. When Didius Julianus outbid all his rivals by promising each man 6,250 drachmas, the guard declared him emperor. After Didius had been in power for only two months, however, the legions under the command of Septimius Severus seized the capital and beheaded the emperor.[7]

Even less is known about auctioning in other ancient civilizations. In China, four institutions were utilized to raise money for Buddhist temples and monasteries: pawnshops, mutual financing associations, lotteries, and auction sales.[8] Apparently the personal belongings of deceased monks were auctioned off as early as the seventh century A.D. The monk who acted as auctioneer had to know the normal price and announce whether the item was new, old, or worn out. If bidding went too high, he reminded his fellow monks: "Better be thoughtful. You might regret it later."

Despite the paucity of information, it is clear from the foregoing that the auction was employed as a sales mechanism in ancient times. Precise auctioning methods and the extensiveness of their use, however, remains shrouded in mystery. All we really know is that this way of selling property is not a modern phenomenon, but has its origins in antiquity.

Early-Day Auctioning in England

It is difficult, if not impossible, to determine when the auction method of selling was first employed in England. The earliest reference to the term in the *Oxford English Dictionary* is dated 1595, although admittedly this is simply a straw in the wind. It is known, however, that toward the end of the seventeenth century sellers of pictures frequently met in coffeehouses and taverns to

7 Will Durant, *Caesar and Christ,* The Story of Civilization, Pt. III (New York: Simon and Schuster, 1944), pp. 620–621.

8 Lien-sheng Yang, "Buddhist Monasteries and Four Money-raising Institutions in Chinese History," *Harvard Journal of Asiatic Studies,* XIII (June, 1950), 174–191.

auction their wares. A 1682 issue of the *London Gazette* referred to the "daily attendance" at the "Auction-house," clearly suggesting an auction operation. Before such sales, catalogs were often issued. The announcement in one of them reads:

> [The goods] will be exposed to sale . . . on Thursday 12th Friday 13th and Saturday 14th of this instant *March*, at Mrs. Smythers Coffee House in Thames street, by the Custom House: The Sale beginning each Morning precisely at Nine of the Clock. The said Paintings are to be viewed from this day forward until all be sold. Catalogues may be had at the place of sale.
> *Pray read me, but do not take me from the Table.*[9]

Sales of certain types of chattels were also conducted by the auction method, at least occasionally, in seventeenth-century England; for example, Samuel Pepys witnessed an auction sale of ships in 1662.[10] It may reasonably be assumed that other types of property were auctioned as well.

The firm of Sotheby's, world-famous auctioneers, was established in 1744, and Christie's, similarly renowned, had its beginnings in 1766. These firms may, of course, have conducted business in other ways than auctioning, and may have been antedated by other auction houses of which we have no knowledge. It was not until years later that announcements of auctions appeared in the public prints, although posted announcements may have been prevalent. The oldest English legal action developing from an auction of any kind appears to have been *Daniel* v. *Adams*, 27 Eng. Rep. (Amb.) 495 (1764).[11]

Little is known about the methods of auctioning in early-day England, but it appears that conditions of sale were as common then as they are today. One extant list of eighteenth-century operating rules indicates the type of auction employed as well as the terms of sale:

9 Quoted in Peter Ash, "The First Auctioneer: Origin of Sales by Auction of Real Property," *Estates Gazette* (Centenary Supplement), May 3, 1958, p. 33.

10 *Diary and Correspondence of Samuel Pepys, Esq., F.R.S.*, with a Life and Notes by Richard Lord Braybrooke, Deciphered, with Additional Notes, by Rev. Mynors Bright, M. A. (New York: Dodd, Mead, 1887), II, 327.

11 Ash, *op. cit.*, p. 33.

1. The high bidder is the buyer and, if any dispute arises as to which bid is the highest, the goods will be put up for sale again.

2. No bidder may advance another's bid by less than sixpence when the amount offered is less than £1, or by less than one shilling when the price is £1 or more.

3. The merchandise for sale is warranted as perfect, and before removing the goods from the premises any buyer may accept or reject them.

4. Each buyer must give his name and make a deposit of 5 shillings on each pound sterling (if demanded); no deliveries will be made during the sale.

5. All purchases must be taken away at the buyer's expense, and the amount due must be paid at the place of sale within three days after the purchase.

6. Any would-be buyer who is unable to attend the sale may have his commission executed by a representative of the auction firm.[12]

A statement found at the beginning of an early-day catalog may throw further light on early English auction operations: "And that I may remove the Prejudices of some, and the Misapprehensions of others, as to the sincerity of the management, I have printed the Conditions of Sale with an additional one, that no Person or Persons shall be admitted to bid for his, or their own Pictures. . . ."[13]

As to the type of auction employed in the eighteenth century, it cannot be assumed that the English, or ascending, system was always used simply because of its prevalence today. Certainly some sales were conducted on that basis, as evidenced by the original wording of the second rule listed above: "That no Person *advances* less than Sixpence each bidding, and after the Book arises to One Pound, no less than One Shilling [emphasis added]."[14] There is little question, also, that in some early auctions the candle method was utilized. For example, Samuel Pepys reported such an auction: "After dinner by water to the office, and there we met and sold the Weymouth, Successe, and Fellowship hulkes, where pleasant to see

---

12 Adapted from the original as given in James Brough, *Auction!* (Indianapolis and New York: Bobbs-Merrill, 1963), pp. 26–27.

13 Quoted in Ash, *op. cit.*, p. 33.

14 Brough, *op. cit.*, p. 26.

how backward men are at first to bid; and yet when the candle is
going out, how they bawl and dispute afterwards who bid *the most
first* [emphasis added]." [15] This type of auction was evidently the
English type, with the added feature of an allowance for a specified
time interval. To a limited extent, it is still used today when speed
of transaction is not requisite and when it is helpful to buyers to
know approximately the amount of time they will have to consider
the maximum amount they wish to bid.

One seventeenth-century catalog mentioned "mineing," a
"Method of Sale not hitherto used in England," [16] undoubtedly
imported from Holland. In this type of auction, the auctioneer
apparently put up each lot at a high price and kept reducing the
price until someone called "Mine!" In the early British system,
however, another bidder presumably could advance on the bid, so
that a blending of the Dutch (descending) system with the English
(ascending) system would have resulted. The available evidence
suggests that auction fees were charged on a percentage basis, and
that they were upward of 5 percent, graduated downward with the
increase in sales prices.

Between 1660 and 1740 auctions in the form of "peremptory
sales," held either by court order or privately, were apparently quite
common in England. Although the auctioning of chattels seems to
have preceded the auctioning of land, both types of property were
offered in an advertisement appearing in the *London Evening Post*,
March 8–10, 1739. After listing some merchandise items (including
threads, sacks, gold and silver lace, and brocaded waistcoats), the
auctioneer announced that in "the first Day's Sale will be sold two
Houses belonging to the said Bankrupt's Estate, situated at Pad-
dington, and adjoining to the Churchyard." [17] The first announcement of a sale devoted only to land appeared in the same newspaper in the 1740's. It is not known what method was employed in
auctions of real property.

The best evidence is that auctioning of estates in England originated with a gentleman named

Christopher Cock, of the Great Piazza in Covent Garden. This man seems
to have been a "live-wire." . . . We are lucky to possess the Daily Ad-

15 *Diary and Correspondence of Samuel Pepys*, p. 327.
16 Quoted in Ash, *op. cit.*, p. 33.
17 Quoted in *ibid.*, p. 35.

vertiser of April 25, 1735, because it contains the earliest advertisement of his I have been able to discover. This announces three chattel sales "at Mr. Cock's *Great Room, in the Piazzas, Covent Garden.*" One of the sales was by order of the South Sea Company, and another was a postponed sale of Arabian horses. The contents and style of the advertisement make it plain that Cock was already in a very substantial way of business.[18]

Auctioning in Early-Day America

It might be expected that institutions as well as ideas would emigrate with the people who move from one country to another. In this way, no doubt, the auction found its way from England to America, where from an early date the colonists used this method of selling to dispose of property under the judicial process or to close out stocks of merchandise. In early-day America the auction was used to liquidate capital goods and inventories, to unload unsalable goods remaining in importers' hands at the end of the season, and to sell secondhand household furnishings, farm utensils, and domestic animals. As auctioning was evidently considered a discreditable way of selling goods, various methods of concealing the owner's name were employed.[19]

Use of auctioning by American importers.—The use of auctioning in early-day America was widespread, particularly at the primary market level.[20] As population increased and larger areas of the East Coast became settled, auctioning made rapid progress. Information is lacking as to which auctioning method was most prevalent, although apparently it was the English or ascending-bid system.

In the early eighteenth century, a British manufacturer or exporter customarily consigned his goods to an agent in some American port. The agent then bonded the merchandise, landed it in the United States, and sold it at auction, usually accepting in payment promissory notes which were discounted at banks. The agent then would deduct his commission and remit the remainder of the

18 *Ibid.* For a discussion of early-day auctions in France, see Octave Uzanne, "The Hotel Drouot and Auction Rooms in Paris before and after the French Revolution," *The Connoisseur,* III (Aug., 1902), 235-242.

19 Ray Bert Westerfield, "Early History of American Auctions: A Chapter in Commercial History," *Transactions of the Connecticut Academy of Arts and Sciences,* XXIII (May, 1920), 164.

20 *Ibid.,* p. 165.

money to his principal in Britain. The usual procedure in these auctions was to exhibit the goods for a day or two prior to the sale, giving prospective purchasers a chance to appraise the articles in which they were interested and check them off in the catalog provided by the auctioneer. Most auction firms of any size held sales on two or more days each week.[21]

When American ports were closed to direct importations from Europe during the War of 1812, British merchants established extensive depots of goods in Halifax, Bermuda, and other British possessions so that they might be ready to supply the American market as soon as peace was declared. After the close of the war, the British found auctions the most profitable and the quickest way to turn their goods into cash. The market was soon glutted with merchandise, and by 1816 prices had fallen so far that they scarcely covered the duties.[22]

As auctioning became prevalent in early-day American commerce, orthodox importers and jobbers were circumvented; they raised loud cries of protest and began to demand protective legislation. To complicate matters, prices were much lower in Britain than America, enabling foreign merchants to undermine American production and marketing operations by exporting British goods to America. The dumping of foreign goods on American markets, which was merely expedited by use of the auction method, created serious public resentment and culminated in a strong campaign against auction sales generally.

The auction system, however, did have some advantageous commercial effects in America. For one thing, auctions facilitated the introduction of new foreign and domestic products; goods were forced onto the market by the simple expedient of price-cutting, and in time the prejudices against the introduction and promotion of such goods were overcome.[23] Auctions also assisted small domestic manufacturers to gain a position in the market. Finally, merchants and retailers from the interior increasingly patronized auction sales in the port cities, especially those in New York, and thus made imported items available to inland markets.

Auctioning of slaves in the Old South.—Any historical account

21 *Ibid.*, pp. 173–177.
22 *Ibid.*, p. 165.
23 *Ibid.*, p. 181.

of auctioning in America would be incomplete without mention of the infamous sale of slaves in the Old South before the Civil War. At that time slaves were considered as chattels and were sold at auction, though occasionally they were bought at a fixed price set by the vendor, or after individual negotiation between seller and buyer.

The demand for slaves varied, depending on sex, age, and physical condition. Healthy young men were much sought after and thus commanded high prices, sometimes as much as $1,750; men who were not so young but who had been trained in a trade were also very desirable. Women, too, were in demand—some as mothers of future children, some as servants, and some as fancy women. Children were acquired for the purpose of keeping families together and as speculative purchases which were expected to pay off at a later time.

Slave trading was unrestricted until 1808, when a federal statute was passed proscribing the importation of slaves into the United States. Up to that time importers offered slaves for sale to plantation owners, their agents or brokers, or secondary traders who acquired the property for subsequent resale. After 1808, or at least after 1818 when the penal clauses of the restrictive legislation were strengthened, the primary slave market presumably ceased to exist. Trading in slaves did continue, however, among hard-pressed plantation owners who had to sell to professional traders, the latter were in the business of buying slaves and selling them to farmers needing additional help or to dealers acquiring the property for resale. After the Emancipation Proclamation, the slave trade was completely outlawed, at least in most jurisdictions.

Available descriptions of the slave-auctioning process, though sketchy, suggest that the English, or ascending-bid, method was used. The auctioneer gave his opening spiel to a crowd gathered in the marketplace, and the first lot, consisting of one person or possibly of a whole family, was put up for sale.[24] He also made full use of the practice of displaying the "merchandise," even at the cost of embarrassing the individual up for sale, and much good-natured but often crude banter was engaged in by the crowd. The auctioneer would suggest an opening bid, but sometimes had to slip

24 Frederic Bancroft, *Slave Trading in the Old South* (New York: Frederick Ungar Publishing Co., 1959), pp. 109–110.

back in order to obtain a firm offer; after receiving a starting bid he would lead the buyers upward, enunciating not only the actual bids that were made but the advance he was aiming for.

When slaves were sold in family groups, the bidding was often based on an average price per person. The value placed on the father might be $1,200 and that on the mother $950, and three children might be valued at $725, $650, and $475, for a total estimated family value of $4,000. Actual bids might start at $200 per person and move up to approximately $700, or a total of about $3,500 for the family. This method of selling multiple units, not uncommon today, was undoubtedly adopted because it was expected to maximize returns. Not only did it emphasize the smaller individual figures instead of the larger total amount, but it placed the "value of the best slave in the group . . . uppermost in the bidder's mind." [25]

In slave auctioning, when the price approached the maximum demand prices of the buyers, it was the practice of the auctioneer to narrow the amount of the advance from, say, 50 dollars to 25 to 10 or even 5 dollars. Finally, when it was apparent that bidders had about reached their limit, the auctioneer would say "Ah you-all *done?* Seven—hundud—an'—five—dollahs! Once—twice—third—an'—*last*—call; goin', *goin','*" and then *"Sold* fo' *seven hundud an' five dollahs* to Mr. Jenks." [26] Although the existing superficial descriptions of American slave auctions give no information about the use of a reserve price, it is clear that lots were withdrawn from sale when bids were considered unreasonably low.

Latter-Day Developments in Auctioning

Despite the long tradition of price making by the auction method, the use of auctioning is relatively new in many areas and fields.

Netherlands.—The practice of auctioning fruits and vegetables in the Netherlands, so prevalent today, is only eighty years old, even though the method had been previously used in other fields (for example, the sale of porcelain ware). It was in 1887 that the sale of produce by auction first replaced sale by private treaty in

25 *Ibid.,* p. 230.
26 *Ibid.,* p. 111.

Holland. Before the days of auctioning, produce dealers would either buy from the grower, acquire goods on commission, or make advances to producers for crops still in the ground. Often the grower needed cash advances to enable him to implement cultivation, but this practice obviously placed him at a disadvantage in relation to the dealer, and "he frequently could do nothing but wait passively for the final settlement which might bear no relation to current prices." [27] As in certain localities and commodity areas today, the distributor controlled the producer.

In 1887 there occurred a significant event that was to have a tremendous effect on the production phase of the industry. One midsummer morning a grower by the name of Jongerling arrived with his bargeload of vegetables at the quay of the inland harbor Broek op Langendijk in North Holland. Here it was customary for producers to sell to dealers or to physically transfer the produce for sale on a commission, but on this particular morning demand was very brisk and the farmer-vendor found it difficult to decide to which of the eagerly competing buyers he should allocate his limited supply of goods. A passing boatman reportedly suggested that Jongerling put his produce up for sale at auction, which he did with gratifying results. Thus it was that the first auction of horticultural produce in the Netherlands took place. From that tiny beginning developed the present-day vast system of auction markets, with all their auxiliary services.[28]

Germany.—Auctioning of fish developed in Germany at almost precisely the same time as auctioning of produce in the Netherlands. Until the latter part of the nineteenth century, German fishermen personally delivered their catches to consumption centers. At first they sold the fish themselves, often having to stay in port for long periods of time in order to do so; later the middlemen took over the selling, thus releasing the fishermen for more productive work.

Although this specialization of effort was basically sound, the distributors frequently took advantage of the absentee owners, using their strong position in relation to that of the individual

27 *The Auction System of Horticultural Marketing in the Netherlands* (2d ed.; The Hague: Central Bureau of Horticultural Auctions in the Netherlands, 1959), p. 6.

28 *Ibid.*, p. 7.

fishermen to bring primary market prices down. Sometimes whole lots spoiled after fishermen refused to deliver their catches to the dealers at the going prices. Eventually, however, a system of firm contracts between fishermen and distributors developed, but the sale of fish by private treaty was still unsatisfactory.

Some type of open-market operation was required to establish a price that would reflect current and prospective demand and supply conditions, and thus eliminate the price-depressing tactics of the distributor-buyers. Consequently, the first fish auction took place in Hamburg on May 1, 1887, when the fishermen sold their catches to dealers on a competitive-bid basis.[29] Other fish auctions soon followed—in Geestemunde in 1888, in Bremerhaven in 1892, and in Cuxhaven in 1908. The Kiel market apparently was not established until 1947.

Japan.—The problem of distributor-dominated selling of fish by private treaty is brought into bold relief by examples from the Orient. Until about a century ago, exploitation of Japanese fishermen by their distributors seems to have been a common, if not universal, phenomenon. Under Japan's feudal organization the rulers gave fish merchants a monopoly of marketing, the so-called *Ura-ukeoi* system, which intensified the dominance of large capitalist-distributors over scattered small-scale fishermen. The favored merchants paid tribute to the overlords as a *quid pro quo* for the exploitation rights they enjoyed.

The first step in the reform movement came with the collapse of feudalism and its monopolistic structure. The process, beginning in 1869, was accelerated during the period 1910–1930, and formerly monopolistic activities were opened to competitive enterprisers. The old market system was replaced by keen competition among dealers for markets and supplies, which might well have paved the way for another type of control—capital advances to fishermen by distributors in exchange for exclusive purchasing agreements at distributor-determined prices during the period of the obligation. Under this system, exploitation of the fisherman developed through distributor credit control and private-treaty buying and selling negotiations.

When control over suppliers is effected through a debtor-

29 Klaus-Hinrich Krohn and Arnold Alewell, *Sea-Fish Marketing in the Federal Republic of Germany* (Rome: Food and Agriculture Organization of the United Nations, 1957), p. 105.

creditor relationship, there is little or no competition for the goods produced; there would exist, in fact, numerous little monopsonies, or "buying monopoly" situations, for suppliers would be permitted to trade only with those to whom they owed money. The buyer-creditor might be able arbitrarily to set the price and thus gain the advantage not only of keeping supply costs low but of depressing prices to fishermen. The latter would find it difficult, if not impossible, to extricate themselves from their predicament,[30] especially in the absence of antitrust laws.

Not until after World War II was the modern wholesale market system established throughout Japan. The key to equitable treatment of producers by distributors is an open-market system, such as the auction, which permits buyers to sell their goods at market prices and thus prevents exploitation by distributor-buyers. In Japan, the relationship between seller and buyer, an important aspect of which is the auction system of selling goods at the primary level, is completely free.

Hong Kong.—Control of the fishermen by the *laan,* or middleman, prevailed in the Hong Kong market until just after the termination of World War II. The merchant-capitalist provided the fishermen with needed supplies and credit and, in return, required the fishermen to bring their catches to him, the creditor, until the debt was paid—which, of course, might never happen. Legislation enacted in the Crown Colony in 1940, however, subsequently led to the replacement of *laan* control by self-governing cooperatives.[31] The latter assumed the fishermen's financial obligations and paid off debts owed the merchant-distributors, many of which had been passed on from father to son and might have gone on forever in the absence of such legislation.

The producers were thus free to sell their goods under competitive market conditions rather than to the monopsonist. This open-market mechanism took the form of public auction for the sale of fish and, oddly enough, of individual negotiation (bargaining be-

30 See Akira Hasegawa and Hirohiko Watanabe, "Distributive System and Cooperative Marketing of Fishery Products in Japan" (Tokyo: Fisheries Research Institute, 1958), mimeographed.

31 "The Hong Kong Fish and Vegetable Marketing Schemes" (Hong Kong: Co-operative Development & Fisheries Department, Dec., 1962), mimeographed, p. 1.

tween the buyer and the cooperative salesman) in the sale of produce. Because all producers were required to distribute their goods through the public market, forestalling was precluded. The auction had become an effective tool in implementing a program of market reform.

Future Developments

Despite significant developments in the application of auctioning to distribution, its potential is still unfulfilled in various parts of the world. In many emerging countries, distributors still control producers. In one African area, for example, fish is caught at night and delivered to distributors, who market it during the day. As they control sales, they can dominate the fishermen, who, once they are financially obligated to the distributors, must sell to them. Because there is no effective competition for their supplies, producers must take whatever the distributors wish to pay them, an amount that is, conceptually at least, just enough to keep supplies flowing.

If underdeveloped countries experience the same thing as Hong Kong and Japan, some organization, perhaps an international agency, may lead the producers out of economic slavery by (a) advancing funds to pay off obligations to distributors, and (b) creating an open-market mechanism, such as an auction, from which the old-type distributors may have to be banned. In this way fishermen would be able to obtain the full market price for the goods they produce. In my opinion such a development is bound to occur in time, and if it does the auction will have served as a social as well as an economic instrument.

Supply, Demand, and Competition

4 THE FORCES of supply, demand, and competition fundamentally determine the prices of goods in a free market economy. The relationship of these factors to price making by the auction method is of vital importance.

The Supply Factor

The term "supply," in its technical sense, refers to the amounts of a commodity or service which would be available at different hypothetical prices. Not only, then, does supply vary with price, other things being equal, but the supply of a commodity has a strong influence on price. The supply factor in relation to auctioning may mean either the supply of the relevant item available generally or the supply available for sale in a particular auction.

Supply in general.—The nature of the property available for sale is a key factor in determining whether the auction system is applicable. Goods typically sold at auction are basic commodities, such as wool, or used manmade goods, such as antiques or secondhand machinery. The distinguishing feature of these items is that the supply is irregular in quantity, quality, and variety, in contrast with supplies of most manufactured products, which are standardized and reproducible in accordance with consumer demand. The sources of the types of goods sold at auction are shown in table 2, derived from observation of auction operations.

The supply of goods for sale at auction is usually part of the total supply available from alternative sources. In some instances, supplies of goods sold at auction are only a fraction of the total supply, although even then the auction price may become the reference price used by traders in negotiated deals. On the other hand, the total supply in a particular market area may pass through the auction, as in the sale of fish at the primary distribution level in certain markets. Because the supply of goods is an important factor in the making of prices in an auction, intelligent buyers and sellers obviously should have some knowledge of the total supply of goods in which they are trading as well as of the amount available for sale at a particular auction. The amateur who wishes to purchase intelligently as well as the dealer who is to survive economically must be so informed.

The prices of goods at auction, compared with those outside the auction, need not, however, be identical. For example, the absence of adequate information would make possible variations in the prices paid, even for identical items at the same moment of time. Furthermore, differences in the quality of the goods in the two markets are reflected in the prices that the goods fetch. Still another reason for disparity is the availability factor: goods sold at auction are immediately available in contrast with others that may require a waiting period. Finally, variations may develop in the price of a perishable commodity, in short-run terms at least, if a certain market is momentarily oversupplied, because market imbalances cannot immediately be corrected by moving a portion of the supply from the glut area to a deficit supply area.

Supply available for sale at auction.—Although the supply of goods available in general is the basic concept, the amount and nature of goods available at auction also possess significance. This information may be given in a catalog, for which a charge may or may not be made. The catalog describes the items to be sold and indicates the order for sale.

While the supply of goods available at auction is often quite broad, including wide varieties of goods from numerous vendors, the number of units of each type of item is usually limited. In fact,

TABLE 2   43

SOURCES OF SUPPLY OF PROPERTY SOLD AT AUCTION

TYPE OF PROPERTY	BASIC SOURCE OF SUPPLY	SUPPLEMENTARY FACTORS AFFECTING SUPPLY	
		MANNER OF REACHING MARKET	INFLUENCE OF AUCTION FIRM
Agricultural products	Growers	Regular marketing of irregular supplies	Little if any influence on total supply, but some on use of auction and selection of particular firm.
Antiques	Former owners	Voluntary or enforced liquidation	Some influence possibly on total supply as well as on use of auction and selection of particular firm.
Fish	Catchers	Regular marketing of irregular supplies	Little if any effect on total supply or on use of auction method, but some on selection of firm.
Household goods	Former owners	Voluntary or enforced liquidation	Some effect possibly on total supply as well as on auction method and selection of auction firm.
Real property	Former owners	Voluntary or enforced liquidation	Little influence on total supply coming into market; considerable influence on use of auction method as well as selection of firm.
Used merchandise and equipment	Former owners	Voluntary or enforced liquidation	Little influence on total supply coming into market, but some on use of auction and particularly on selection of firm.

only one of a kind may be available for sale. Moreover, the total
supply of a particular item, such as a fine painting or an outstanding piece of real estate, may be put up for sale in a particular
auction. On the other hand, several, or even numerous, items may
be identical or nearly identical in certain or all respects. The auctioneer, however, may decide not to disclose this fact to the buyers, especially if the assemblage is made up mostly of householders.
By feeding the goods onto the market over a period of time in an
orderly fashion, he may obtain a higher average price for them than
if they had been dumped at one time. If this course of action is
not practicable, the auctioneer may have to find dealer-buyers
who are willing to acquire numerous units of such merchandise
for resale. In this instance the multiple supply may be an advantage
rather than a disadvantage.

The existence of a large supply in relation to demand undoubtedly affects the price of goods available for sale in an auction,
assuming that there is more than enough to satisfy all potential
buyers and that this fact is known to them. Why would one bid
against another if he knew that he would be able to satisfy his requirements at much lower prices simply by waiting? In certain
situations, therefore, it may be better to send only a fraction of the
total supply through during each auction period, thus avoiding a
short-term glut. If a season's whole supply is sold at auction, as is
the Sudan cotton crop, for example, decisions must be made concerning the proportion of the total supply to be offered at each
auction session.[1]

The close relationship between auction prices and prices for
similar merchandise sold elsewhere does not necessarily mean that
the prices are identical. In addition to the factors that, as noted
above, serve to offset the tendency toward price identity, such as
absence of market knowledge, the goodwill possessed by the firm
handling the sale is important. A name like Sotheby's or Christie's
could lend an aura of distinctiveness to an otherwise ordinary item,
which could perhaps be readily duplicated elsewhere for considerably less money. A psychological factor may enter into the auctioning of antiques, for some buyers will pay more for an item that has
been in the possession of a well-known public figure.

1 Mohamed Hashim Awad, "The Export Marketing of Sudan Cotton since
the War" (unpublished M.S. thesis, University of London, 1964), pp. 54–64.

One further question remains in connection with the supply of goods for sale at auction: How do such goods get into this particular channel? The stock of goods that the auctioneer has for sale is typically owned by others, and even more important, in any one field the auctioneer may be representing numerous vendors. In some instances it is easy for an auction firm to obtain consignments. For example, in auction firms that are cooperatively owned, the agent of the producers routinely consigns his supplies to the auction for resale. The problem of the cooperatives is simply to obtain members. But in some auctions the supplies must be sought for each session from relatively obscure sources (such as the owners of antiques), and in others they are acquired from known growers (the producers of livestock, for example). The problem of obtaining supplies like antiques, which are not reproducible but must be located, is a very complex one. Much effort is often expended by firms in ferreting out and acquiring commissions for the sale of art treasures. Auction houses may even resort to espionage to find likely sources of supply.[2]

Peter Wilson, star auctioneer and chairman of the board of Sotheby's, spends much time and effort in acquiring consignments. The three essential aspects of this important function are: (1) to procure consignments, an auction firm has to inform itself of the location and availability of relevant property; (2) a representative must therefore travel widely and become acquainted with many people; and (3) he must persuade those with whom he comes in contact to sell their property through his firm.[3] The last requirement may call for a bit of hard selling.[4]

Another complication in obtaining supplies for auctioning arises when the property to be sold is not under the control of the owner; for example, real property or chattels may have to be sold by court

2 See S. N. Behrman, *Duveen* (New York: Random House, 1951), pp. 246–248, for a description of the espionage operations of the great art dealer, Lord Duveen, and James Brough, *Auction!* (Indianapolis and New York: Bobbs-Merrill, 1963), p. 34, for information on the undercover activities of a dealer named Wildenstein.

3 After two days of quiet negotiation with a Sotheby representative for the sale of his art collection, Somerset Maugham is reported to have said, " 'I wouldn't trust my pictures with anyone else' " (Brough, *op. cit.*, p. 40).

4 Peter Wilson is quoted as saying: " 'Once we know a collection is going on the block' . . . 'getting the sale is high-pressure business' " *(ibid.)*.

order to liquidate bankrupt firms or to settle estates. Some auction sales are held by order of an assignee to whom the property has been transferred for conservation and/or liquidation, whereas others develop when taxes are delinquent, customs fees are unpaid, or goods are unclaimed. Such sales are often held at the instigation of agencies that have a lien against the goods; they may be conducted by the interested agency itself or by an auction firm appointed by the agency. It goes without saying that auction firms are alert to such opportunities and pursue them vigorously.

The Demand Factor

The second important basic factor in price making by the auction method is the demand for the goods that are being sold. Technically, demand has to do with the precise relationship of prices and amounts taken at such prices, but in this context it may be thought of in the broader aspects of interest and desire to purchase without reference to particular prices. Even in this sense, demand may be considered in general terms or in relation to goods being put up for sale at a particular auction.

Demand in general.—Since the demand for a specific commodity or item at an auction is closely related to the demand for such items generally, it is important to consider the latter first. Some consumer wants stem from biological requirements, some from intellectual needs, some from aesthetic desires, some from religious convictions, and so forth. In a free society values are put on the needed products and services in the marketplace through the forces of demand and supply, conditioned by competition among vendors. The demand of ultimate consumers is largely direct, whereas the demand of dealers is derived from that of consumer-buyers.

More desirable consumption items tend to bring higher prices than others less desirable. Moreover, some types or styles of items may be in favor at one time but out of favor at another time. Although goods that are not in favor usually lack value, in the market sense, they may be very desirable to individuals who collect such items. For example, a collector may be willing (although it may not be necessary) to pay a very high price to acquire an outmoded item like a horse-drawn surrey.[5]

5 At a recent auction of antique cars held in Royan, France, a "plain old, everyday 1906 Peugeot automobile" brought $40,000, a rare steam-powered De

Demand in its technical sense is not just another term for *desire;* it is, rather, related to the monetary value that consumers place on goods. In general, the quantity that consumers will take is in inverse relationship to the price of the goods. A strong demand means that buyers stand ready to pay a high price for goods, amount taken remaining the same, or that they will take a larger amount of the commodity, price remaining the same. A strong demand for nonreproducible goods, whose supply is not expansible, is usually reflected in a high price.

The auction per se does not create demand, as goods for which there is no demand would hardly be offered in this type of market. The announcement of an auction may, however, be the best way of bringing an item to the attention of those desiring it, or even of awakening a latent interest in other potential purchasers.

Demand for goods at auction.—Because buyers are an essential part of auctioning, they must be available if this price-making system is to function effectively. The seller cannot set prices by himself, nor can he do so with the help of only one buyer. The auction is clearly a buyer-competitive pricing scheme that depends on rivalry among those wanting to purchase the goods.

In an auction, except when a single item, such as a piece of real estate, is being offered for sale, the individual demands for the different items must be considered, rather than the demand for the total stock of goods. It follows that (a) the demand for each item is composed of demands of different combinations of individual buyers, and (b) the individuals making up the demand for a particular item are likely to possess different demand prices. The auction company, then, must do its utmost to attract all potential demanders who may be interested in the goods being offered for sale. A firm's clientele may include thousands of individual collectors and/or dealers with varying requirements and buying power. Although buyers who represent museums may pay as much as a million dollars, or more, for a rare old master, the bread-and-butter business of most auctions depends on more modest demands. Multimillion dollar purchases are highly dramatic and well publicized, but the major portion of auction-house transactions consists of sales to small purchasers. "Of the 250,000 items sold at Sotheby's

Dion Bouton tricycle built in 1895 fetched the same price, and a ceremonial carriage built for King Louis XIV brought $4,400 ("$40,000 Bid for Old Auto," *Christian Science Monitor,* Aug. 13, 1966, p. 3).

auctions last year [1965], three-quarters sold for $280 or less, and a third of the items cost under $56." [6]

Perhaps the most significant aspect of demand at auction sales is the existence of separate demands for each of the items making up the total stock. Of 150 persons, say, at an auction, probably only a few are interested in any one item. Thus the auction is really a series of sales in which limited numbers of bidders—two, at a minimum—want to buy each item. A large number of people in attendance is significant only to the extent that it increases the chances that there will be two or more individuals to bid on each item.

Figure 3 depicts the segmented demand situation characterizing most auctions. Each square, identified by a different roman numeral, indicates one bidder. It is important to note that this chart represents only one individual sales transaction, the sale of item X. The chart reveals that only a few individuals—buyers I, VII, XI, XXIV, XXVI—are interested in item X, though buyers XXII and XXVIII may also enter bids. Moreover, those who do exhibit interest possess differing intensities of desire.

Obviously, the interest of would-be buyers varies considerably from one item to another. If the suggested starting price evokes no bidding, the auctioneer will pass the item, or, if no interest at all develops at any price, the item will be withdrawn or may even be given away. For example, in an auction of unclaimed merchandise held by a storage company in the Los Angeles area, a mattress was offered for sale. When it called forth no bids, the auctioneer offered it in exchange for payment of the sterilization fee. Receiving no response, and having been instructed to get rid of everything, he finally gave the mattress away to a member of the crowd who was willing to accept it.

Sometimes the demand for items offered for sale is so small, and so little interest is expressed, that the auction fails as a price-making mechanism. In an auction of carpets which I attended, the few customers were spread so thinly over the various offerings that within a few minutes the auctioneer switched to a fixed, or take-it-or-leave-it, price sale. Each customer for a particular item was dealt with on an individual basis. Had the few customers present been

6 Ray Vicker, "How To Sell a Seurat: London Art Houses Thrive as Prices Soar," *Wall Street Journal*, June 24, 1966, p. 22.

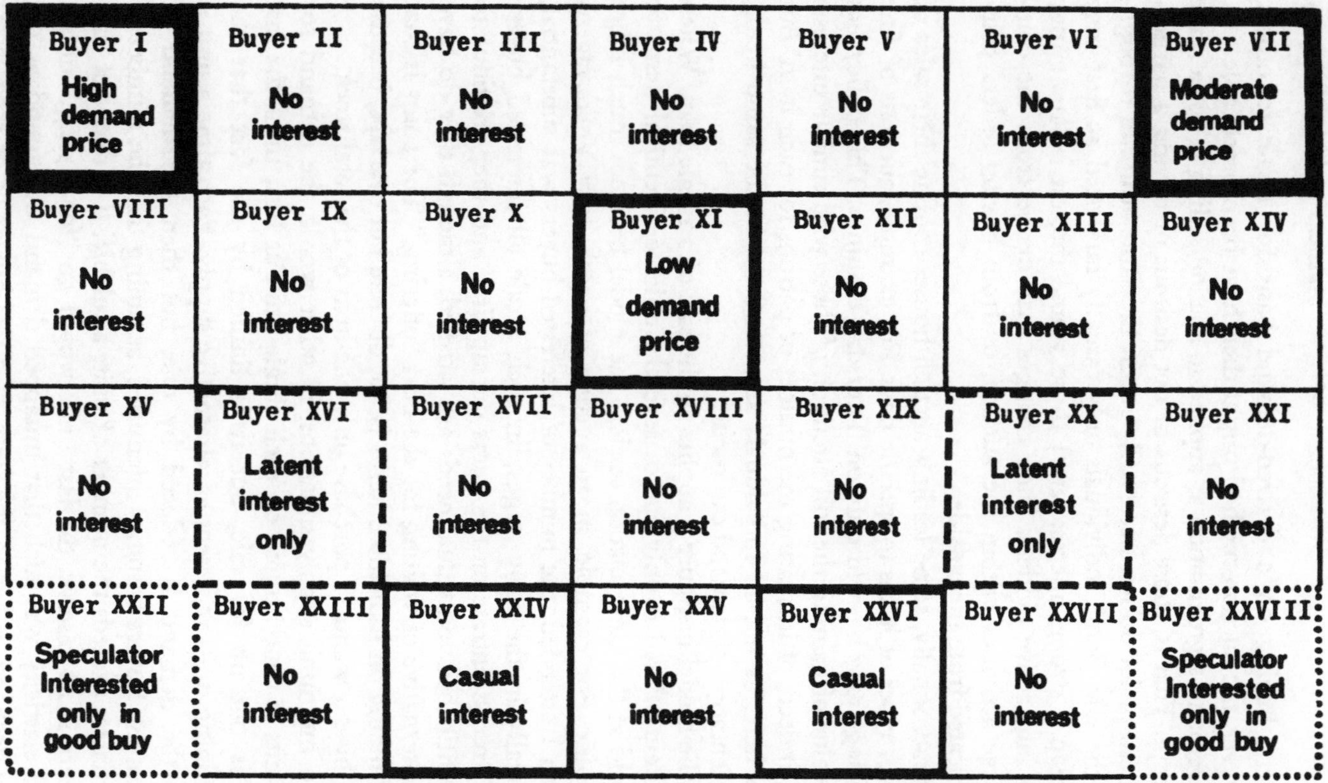

Buyer I High demand price	Buyer II No interest	Buyer III No interest	Buyer IV No interest	Buyer V No interest	Buyer VI No interest	Buyer VII Moderate demand price
Buyer VIII No interest	Buyer IX No interest	Buyer X No interest	Buyer XI Low demand price	Buyer XII No interest	Buyer XIII No interest	Buyer XIV No interest
Buyer XV No interest	Buyer XVI Latent interest only	Buyer XVII No interest	Buyer XVIII No interest	Buyer XIX No interest	Buyer XX Latent interest only	Buyer XXI No interest
Buyer XXII Speculator Interested only in good buy	Buyer XXIII No interest	Buyer XXIV Casual interest	Buyer XXV No interest	Buyer XXVI Casual interest	Buyer XXVII No interest	Buyer XXVIII Speculator Interested only in good buy

Fig. 3 Model of the demand for item X, one of various types of items up for sale at a single auction session.

dealers, buying on a derived-demand basis for resale to others, however, the auction method might then have been practicable.

Demand segmentation as applied to auction selling is not a static concept. That is, those desirous or not desirous of buying a particular item or lot do not necessarily retain the same attitudes throughout the sale. Some individuals only casually interested at first may develop a strong interest later; those whose interest is latent may turn into active bidders. Such changes may derive from the competitive activities within the auction, or from buying orders communicated from the outside.

Traditionally, some leading auction houses confine their sales of certain types of items to specific days. For example, auctions of fine paintings may be held only on Thursday evenings. This policy has the value of gaining the full attention of those with similar interests and, indeed, of increasing the number of patrons for each item. But even here, as not all individuals are interested in the same items, segmentation of demand can occur.

The model in figure 3 applies to the sale of a single item. When the item offered is only one of several similar or identical items to be sold at the same auction session, the model becomes much more complex. For example, in an auction of nearly new Volkswagens which I attended, the number of interested buyers was substantial, especially in the early stages; in such a sale all interested buyers tend to concentrate on the items put up first, and they continue to bid until their individual needs are satisfied, although they do have the alternative of waiting for the next "offering." The point is that the bidding on individual items is not discrete but overlaps, because each bidder wants to purchase only one item of the total stock.

In multiunit supply situations, in other words, the demand for all units is concentrated on each single unit, at least until the last one is put up for sale, but it is limited by the fact that the remaining units represent an alternative supply. Each time a unit is sold the demand is reduced by one, but then the demand of remaining buyers becomes intensified, assuming that the number of purchasers exceeds the number of units available. If it does not, and if there is no reserve, the last units would go "for a song," unless price elasticity was such that untapped demand was found as the price declined, either in the form of direct buyers or of speculators purchasing for resale. No precise analysis is possible, because the number of would-be buyers, the intensity of their desire, and their strategies are unknown. Figure 4 depicts this complex behavioral pattern in graphic form.

Some individual buyers have higher demand prices than others, even though they perform similar functions (that is, they may all be dealers). When both dealers and collectors are present at an auction

Buyer I Intensive interest	Buyer II Some interest	Buyer III No interest	Buyer IV Moderate interest	Buyer V No interest	Buyer VI Intensive interest
Buyer VII Moderate interest	Buyer VIII Latent interest	Buyer IX Some interest	Buyer X Some interest	Buyer XI No interest	Buyer XII Latent interest
Buyer XIII Moderate interest	Buyer XIV Intensive interest	Buyer XV Some interest	Buyer XVI Latent interest	Buyer XVII Intensive interest	Buyer XVIII Moderate interest
Buyer XIX Some interest	Buyer XX Moderate interest	Buyer XXI Latent interest	Buyer XXII Some interest	Buyer XXIII Moderate interest	Buyer XXIV Latent interest
Buyer XXV Speculator Interested only in good buy	Buyer XXVI Intensive interest	Buyer XXVII Latent interest	Buyer XXVIII No interest	Buyer XXIX Intensive interest	Buyer XXX Speculator Interested only in good buy

Fig. 4 Model of the demand for a particular unit of the total of similar items up for sale in a multiunit auction.

of antiques, for example, the demand prices of the latter are likely to be higher than those of the former, who have to add on a commission, assuming that each is fully informed. The strategy of some collectors, indeed, may be to watch astute dealers and then outbid them at the crucial moment, knowing that they must allow for the dealer's margin in the price they bid.

In attempting to purchase goods at an auction, the would-be buyer should be aware of the number of items on which he is bidding. It is the custom of some galleries to display only a small sample of a lot composed of numerous identical objects. When the contents of the old Ritz-Carlton Hotel were sold at auction in New York several years ago, a newspaperman bid on a lot consisting, he thought, of two small smoking stands, but upon settling his bill discovered "to his dismay" that he had actually purchased more than a hundred of them.[7]

Competition

Competition, the third key factor in price making by the auction method, is in some ways the most important of all. It manifests itself in two ways: as competition among sellers for consignments and clients, and as competition among buyers for the goods that are up for sale.

Competition among sellers.—Competition on the selling side is of two different, although related, types. First, auction houses must compete for consignments from vendors who want to sell their property. This type of competition is usually very keen, and liberal use may be made of various types of sales promotional efforts. Heavy reliance is placed either on direct personal contact with owners of goods or other property, on telephonic communication with them, or on both. Sometimes, as in the case of livestock, most of the efforts are made before the owner-vendor has sold any goods through the auction company; from then on the negotiations may be more or less routine. On the other hand, the problem of obtaining consignments of antiques is a recurring one, and the competitive action is likely to be incessant. In a cooperative operation (such as selling fish at auction), after the original effort to obtain members the flow of goods through the auction is almost automatic.

In the obtaining of consignments, auction firms may employ price competition to some extent by adjusting the fees they charge for selling merchandise. The standard list of charges may be adjusted in accordance with changing competitive conditions, but concessions may also be made if they appear advantageous to the auction company. Some auction firms probably adhere strictly to schedules of commission rates, but a new company attempting to get a foothold in a market or to increase its share of business is likely to resort to discriminatory treatment favoring reluctant con-

7 "How To Go to an Auction," *House and Garden,* CIX (May, 1956), 208.

signors. Intensive competition, extending to the departure from normal rate charges, prevails among top auction houses seeking the consignment of art treasures. When Sotheby's and Parke-Bernet were competing for the sale of the Erickson paintings, including Rembrandt's "Aristotle Contemplating the Bust of Homer," it is said that Parke-Bernet, in order to obtain the selling commission, made a substantial concession to the Erickson estate in the form of a lower percentage fee.[8]

Although the quality and the quantity of the goods assembled for sale by an auction firm help to attract interested dealers and direct buyers, the success of a sale is not assured simply by having outstanding offerings. Competition for patrons exists among auction houses as well as between auction houses and other types of marketers. It is not usually manifested in the prices charged for goods, as in nonauction sales, because auction prices are buyer-made.

Competition for patronage at auctions has to take a different form. Some auction houses attempt to outdo their competitors in providing comfortable facilities for patrons.[9] Choice of location and the timing of the sale are extremely important, as is also effective publicizing. Various forms of advertising may be employed, including the use of newspaper space, appeals by mail, and direct contact with key dealers and buyers. If the auction is a regular event—weekly or even daily sessions are held during the season—and a more or less standardized commodity is to be sold, publicity is less essential.

Competition among buyers.—Of the large number of would-be buyers assembled at a typical auction, a relatively small proportion are likely to be interested in a single item. If the seller is to obtain maximum returns for his offerings, however, there must be at least

8 According to Brough (*op. cit.,* p. 14), "Unquestionably, Hyam [of Parke-Bernet] surrendered a considerable part of his galleries' usual commission, which would otherwise have amounted to a staggering twenty per cent of the $4,679,250 which the collection brought under the hammer. . . . In London, aggrieved national pride led one national newspaper to speculate that Hyam had sacrificed every dime in commissions and was willing to carry out the job for the sake of prestige alone. When confronted with this, Hyam snapped, 'Nonsense!' "

9 "Cattle Auction Barn Profits by Keeping Customers Cool—and Warm," *Air Conditioning, Heating & Refrigeration News,* Sept. 11, 1961, p. 12.

two competing buyers. Indeed, there should be two or more with high demand prices, for a would-be buyer will pay no more than necessary for an item he wishes to acquire, no matter how high his demand price. Competition between or among bidders is thus the key factor in forcing auction prices upward.

Nevertheless, the optimum results may not be achieved in any one transaction, because interested buyers have different demand prices, and the demand price of the underbidder may be well below that of the high bidder. If the former drops out when his level is reached, the high bidder does not have to go to his maximum demand price. Underbidders, however, may have supplementary motives for bidding the price up. Some dealer-bidders want to force competitors to buy at high prices at auction, and thus bid up an item or lot considerably above the underbidder's highest demand price. This tactic is found in antique auctions, but it is particularly prevalent in the sale of commodities such as fish, for a dealer who has just purchased goods at a particular price cannot afford to allow competitors to acquire supplies at a lower price and undersell him in the secondary market. Such individuals, of course, take a chance that this tactic will backfire, and they will find themselves in possession of unneeded merchandise at a disadvantageous price. Some auction systems (to be described in detail in chaps. 5 and 6) exert more pressure than others in forcing prices toward the highest demand price of the high bidder.

Under certain conditions there is no buyer competition at auctions. A lack of buyer interest in a particular item may manifest itself in the presence of only one buyer, or indeed of no buyers. In an oligopsonistic situation it is unlikely that buyers will bid against one another. The failure to bid competitively may be due to collusion among interested buyers (to be discussed later). Whatever the reason, the absence of intensive buyer competition, though bound to have a depressing effect on prices, does not necessarily mean that prices will collapse. Buyers realize that in the longer run abnormally low prices tend to reduce, or dry up, the flow of supplies (of fish, for example).

In some markets, however (the British country auctions, for example), a buyer representing a ring is apt to give little thought to an adverse effect on supply, and thus may attempt to depress the price to very low levels. Yet even in such instances competition, by ring members or others, may be promoted at lower price levels in order to prevent auction officials from suspecting the existence of collusive activity. As a result, of course, the ring may have to pay a slightly higher price than would have been necessary without the simulated competition.

It is characteristic of auctions that buyers seek to reduce competition, and sellers, to intensify competition. Buyers try by various means to relieve the competitive pressure so as to keep prices under control, whereas sellers seek to enhance such pressure. The resulting tug-of-war may go first one way and then the other; the outcome is difficult to predict. On the one hand, competition may tend to smooth out price fluctuations because of the attempt to resist an adverse change; or, on the other, it may accelerate fluctuations because of the continual jockeying of contending parties for better competitive positions.

The Principal Auction Systems

5 OF THE innumerable auction systems in use throughout the world, none is precisely the same as any other. The systems are, however, classifiable into a limited number of types,[1] of which three are the most important.

The English (Ascending-Bid) Auction

The most familiar type of auction—at least in the United States—is the English system; it is the most commonly used auction scheme in English-speaking countries. Interestingly enough, many Americans, even those actively engaged in auctioning, are not aware of the existence of other systems.

The principle of the ascending-bid selling scheme is very simple: the auctioneer seeks an initial bid from one of the assembled buyers with the expectation that those interested in the item or lot will bid against one another

---

[1] Some students of auctioning choose to classify auctions, not in the broad sense I am here employing, but in much narrower terms. They would include among their categories auctions advertised as reserve-price sales, those advertised as unreserved sales, and those not indicated as either. This scheme is perfectly sound, but inasmuch as the reserve-price criterion is applicable not only to the English-type auction, but to others as well, it is not a proper basis, in my opinion, for the classification of auction systems.

until all but the highest bidder are eliminated. If there is no reserve price, or if the last bid equals or exceeds the reserve figure, the item or lot is knocked down to the one remaining bidder. Figure 5 depicts the functioning of this system.

Despite its basic simplicity, in practice the English auction system is quite complex. Bidders vie with one another at successively higher prices for the right to purchase property that is up for sale. There may be numerous bids at lower price levels, with the number of competing bidders normally declining as the bid level increases. It is the auctioneer's duty to recognize one bidder at each level, and to announce the amount of the bid, in order to establish a basis for increased bids. As the auction progresses toward the climax, all but one would-be buyer usually retire, and the high bidder then acquires title to the property, although tie bids are possible.

The initial step is to obtain an opening bid by soliciting a bid from the audience and waiting for an offer to be made. As this process may be very time-consuming, an auctioneer often suggests a specific amount—for example, "Who will give me fifty dollars?" If he gets no response, he may lower the figure until he obtains a starting bid. He then obtains further bids, ultimately advancing the price considerably beyond the point at which he first attempted to open the bidding. When the auctioneer is proceeding on a reserve-price basis, he will withdraw the item if no bid he deems adequate is forthcoming; when there is no reserve price, he will do the same if he receives no bid within a reasonable length of time.

Although the auctioneer usually tries to find a starting price that is acceptable to some buyer, he may instead start at a specific price and move up without regard for actual bids in the hope of bringing in one or more traders at higher levels. In fact, an outstanding continental auctioneer with whom I am acquainted uses precisely this procedure, perhaps because he is an excellent judge of values and obtains the finest consignments in his market. An auctioneer operating in this manner must, however, occasionally withdraw items because they remain unsold by the time the reserve-price level is reached.

A complicating factor in an ascending-bid auction is the fact that often the bids are not made by open outcry, but are indicated surreptitiously. Signaled bids (discussed at length in chapter 11) take various forms, such as "a tug at the ear, a wink of the eye." The use

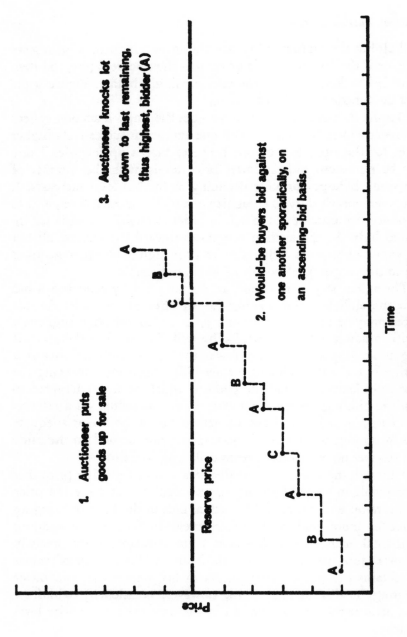

Fig. 5 English (ascending-bid) auction.

of signals in bidding has numerous advantages. Auction rooms would be bedlam if bidders' voices were relied on to execute bids. Also, audible bids increase the chances of error, for it is difficult to catch all the bids when everybody is calling out at the same time. Moreover, some traders may not wish to disclose their hand.

Once the decision is made to employ signals, a system of price intervals must be introduced so that the seller and the buyer know exactly what the signals mean. Sometimes the intervals are fixed in amount, as in tobacco and livestock auctions in the United States. Advances, however, may vary at different price levels, or even at the same price level for different offerings. In certain situations the auctioneer has wide discretion in the advances sought. For example, in antique auctions in London he calls actual bids only, and, when a bidder offers to advance, determines the amount of the increment and enunciates the bid. The advances are determined on a basis of the price level at which the bidding is taking place, combined with the prospective sale price of the item. In a sense, a would-be buyer is bidding blindly, because he does not know, until the auctioneer announces it, the exact amount of his bid or what the advance in fact was.

Much of the complexity of a signal system is eliminated by the technique of leading the bidder, particularly in American auctions that are heavily patronized by collectors. The auctioneer leads the bidders by calling out not only the amount of the bid he has in hand but the amount he is seeking as well. Even the tyro may intelligently participate in this kind of bidding. On the contrary, in some auctions, especially those in England, the auctioneer makes no attempt to lead the bidders, but relies on the market knowledge of the participants to guide them in their bidding.

In the ascending-bid auction, buyer competition is at its maximum intensity level. (Buyers may, of course, decide to collude rather than compete. See chapter 13.) Moreover, an auctioneer can exert considerable influence on the price achieved, possibly more than in any other type of auction. The English-type auction is so structured that competition among individual buyers is more overt than in other auction systems, and the auctioneer has more opportunities to use manipulative tactics. The auctioneer's influence depends in part on his personality, his voice, and his imperturbability, but he must also know values, must be skillful in stimulating competition, and must be able to accelerate the selling pace when the occasion requires it.

The Dutch (Descending-Price) Auction

The Dutch system, instead of starting at a relatively low price level and ascending by steps until only one bidder remains, follows a descending-price pattern. The auctioneer determines the starting figure and quotes prices at descending intervals until someone bids the item in. The prices enunciated are thus simply invitations to buyers to bid, and the first bidder is the high, or the successful, bidder. In this system would-be buyers vie with one another just as they do in the English system, for the individual having an intensive desire for the item must register his bid before others similarly motivated have a chance to do so. Each bidder is competing against his perception of the competitive structure facing him at the moment. The Dutch auction system is shown in diagrammatic form in figure 6.

The descending-price scheme may be implemented either by the human voice, or electronically by the Dutch clock, so called, although the two methods are identical in principle. (Discussion of the electronic method is reserved for chapter 14.) The oral method is used not only in Holland, but in some other Continental, and even British, communities, in certain Middle Eastern countries, and elsewhere. It is interesting that the Dutch auction method is utilized in the sale of fish in Hull, England, while the English system is employed in Grimsby, just across the Humber River.

The key aspect of the Dutch auction system is the calling of hypothetical prices on a downward scale at predetermined intervals with the expectation that a would-be buyer will bid the item in before the prices decline too far. The auctioneer must start the quotation at a sufficiently high level to permit the bidder with the highest demand price to register his maximum bid. On the other hand, he should not start too high, particularly in market situations where speed is essential. Normally the auctioneer does not cajole or otherwise influence the bidders. After selecting the starting point, he calls out the prices at successively lower levels, recognizes the first and high bidder, and announces the amount of the successful bid and the name of the buyer. Ordinarily, the first bid is the only

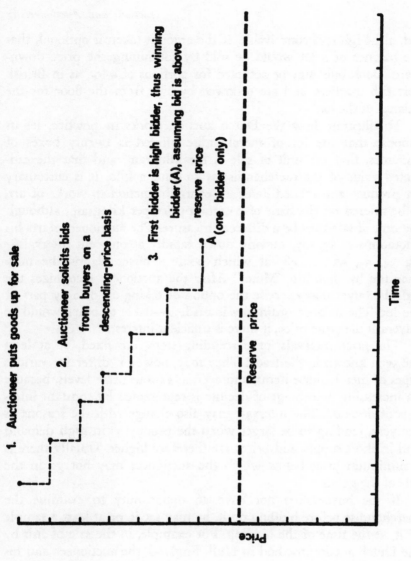

1. Auctioneer puts goods up for sale

2. Auctioneer solicits bids from buyers on a descending-price basis

3. First bidder is high bidder, thus winning bidder(A), assuming bid is above reserve price

A (one bidder only)

Reserve price

Price

Time

Fig. 6 Dutch (descending-price) auction.

bid, although it is conceivable, if the amount taken is optional, that the balance of a lot would be sold by continuing the price downward. Book bids may be accepted for portions of a lot, as in British port fish markets, and are followed by bids from the floor for the balance of the lot.[2]

To illustrate how the Dutch auction works in practice, let us suppose that the lot of merchandise offered is twenty boxes of tomatoes, that the unit of sale is the kilogram, and that the estimated value of the merchandise is 50 cents a kilo. It is customary for produce and related items, in contradistinction to works of art, to be offered on the basis of a certain price per kilogram, although the unit of sale may be a different measure. The auctioneer starts his quotations at 55, say, moving down rapidly at one-cent intervals—55, 54, 53, 52 . . . 48—at which point a buyer claims the merchandise by shouting "Mine!" After the auctioneer recognizes the bid, the buyer may exercise the option of taking all or only part of the lot. The balance ordinarily is made available to other would-be buyers at the same price, if there is sufficient interest.

The price intervals, or descending steps, are fixed, or at least are well known in the trade. They may, however, differ for various types of merchandise items, and even at various price levels, because an increasing percentage of decline is represented by constant intervals of decrease. The intervals may also change with the seasons of the year, tending to be larger when the product is in high demand and in short supply and prices are therefore higher. Usually there is a minimum price below which the auctioneer may not go in the sale of the goods.

If the buyer does not have an opportunity to examine the merchandise before bidding on it, he may see it, or at least a sample of it, at the time of the bidding. For example, in the sale of fish by the Dutch auction method in Hull, England, the auctioneer and his staff and the buyers move from one lot to another as the auction progresses, some standing in aisles, some on boxes of fish. In Dutch auctions in Holland, the goods are displayed in front of the seated

2 By the use of book bids, the auctioneer may practice a form of running by announcing the award to the book bidder before he gets to the book bidder's price level. This procedure gives the assembled buyers the impression that the bid was higher than it actually was, and may enhance the prices bid by subsequent purchasers.

buyers as the bidding takes place. In a descending-price auction of fresh fish in Israel, the merchandise is offered in lots consisting of boxes containing a certain number of kilos of a specified variety. The fish are carried on a moving belt from the storeroom past the buyers, who can thus see the offerings as the auctioneer starts calling the descending numbers.

The oral method of the Dutch auctioning system (but not the clock method) is used mainly for the sale of nonstandardized items where quality differences require flexibility. In the early days, the descending-price system was more commonly employed in Holland than it is today in the auctioning of art treasures. Now the English or ascending-bid system is preferred, except by a few firms.[3]

It has been argued that one advantage of the descending auction system is that it makes impracticable the colluding of buyers to depress prices. This contention is, in my opinion, without merit. Theoretically, it is quite possible for buyers to cooperate by the same sort of agreement that is utilized in the English system—merely an understanding among several buyers that they will not compete against one another. Because the bidder acting for the combination knows the others will not attempt to get ahead of him, he may let the price slip to levels that would be impossible without the agreement. As a practical matter, however, buyer collusion, although not unknown in Dutch auction markets, poses no serious problem.

One question remains: Are buyers subject to competitive pressure under the Dutch system? The answer is that they experience as much pressure as do buyers in the English system, although it is covert rather than overt. It may even be argued that competitive pressure is stronger in the Dutch system than in the English, because a buyer in the descending-bid system, especially one who is determined to acquire an item, may overestimate his competition.

The Japanese (Simultaneous-Bidding) Auction

One of the auction schemes utilized in the sale of fish in Japan, at least in Greater Tokyo, is what I have designated the "simultaneous-bidding" system. Its distinctive aspect is that all bids are

3 See James Henry Duveen, *Art Treasures and Intrigue* (Garden City, N.Y.: Doubleday, Doran, 1935), pp. 27, 28.

made by prospective buyers at the same time, or approximately the same time, using individual hand signs for each monetary unit. Theoretically, all the bids are made simultaneously, but as a practical matter it takes several seconds for bidders to get their hands in the air and the auctioneer to read the signs. The bidding starts as soon as the auctioneer gives the signal, and the highest bidder, as determined by the auctioneer, is awarded the lot. This auction system is shown in figure 7.

Bidders are expected to register their maximum bids within the limited time provided for the purpose. Although bids are registered simultaneously, some bidders manage to raise their bids within the allotted time after seeing the signals of others. As the rules do not preclude the raising of bids, the time element is crucial in determining whether the system is in fact one of simultaneous or ascending bids.

Before assembling for the auction, buyers in the Tokyo fish market spend considerable time examining the merchandise to be offered that day. The lots of fish, identified by number, are displayed on the docks; each buyer may record in a notebook the lots in which he is interested, including alternative choices. The simultaneous-bidding auction, more so perhaps than either the English or the Dutch auction, is characterized by a great deal of noise and confusion, much of it stemming from the efforts of scores of bidders to gain the attention of the auctioneer. The din is increased by the auctioneer's attempts to get the bidding underway and then designating the high bidder by repeatedly announcing his name and the amount of his bid.

At the time set for starting the auction, which may be as early as 5 A.M., would-be buyers take their positions in an amphitheater made of roughhewn timber. When the buzzer rings for the beginning of the sale, all assembled buyers are given an opportunity to bid on successive lots as they are put up for sale. The auctioneer importunes the buyers to bid as he auctions each lot, and each buyer orally attempts to draw attention to his own bid which he is registering by finger signs. The confusion calls to mind the frenzied trading by brokers in the stock market, except that there is only one auctioneer in the simultaneous-bidding system.

Each of the hand signs used in a Japanese auction represents a number from 1 to 9 (see illustrations). Two- or three-digit numbers

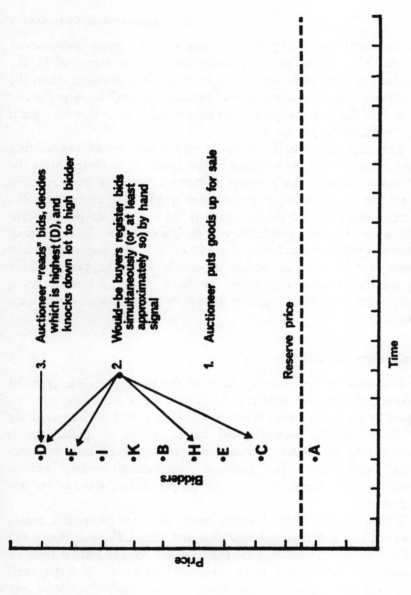

3. Auctioneer "reads" bids, decides which is highest (D), and knocks down lot to high bidder

2. Would-be buyers register bids simultaneously (or at least approximately so) by hand signal

1. Auctioneer puts goods up for sale

Bidders

Price

Reserve price

Time

Fig. 7 Japanese (simultaneous-bidding) auction.

are indicated by rapidly repeated signs, or by more complicated signals. The use of two-digit numbers is quite common in the purchase of fish, but is not always necessary. For instance, when the auctioneer and the bidders know the bidding level for a particular lot of fish, the bids may be in part inferential. The man who signals a 3 may be bidding at 300 yen.

This auction system is potentially very fast. Simultaneous bidding saves time, and no examination of the goods is permitted after the preauction display. An inexpert auctioneer could, of course, cause delay, but it is amazing to realize how quickly the auctioneers can interpret the bids and decide which is the highest, simply by scanning a sea of hands, particularly if double or triple signs are used. Because speed is essential in the sale of fish, the auctioneer must knock each lot down as quickly as possible. In Osaka, Japan, where the simultaneous-bidding system has been utilized for some years, finger signs have been replaced in part by an electronic device (see chap. 14).

Applicability and Efficiency

Empirical evidence reveals that, of the three principal types of auctions, the English system is by far the most common. An estimated 75 percent, or even more, of all the auctions in the world are conducted on the ascending-bid basis. Second in popularity is undoubtedly the Dutch auction, with its heavy reliance on electronic mechanisms. The Japanese simultaneous-bidding system comes in a poor third, although its full potentialities are as yet untapped.

The prevalence of the English system does not necessarily mean, however, that it is more efficient than the others. For one thing, the tasks to be performed may be better suited to one system than to another. In the second place, environmental and perhaps even hereditary conditions in certain countries may make the use of one system more practicable than the use of another.

The relative effectiveness of the three systems may depend also on their price-level potentials. From this point of view the English system may be inferior to the Dutch system, in at least one particular. The key to a successful auction is the effect of competition on the bids of would-be buyers. Usually the underbidder in the English system forces the bidder with a high demand price up only one step, or increment, above his own highest demand price, which may be considerably below the high bidder's maximum. In the Dutch system, however, if the bidder with the highest demand price really wants the goods, he cannot wait too long to enter his bid lest he endanger his chance of gaining the award. He thus may bid at or near his highest demand price. The difference may not be significant if bidders are numerous and their highest demand prices do not differ widely. In this situation there may be little choice between the two systems, at least from the seller's point of view.

Another element that makes it difficult to assess the relative price levels attainable under different systems is the effect of open competition in bidding. At this stage of our understanding of a complex subject, it is impossible to say that the open bidding of the English system is better than the covert bidding of the Dutch system. Japanese simultaneous bidding is also a kind of "blind" system, although, where hand signs are employed, bidders can determine the amounts of rival bids if their eyes are quick enough. If they do not have time to look, they bid without knowing how much they *must* bid in order to beat the other fellow. The Japanese system, then, would appear to be much like the Dutch system, insofar as resulting price levels are concerned. Theoretically, the former may yield higher prices than the latter because of the excitement it generates.

Despite technical differences, each of the three principal auction systems has a high-speed potential, and thus presumably can be used for sales tasks when the time element is important. This feature comes into bold relief in contrast with the inherent slowness of most other auction schemes.

Other Auction Systems

6 IN ADDITION to the three principal auctioning systems, there are a number of others which I have termed "haphazard" bidding schemes, including written-bid, handshake, and whispered-bid procedures. There are also miscellaneous auctioning methods that do not readily fall into any one category.

Haphazard Bidding Systems

In these haphazard bidding schemes, bids are secretly communicated by would-be buyers to the auctioneer, who considers them but does not publicize them to the other bidders. Each entrant is thus bidding blindly. Figure 8 illustrates the operation of this type of auction.

Written-bid auction.—In this system, sometimes called the "tender" scheme or, in other contexts, the "dumb"-bidding auction, all bids are made in writing and deposited with an auction official. In principle the method resembles the sealed-bid system used in the awarding of construction contracts. Those who bid for construction jobs, however, are sellers, not buyers, and they have a longer time to decide on the size of their bids. Weeks or even months may elapse between the invitation to bid and the awarding of a contract, whereas those who submit written bids in an auction have at most a few minutes.

The written-bid auction system is utilized in several primary fish markets in Japan. The procedure at one of them, in Tokyo, shows how this type of auction works. Wholesale vendors who specialize in dried fish display their wares, and would-be buyers are invited

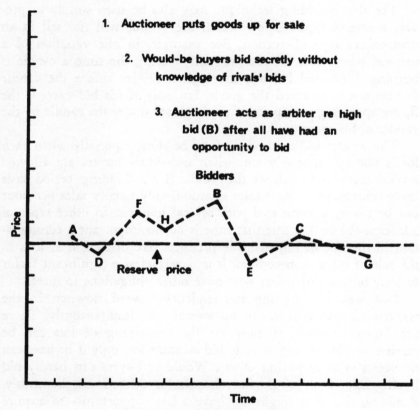

Fig. 8 Haphazard-bidding auction.

to make offers in an orderly manner on any lot within a particular group. Each potential purchaser writes the amount of his bid and the lot or lots to which his offer applies on a slip of paper containing an identifying watermark. The bids are then deposited in a box or handed to the auctioneer. After the time interval allowed for filing the bids has expired, the auctioneer announces the successful bidder, provided that the maximum bid equals or exceeds any reserve price that may have been set on the goods. Bidders may or may not bid on all the lots within a particular group, but the auctioneer is expected to maximize the total revenue for all the lots. Hence, the prices paid by a successful bidder on certain individual lots within the group may be lower than those paid by bidders who bid on only one lot.

The dumb-bidding technique may also be used simply to provide a reserve figure below which the vendor will not sell in an open-outcry type of auction. For example, in one variation of a method where bids are accepted only during the time a candle is burning (discussed below), the highest bidder before the candle flickers out is awarded the goods, but only if his bid exceeds the figure appearing on a piece of paper placed under the candle by the vendor or his agent.

The written-bid method tends to be slow, especially when each lot is put up separately and when individual buyers are allowed several minutes to submit their bids. If the bidding period lasts three minutes in a single sales situation, only twenty sales per hour can be made, as compared with several hundred in other types of auctions. While it is true that time is not so important a consideration in the sale of imperishable products like dried fish as it is in the sale of other commodities, it is nevertheless a significant factor to busy buyers and sellers who have other obligations to meet.

One way of offsetting the tendency toward slowness in the written-bid system is to put up several lots simultaneously. There are limits, however, to how far the combining of lots can be carried, as a buyer may want to bid on some lots only if he has been unsuccessful in acquiring others. Would-be buyers can hardly bid intelligently if all of the merchandise is offered simultaneously. Realizing that they might not have a later opportunity to acquire needed supplies, they may overbid on some or all of the lots.

Written bids are occasionally utilized in auctions of art treasures in the United States, and even in the sale of real property. The technique does appear to have limited applicability, however. One disadvantage is that the bidder has no flexibility; if he wants to be sure of obtaining the goods, he must bid high. In contrast, he could probably obtain the goods for less under the English system, for he would have to bid only one step higher than his competitors' highest bids. Some flexibility is introduced under a plan, which is actually utilized in certain market situations, permitting each bidder to submit two bids rather than one. His higher bid goes into effect only if his lower bid does not exceed the bids of competitors,[1] but the award is made on the basis of the lower figure if it is higher than the highest bid of competitors.

This principle might be extended to provide for three or even more bids from each bidder, thus giving the bidder wider latitude. For example, three bidders—A, B, and C—each bidding at three price levels, might turn in the following amounts:

Level of bid	Bidder A	Bidder B	Bidder C
Highest	$4.00	$4.50	$6.00
Medium	3.00	3.50	5.00
Lowest	2.00	2.50	4.00

Obviously bidder C is the winner with his second-highest bid of $5.00, as this figure exceeds the highest bids of A and B.

The contention that the written-bid or tender scheme is not actually an auction carries little weight, unless it can be successfully argued that no secret-bid system of any kind is an auction. The written-bid system appears to be just as much of an auction as the whispered-bid or the handshake method. In my opinion they are all auction systems of a sort, although admittedly it is difficult to differentiate precisely between competitive-bid systems and auctions.

Handshake auction.—One of the oldest auctioning schemes I know of is that in which would-be buyers communicate their bids to the auctioneer by the squeezing of fingers. Said to have had its origins in China centuries ago, this method was utilized until recently in the sale of dried fish in Karachi, Pakistan. One can picture a group of potential buyers arranged in a semicircle, each in turn having an opportunity to clasp the hand of the auctioneer and register his bid. Under cover of a piece of cloth, the bidder indicates the amount he is offering by pressing a certain number of the

1 See *Rex* v. *Taylor*, M'Cle. 362, 148 E.R. 151 (1824), in which such a scheme was employed in an auction operation, the case turning on whether the sale was, in fact, a public auction. See also *The King* v. *Chapman*, 3 Anst. 811 (1796–97), involving a similar issue.

auctioneer's fingers at the same moment that he announces a monetary unit, first "tens," then "rupees," then "anas." The auctioneer mentally calculates the amount of each bid, and then, after each participant has had a chance to make an offer, announces the successful bidder. As the sale price may be kept secret, the auctioneer has a great deal of discretion; not only may he make arbitrary decisions favoring one buyer over another, but he may not always act in the best interests of the producer.

It might be supposed that buyers would be restricted by the five-finger limitation in registering the amount of their bids. Bidding flexibility can be obtained, however, by the use of multiple squeezes. Because the auctioneer does not reveal the bids he receives, would-be buyers do not know whether their offers are lower or higher than others. The pattern of bidding is therefore haphazard.

In order to mislead competitors, who can hear the words spoken and thus draw certain inferences, a bidder in the handshake system may resort to subterfuge. For example, if he wants to give the impression that his bid is lower than it actually is, he may grasp the whole hand including the thumb, instead of just the fingers as in the normal practice, while repeating the denomination (for example, "tens"). Conversely, he may grasp fewer fingers but repeat the squeezing process if he wishes to suggest that he is making a higher bid. If the bidder wants to convey the idea that he is bidding when he is not, he may take the auctioneer's hand and make a bid, but may cancel it by scratching the hand with his index finger as he announces the denomination.

Dealers in Karachi strongly contend that the handshake system is fair to both buyers and producers and that it protects their respective interests. The only purpose of the secrecy, they say, is to avoid "unhealthy competition" among fish experts and merchants. One knowledgeable informant, however, long familiar with the Karachi fish market, feels that auctioneer-agents can manipulate prices in their favor and against producers, and that they can perhaps designate successful purchasers in advance by prior collusive arrangements.

Even when completely straightforward, however, this auction method possesses serious limitations for the buyer. Most important, perhaps, is the time-consuming aspect of the procedure, which in many markets would be a fatal flaw. For various reasons, including opposition by government authorities, the handshake auction was discontinued in Karachi in 1959, and was replaced by the English, or ascending-bid, auction.

Whispered-bid auction.—In this system the auctioneer announces that the goods are up for sale, and would-be buyers approach him and whisper offers in his ear. The fact that bids are whispered rather than called out or signaled is very significant, because each bidder makes an offer without any information about the bids of others. Again the bids, having no pattern, are haphazard.

I found the whispered-bid auction system only in fish markets in Singapore, Manila, Venice, and Chioggia, where it was practiced by numerous competing vendors rather than by a centralized sales agent. Because buyers can acquire supplies from a large number of sellers, it is not easy to assemble an auction crowd. Vendors often have to importune buyers to come and register their bids.

In a whispered-bid auction, as in a handshake auction, bidders transmit their bids to the auctioneer for the particular lot that is up for sale, and the auctioneer sorts them out in his mind and finally knocks the goods down to the successful bidder. The process is repeated as each lot is put up for sale. In its pure form, then, this type of auction is very time-consuming, and is practicable only in certain market situations. Speed, however, does not seem important in places where the whispered-bid scheme is practiced. The process could be hastened if the auctioneer entertained bids for several lots at one time, but then the prospective purchaser would lack information on his success or failure in bidding for some lots, information he needs in order to bid intelligently on other lots. Without such information, he may either overbuy or end up without adequate supplies.

It is difficult to isolate the reasons for the employment of whispered-bid auctioning. It is used in Singapore, allegedly at least, to enable the auctioneer to ignore the bids of particular dealers (for example, bad credit risks). Some informants have contended that the strength of the system lies in the facts that all bidders have an equal opportunity to enter their bids, regardless of their buying strength, and that the auctioneer is better informed about the demand situation. It is argued in Manila that a secret-bid system is more likely to preclude emotional reactions, but this argument suggests that the buyer has some influence on the type of auction system employed, which may not be true.

According to a fish company executive in Venice, the main, if not the only, purpose of the whispered-bid system is to give the auctioneer market information about the demand for fish, so that he can intelligently price his goods on a take-it-or-leave-it basis. In his view, it is not so much an auction as a sales plan designed to assist the vendor. The weakness in this argument is that, while the whispered-bid auction may change during a sales session to either a fixed-price or a negotiated-price system, apparently some sales are always made on a whispered-bid basis.

A competent observer in Manila has reported that the "bids are always whispered except (as far as we have observed) when a buyer may offer to buy a portion of a lot of the same class of fish, a part of which is already sold, at a price set by whispered bid in the consummated sale. This is done by a buyer pointing to a definite number of fish containers within the lot from which a number of containers are already sold by the usual whispered bids and saying something like: 'I will buy this (pointing to the containers desired) at the same price.' Other buyers may follow in the same manner and at the same price until the lot is sold out. This usually occurs when a lot of the same class of fish is big and, especially, when the morning is getting late and the remaining buyers are not as many as the auctioneer believes necessary to finish his sale for the day."

It is interesting to note that in Singapore and Manila the whispered-bid system is used at only one of the several fish markets where auctioning is employed. In Singapore the English system is utilized in one market, but with a variation from the orthodox method. When the number of traders declines to one or two, the auction is discontinued and prices are individually negotiated between buyer and seller. After a brief period of auctioning for market-testing purposes and then of individual negotiation, take-it-or-leave-it pricing may be practiced, particularly in a seller's market.

Miscellaneous Auction Systems

In addition to the ascending-bid, descending-price, simultaneous-bidding, and haphazard auctioning systems, there are some that do not clearly fall into any of these categories.

Time-interval auction.—Some ascending-bid auctions carry a proviso that all bidding must be completed within a certain time interval. The time-interval auction allows bidders a reasonable period in which to consider their bids, rather than forcing them to move precipitately. It could be used to advantage in sales of real property, where speed is not important and time for consideration may yield more and higher bids. The interval may be determined by burning a candle of specified length, or by using a sandglass or a time clock. These time-measuring devices, although relatively rare, are still used in some auction markets today. For example, in a fish auction in New Bedford, Massachusetts, would-be buyers may bid on boatloads of fish during a time limit of half an hour, the end of the period being signaled by the ringing of a bell.[2]

One of the oldest time-interval auctions is that in which a burning candle is used to measure the time within which bids may be registered by public outcry or signal. Bids are openly made on an ascending basis, in a period that may extend to thirty minutes. Under an alternative method, used in a Cornish auction, the clerk was required to insert a pin one inch from the top of the candle; as long as the pin was held firmly, bidding was permitted, but when it fell out the merchandise went to the last bidder,[3] who would presumably be the highest bidder. If, however, prospective buyers all wait until the last moment to bid, the first bidder could also be the last and high bidder. The burning-candle method of auctioning, which was prevalent in Great Britain in the latter half of the seventeenth century, was used recently in certain types of auctions. In 1932, for example, it was applied to the auctioning of an estate: "After supper an inch of candle is lit, and bidding continues until it dies out, the last [and thus highest] bid before the final flicker securing the tenancy for the ensuing year."[4]

One of the most interesting aspects of burning-candle auctions is the bidding strategy that may be employed by the would-be buyer. For example, he may offer a high price at an early stage in the proceedings in the hope of scaring off competitors.[5] In a quite

2 Donald J. White, *The New England Fishing Industry* (Cambridge, Mass.: Harvard University Press, 1954), p. 35.

3 "A Curious Survival," *The Conveyancer*, XVII (Dec., 1931), 76.

4 "A Curious Survival: Sale by Candle," *The Conveyancer*, XVII (May, 1932), 138.

5 The same strategy may be applied in a sandglass auction: "At the auction held on Tuesday last a bid of £800 was made shortly after the sand

different stratagem, he may wait until the last second to bid, hoping to get the high bid in just before the time runs out. The bidder may, in fact, be able through careful study to anticipate the final flicker of the candle, and hence prevail in the competition by topping the previous high bid at the very last moment. Indeed, Samuel Pepys mentions the use of such a strategy in his diary.[6]

In most instances, however, bidders are likely to bid actively against one another throughout the allotted time period, though there is the difficulty that all of them may adopt the strategy of waiting, with a possible jamming of bidders at the end. In an auction of toll collection rights, as "the bidders consumed free beer meantime, no advance was made on a bid [made earlier] until the sand had nearly run out for the third [and last] time."[7] If this happens, it may be very difficult to recognize the highest bidder among all those bidding at the expiration of the bidding period. It is important, in time-interval auctions, to establish a standard or minimum price advance; otherwise a buyer hoping to be the last and highest bidder might be encouraged to wait and bid the price up by only a trivial amount.

   Combination English-Dutch auction.—An interesting subtype of the Dutch auction, though basically a descending-price scheme, employs the ascending-bid principle to establish a starting position for the descending process. In Dutch auctions an important, if not the key, element is the starting figure, which ideally exceeds the highest demand price of any bidder present in order to enable the auctioneer to get the highest possible bid. The problem is not serious in commercial markets because vendors can closely approximate the market value of their goods, based on the preceding day's prices adjusted to current conditions; the quotations are then given in descending order at a price just above that figure. But

had started running through the glass for the first time, and no advance on this sum was offered during the time taken by the sand to complete its three runs—the glass, of course, being inverted immediately [after] each run was completed" ("A Curious Survival: Sale by Sand Glass," *The Conveyancer,* XVII [May, 1932], 139).

   6 See *Diary and Correspondence of Samuel Pepys, Esq., F.R.S.,* with a Life and Notes by Richard Lord Braybrooke, Deciphered, with Additional Notes, by Rev. Mynors Bright, M.A. (New York: Dodd, Mead, 1887), II, 327.

   7 "Sale by Sand Glass," *The Conveyancer,* XVIII (Aug., 1932), 20.

the solution is not so easy when specialty items, such as antiques, are being sold, for a precise market level may be nonexistent.

It is for just such a situation that this subtype of Dutch auction was devised. As a first step the auction is conducted on an ascending-bid, or English, basis, with the understanding that the high bidder will not be awarded the goods unless he remains the high bidder in the second, or Dutch, phase of the auction. To determine the starting figure, the English auction figure is often doubled, or, more precisely, the bidding starts downward from the highest price attained, with the prices in the descending phase including the maximum English-auction bid as well as the amount of the Dutch-auction bid. The attainment of a sufficiently high first-phase bid is so crucial to a successful Dutch auction that sometimes bidders in the ascending phase are encouraged by means of a small bonus, called in Holland *plok* or *plokgelden*.

Although the English-Dutch auction scheme may be useful in the sale of merchandise for which even approximate market prices are difficult to determine, its advantages over the straight English type of auction, insofar as prices are concerned, are doubtful. It is not meaningful to compare the prices established in the English phase with those finally attained in the Dutch phase, for some buyers may not bid in the first phase. If their abstention results in a lower basic price, a bidder may be able to bid the item in at a lower price in the Dutch phase than if he had bid in the initial phase. Thus the combination auction scheme may fail to produce prices higher than those attained in the pure English-type auction, for really interested buyers would not abstain in the latter. The price paid in a combination auction would exceed the price paid in an English auction only if the bidder with the highest demand price overestimated the demand prices of his competitors.

The combination scheme also possesses the distinct disadvantages of being cumbersome and time-consuming, making its use impracticable in most merchandising fields. Probably for this reason the straight English system is frequently employed in the auctioning of antiques in Amsterdam, a city that might be expected to favor some form of Dutch auction. In spite of its disadvantages, however, the combination auction is still used by some firms in the Netherlands in the auctioning of antiques.

Audible-bid rotation auction.—In the handshake auction, as practiced in Pakistan, the bids, though secretly conveyed from bidder to auctioneer, are made in rotation. The same method of receiving the bids is characteristic of some auctions in the United States, but in them the bidding is open rather than secret. This difference is significant enough to place the handshake and the audible-bid rotation systems in entirely different categories, even though the element of rotation is common to both. In the audible-bid rotation auction, where all the bidders hear all the bids, the bidding is not haphazard, as it is in the handshake auction. Rather, it follows an ascending pattern and thus may be thought of as a subtype of the English method.

The audible-bid rotation system is employed in the sale of halibut in Seattle, Washington. The commodity is put up for sale by the boatload each market day during the season to assembled buyers, if there are two or more boats, or by telephone, if there is only one. Bids are taken from individual buyers in rotation on a per-pound basis for each boatload, separate bids being made for large, medium, and small fish. The auctioneer writes the bids on a blackboard as they are received, replacing them with other figures as higher bids are made. Each bidder either raises the previous high, for at least one classification of fish, by a minimum of one-tenth of a cent, or stands firm by saying "I pass." When all buyers but one pass the opportunity to raise the bid, the auctioneer awards the merchandise to the remaining, or high, bidder.

As the buyers of fish in the Seattle halibut auction are distributors who compete with one another for patronage in the consumption market, they try to avoid cost disadvantages by bidding the price up even when they do not need fish, hoping to equalize the buying price today with the price they paid yesterday. This practice possesses the further advantage of enabling a buyer to avoid tipping his hand on a day when he really *needs* fish.

Preauction qualification sales.—Auctions may be organized on the same bidding basis and yet vary from one another in certain respects. Such variation may be in the form of a requirement by the auction firm that would-be buyers must qualify in some way prior to bidding at an auction. The qualification may be on a basis of type of functionary, financial competence, or sincere intent to bid indicated by registration accompanied perhaps by a returnable deposit fee. Preauction registration is often designed simply to increase efficiency by providing bidders with numbers for purposes of quick identification by bid spotters.

There are several possible reasons for requiring preauction qualification. One is that the seller and his agent, the auctioneer, can better plan the sale when they know who the would-be buyers are to be. Another is that, if no prior interest is manifested, an auction that might be aborted can be postponed. The most important reason, however, is to assure the seller that bidders are both serious and competent. In an auction of real property of considerable value, the high bidder was reported to be mentally incompetent and, in fact, an inmate of an institution. A preauction qualifying procedure might have prevented this occurrence.

In the sale of timber rights, the Forest Service of the United States government uses two different approaches. Some sales are conducted on a tender, sealed-bid basis in which the high bidder, if there is one, is awarded the property. Should a tie occur, both bids may be rejected, or the timber may be allocated between the tie bidders or awarded by the drawing of lots. This system is in effect a written-bid auction. In its second, much more common, sales plan, the Forest Service requires preauction qualification. Those who want to bid at an oral auction must first present sealed bids, which usually are identical at the government appraised figure. A potential bidder must also make a 5 percent deposit and must establish his financial responsibility to the satisfaction of the selling agency.[8]

The deposit requirement may be quite important in some auctions. In the auctioning of the vast Van Sweringen real estate empire in the mid-1930's, the company conducting the sale, Adrian H. Muller & Sons, required potential bidders to make an advance deposit with Morgan & Co.[9] This requirement, in addition to revealing the financial competence and good faith of buyers, would also

8 Walter J. Mead, *Competition and Oligopsony in the Douglas Fir Lumber Industry* (Berkeley and Los Angeles: University of California Press, 1966), pp. 138–141.

9 John Brooks, "Annals of Finance: One Dollar for the Lot," *New Yorker*, April 27, 1957, p. 123. For details on the sale of the Van Sweringen railroad empire, see H. Louis Hollander, "Public Auction of Stocks and Bonds," in *1958 Appraisal and Valuation Manual* (Washington: American Society of Appraisers, 1958), esp. p. 129.

bar the small speculators who usually participate in Muller & Sons auction sales.

Silent auction.—A variation of the written-bid system, sometimes called the silent auction, is occasionally used in the sale of paintings in the United States. It differs from the written-bid auction in that participants do not bid blindly, and thus prices move upward in a more or less orderly manner.

At a silent auction of paintings I investigated, each would-be buyer entered his name and address and the amount of his bid on a bidding slip placed beside each item five days before the sale. The slip specified the minimum bid acceptable as well as the minimum increment. An interested party could thus ascertain the last bid on an item and decide if he wanted to increase it by the minimum increment. Each painting was then sold for the highest bid entered on its bidding slip before 7:30 P.M. of the auction day. This particular silent auction was held in conjunction with a regular English-type auction, items for sale under both plans being displayed during the five-day exhibition period. The minimum and incremental bids for some of the items to be sold at silent auction were:

Item	Minimum bid	Increment bid
A	$675	$50
B	450	50
C	115	10
D	75	10
E	55	10
F	50	25
G	50	10
H	45	10
I	20	5
J	15	5

To what extent bids are elicited from patrons by so inert a selling scheme is an open question. The sale described above opened its doors to the public on a Thursday, and by early Saturday morning few bids above the minimum had been entered on the sheets, usually raising the minimum by only one increment. One item with a minimum bid of $15 and an increment of $5 had attracted an initial bid of $25, but this kind of bidding was certainly not typical.

No firm statement can be made about the motives of bidders in a silent auction. One conversation between an interested observer and her husband was enlightening, however. The wife wanted to enter her bid for a small drawing, but her husband advised her to wait until Tuesday, just before the closing of the bidding. Otherwise, he argued, someone might raise her bid by an increment of $5 and she would then have to go $10 higher than her original bid in order to buy the item. It can be argued that the contrary strategy of making a high "keep-out" bid might be a sounder approach for one determined to buy the drawing.

Conclusions

The auction schemes discussed in this chapter, although relatively unimportant from the point of view of general applicability, may be very useful in special situations. Together with the methods described in chapter 5 and the electronic devices discussed in chapter 14, they are a fair representation of all the variations of auctioning in use throughout the world.

Not all auction systems, however, are applicable to all market conditions. One system is undoubtedly superior to another in the sale of a particular type of product; the sale of fish and the sale of real estate, for example, require entirely different auctioning methods. The type of buyer also has an important bearing on the applicability of certain auction systems. Buyers who are very busy with marketing tasks, in contrast with those who patronize auctions as an avocation, strongly prefer a fast-selling scheme.

Measurement of the efficiency of an auction system must, of course, be based on certain criteria, or standards. The most important of these are the price level that can be attained for the goods that are up for sale, the speed of the selling operation, and the acceptability of the scheme to prospective buyers. Thus the selection of a particular type of auction is based to a considerable extent on the applicability of that system to the selling task that is being assigned to it.

Strategy and Tactics of Auction Selling

7 ANY AUCTION firm wants to get as much as possible for the owner-vendor of goods consigned to it for sale, and employs strategy and tactics designed to achieve that purpose. Strategy has to do with the overall plan of the campaign—how best to approach the problem in order to accomplish one's purpose most advantageously. Tactics have to do with procedural matters—maneuvers designed to implement the general plan.

Preliminary Considerations

An auction sale that is not strategically sound is unlikely to be successful, but even a well-planned auction may fail unless it is properly managed at the procedural, or tactical, level.

Strategy.—In planning his strategy of selling, the vendor must first decide, before moving his goods into distribution channels, whether to employ the auction method. He must weigh the strategic advantages of various selling methods as applied to particular distribution problems.

Once sale by auction has been elected, strategy questions take a somewhat different tack. As buyers make prices in an auction, the first problem is to attract a group of potential purchasers. The more financially competent buyers one can assemble, the livelier will be the bidding and, within reasonable limits, the higher the price levels reached. The overall plan of an auction should also include the selection of a time and a place that would be most convenient for interested dealers and private buyers. Furthermore, the quantity of goods is of major importance in some auctions, especially when buyers are professionals who need large amounts of a certain type of goods; it may be physically impossible for huge organizations, such as major packing plants, to supply their needs by purchasing small amounts of goods at many widely scattered points. Some buyers, in fact, must be able to procure at least a truckload of whatever goods they handle.

Proper publicity for an auction sale is another strategic factor of importance in some commodity areas, although in others (for example, fish) the regular occurrence of the auction is well known to all relevant traders in the community. In auction sales of antiques or of used machinery, usually scheduled only occasionally, prospective buyers must be informed of the time, place, and nature of the event through direct mail, newspaper advertisements, or even the telephone. It is extremely important to notify specific individuals known to be buyers of the particular type of merchandise to be placed on sale at an auction, even if the information has to be communicated by wire or special post. In some instances, special provision should be made to attract dealers rather than individual collectors, especially if the goods to be sold include numerous units of a certain type of item. On the contrary, sometimes the main promotional effort is directed toward collectors, who usually offer more for one-of-a-kind items than dealers, if only because the latter must allow for a margin to cover their costs and ensure a profit.

One very important strategic device in auctioning is the provision by the vendor or his agent for a preview of the property to be put up for sale. The preview is an integral part of some auctions, such as Tokyo's primary-level fish auction, where the product is not in evidence during the sale, but it has high promotional value in any auction. An industrial buyer, for example, would want to inspect used machinery to determine whether it would fit his needs. Consumer-buyers, given an opportunity to examine goods before an auction, may become emotionally attached to certain items, and hence more likely to bid, and buy. Furthermore, an auction sale will undoubtedly be more lively if buyers have had a chance to preview the goods—to gain a clear idea of the merits and the value of certain items.

A further strategic consideration in some auctions involves the items or lots to be placed on sale at a given session, or sessions. Vendors or auctioneers have an almost infinite number of alternatives. The questions here concern the advantage of putting up a certain item early or late in the sale, and in conjunction with what other items. The latter point is significant, for some items have little or no market if sold along with unrelated goods, partly because of the composition of the assembled buying groups. In a livestock auction I attended, the morning session was devoted to the sale of dairy cattle, and the afternoon session, to the sale of beef cattle. In the sale of real property, a California auction firm publicizes the approximate time of sale of each parcel.

The choice of auction method is also a strategic matter. Even a vendor who has adequate quantities of high-quality merchandise and a fine crowd of would-be buyers must decide which auction system is best suited to the particular sales task. The Dutch (descending-price) method may be better than the English (ascending-bid) method, or vice versa. Often, however, no consideration is given to this question simply because those in charge are unaware of alternative methods. Usually, then, the choice of the auction system to be employed is not a matter for decision, but a matter of customary procedure.

Tactics.—To make an auction operation successful, wise strategical decisions must be accompanied by effective tactics. One tactical aspect of auctions is the scheduling of individual sales within the auction period. Although some auctions permit no choice, either because the order is determined by the arrival of the goods on the market (that is, first in, first out), or because sellers' products are alternated in the sales schedules, in others those in charge must determine the most advantageous scheduling. For example, the knowledge that certain items arouse more interest than others may be exploited in the construction of a sales schedule, as well as for the elimination of "dead spots" during a sale and for the maintenance of buyer interest until the end of the auction.

One of the most important tactical factors in the success of an auction sale is the development of lively bidding at the beginning of the sale, with the possible exception of sales where the buyers are exclusively professionals who purchase for resale to consumer-buyers. Yet even under such circumstances a good sale depends on the alertness of prospective buyers, and a fast tempo developed in the first few transactions is apt to influence subsequent bidding. Liveliness at the start may be achieved by first putting up for sale especially selected "hot" demand items, or by knocking down an item quickly at a relatively low price with the "fast hammer." Some tacticians, of course, may prefer a gradual warming-up process.

Every auctioneer has to face, at one time or another, the possibility that a dead spot will develop during a sale, which could be disastrous. Here the fast hammer, by increasing the alertness of prospective buyers, may also be effective. Another tactical device used by some auctioneers to stimulate interest is to permit buyers to select the items they would like to have put up for early sale. As one auctioneer has said, "Having set their hearts on these things, buyers are not going to let them get away without some competition." If, despite all efforts, a dead spot *does* develop, an auctioneer may switch to another type of item in which he is reasonably sure buyers would be interested. To solve the problem, one auctioneer with whom I am acquainted occasionally shifts to the Dutch system of selling for one or two transactions. Others create diversions by telling anecdotes or, indeed, by "carelessly" dropping and breaking a "valuable" item.

In a multisession auction, it may be possible to build up the attendance at later sessions by giving away a little in the first session. A small community where word-of-mouth advertising is particularly effective provides a good setting for the use of this tactical device. If buyers find bargains on the first day of the sale, patronage is almost sure to increase on the following day or days. One auctioneer who successfully uses this method believes that bargain prices on the first night of a multisession sale are the "cheapest form of advertising," at least in small communities where news spreads rapidly. Needless to say, no bargains are available after the first night, nor are they usually necessary, for bidding is stimulated by the participation of a larger crowd of potential buyers.

A significant aspect of auctioning is the makeup of a lot. If a lot is too large, small bidders may be excluded; if it is too small, larger buyers may lose interest. Sometimes, as in the sale of fish in England's primary markets, lots are large but the high bidder has the option of taking all or part of a lot. This practice, which satisfies large as well as small buyers, permits flexibility in bidding.

Closely related to the size of the lot is the basis of pricing employed by vendors. Goods may be priced by the lot, or the bidding may be on the basis of a unit of weight (pound or kilogram, for example), the total price being the product of the unit price times the number of units. The latter method may achieve better total price results than the former, especially when goods have no easily determined market value, because a buyer, particularly a nonprofessional buyer, is less apt to be aware of the total price he would be paying for the lot.

It is important to the success of an English-type auction sale that the step-ups in price be set at the right amount. If they are too small, especially when the bidding is at a level way below the reserve, too much time is needed to sell each item, and thus there may be an adverse influence on the interest of assembled buyers. If the advances are too large, on the other hand, they may be difficult to obtain from bidders, resulting in a depressing effect on prices or even in an aborted sale.

Additional tactical sales schemes are discussed elsewhere in this volume. An ingratiating personality, a sense of humor, an attractive voice—all may be thought of as tactical weapons at the disposal of the salesman.[1] The use of price-enhancing devices, such as "phantom bids," also has tactical value in an auction.[2] The effectiveness of any tactic, whatever its inherent worth, depends on its relation to sound strategy and the skill with which it is executed.

Multiple Bids

The lively bidding that is likely to result from the presence of numerous interested buyers at an auction may lead to higher prices than might otherwise have been obtained, but it also poses the

1 See pp. 102–105, 165.
2 See pp. 105–106, 166.

tactical problem of determining who is to be designated as the effective bidder in multiple-bid situations. The term "multiple bids" refers to several, perhaps numerous, bids at the same price level. While multiple bids are equal, as each bidder has made an offer at the same price level, actually the successful bidder is traditionally the one who placed his bid first. In order to determine the effective bidder at each bidding level, therefore, the auctioneer must take cognizance of the timing element.

When several would-be buyers compete at lower price levels, however, the identity of the bidders may usually be disregarded, for it is likely that at least one bidder will go higher, especially if the price is below the estimated value. This course of action may be safely pursued until only two or three bidders remain in competition. Then the identity of the bidders becomes increasingly important, but determination of the winner is easier because there are fewer bidders to keep track of.

Two further aspects of multiple bids should be considered at this juncture:

1. The foregoing analysis does not cover all contingencies. For instance, multiple bidders—at least those who bid in secret and are thus conscious only of their own bids—may bid once and wait in vain for someone to raise the bid because each fears that by raising he would be bidding against himself. The auctioneer may then have to indicate who the high bidder is (that is, the first to bid at that level), so that an opponent will have the opportunity to break the logjam. This may be done simply by saying that the high bid is in a certain part of the room—"The high bid is in the front"—thus notifying others that the bid is against them.

2. In auctions where there is likely to be lively action by would-be buyers who bid surreptitiously, bid spotters may be employed. Two such individuals, each covering a certain area of the room, may communicate identical bids to the auctioneer, so that the latter is able to advance the bid without necessarily knowing the identity of the bidders. The spotters, on the other hand, although presumably able to identify their bidders, would not be in a position to determine the priority of the bids. The auctioneer is undoubtedly guided by his impression of which spotter communicated a bid first, although the decision may often have to be made arbitrarily.

The use of spotters, however, lessens the auctioneer's influence on prices because his relationship with buyers is not so close as it might otherwise be.

Tie Bids

The concept of knocking goods down to the highest bidder assumes that the offer of one bidder will exceed the offers of competing bidders. In most auction systems, however, two or more bidders may be tied, so that a choice must be made as to who is to be declared the successful bidder. How can this problem be resolved to the satisfaction of both buyer and seller?

Tie bids can develop in almost any auction system if bidding is conducted by nonelectronic means. This is obviously true of the English system of auctioning, but it can also happen in the Dutch system, for two or more individuals may simultaneously shout "Mine!" The possibilities of a tie bid are particularly good in the Japanese simultaneous-bidding scheme, as several bidders may tender identical offers. Likewise, in the ancient handshake system two or more individuals may well bid the same figure. And so it is with other systems in which bids are made blindly. Among the few systems that preclude the chance of tie bids are audible bidding in rotation, for each bidder must advance the bid or pass, and the Dutch clock system, which electronically discriminates between split-second differences.

In the English system, the possibility of ties exists at all bidding levels, not only at the high price level. As the price ascends, two or more bidders may call out simultaneously, but there is no difficulty so long as a higher bid is subsequently received. If no higher bid is forthcoming, the auctioneer is forced to decide who is to get the merchandise. A tie bid exists, however, only if two buyers bid exactly the same amount at the same point of time. If there is a time difference of only a fraction of a second, the first bidder is the high bidder and the second one is the underbidder. The latter must either counter the bid of the former by moving up to the next higher level, or drop out of the bidding. If the underbidder makes no move, the first bidder is normally awarded the property.

Ties do occur, of course. Let us suppose that three bidders are competing for a piece of Meissen ware. Number 1 bids $100, number 2 ups the bid to $110, and number 3 raises it to $120. At that point, number 1 and number 2 may easily counter the $120 bid with an offer of $130 at the identical moment, and thus be tied. There can also be a tie if only two bidders are competing, and if one of them, wanting perhaps to indicate bidding strength, advances his own bid at the same time that his opponent is moving to a higher level by the same amount. If either of the two lags behind the other, however, *he* has to move up another notch in order to acquire the goods.

If and when tie bids develop, how are they resolved by the individual who is crying the sale? One way to solve the problem is to decide in advance, on a strategy basis, that there will be no ties, much as an officer may decide to take no prisoners in certain military campaigns! Then, of course, arbitrary tactical decisions as to the identity of the successful bidder are required in doubtful situations. Such a procedure is probably justifiable, assuming an absence of bias on the part of the person making the decision. If the foregoing plan is impracticable or unacceptable, the auctioneer first tries to get one of the tie bidders to move up, thus breaking the tie. When a trader makes such a move, he is in a sense bidding against himself, but actually he is at the same time bidding against another who has an equal stake in the property.

There are various other ways of handling the impasse caused by a tie bid. One way is to reauction the lot, in the hope that a single high bid will emerge. Another is to divide the goods between tie bidders, although this solution is not always practicable. Still another possibility is to use a game of chance, such as the toss of a coin, to ascertain the winner. In Japan the game of Jan Ken Pon ("paper, stone, scissors"), known popularly as "Janken," is used for the purpose of determining the winner. It is not an uncommon sight to see two bidders breaking their tie in this manner.

One of the most interesting cases of a tie developed in the sale of the Idol's Eye diamond at the Parke-Bernet Galleries several years ago. The circumstances leading to the tie are not entirely clear, but the problem was resolved by invoking a traditional rule stipulating that in a tie the bidder nearest the auctioneer is awarded the merchandise. One of the tie bidders for the diamond was a dealer who knew about the rule; the other was a private collector who evidently did not, and possibly assumed that some other method would be used to settle the issue. The former knew that he was in the favored position and did not have to bid higher in order to protect his position, while the other was apparently unwilling to go beyond the high figure of $375,000.[3] Thus, despite the tie, the diamond was awarded to the bidder sitting closer to the rostrum.

Terminating the Bidding

As we shall see later, there are different schools of thought with respect to the prompt termination of auction sales transactions. In some instances—tobacco auctions, for example—bids come so fast that within seconds the climactic high bid is reached and terminating the sale becomes a routine matter. In auctions of antiques and other items, however, those conducting the sale use their discretion in the matter of bringing the transaction to a conclusion.

Some auction operations are by nature speedy, permitting the sale of several hundred lots at a single session. Good examples are auctions of tobacco, fish, and produce (in Holland, at least). Speed is important to buyers who are too busy to spend time in unnecessarily extended operations, and also when the magnitude of the selling job requires that the task be accomplished with expedition.

Some auction operations are much slower paced. In livestock auctions, for example, fifty sales per hour is perhaps average. The time required to move animals through an auction slows down the operation, and the buyers, some of them ranchers to whom time is a more flexible element, tend to be more casual in their bidding. The auctioning of real estate obviously requires considerable time; not only does the property have to be minutely described, but bidders must be given time to consider each bid. One sale an hour may be considered very fast, and several hours may be devoted to a single sale.

When the auctioneer has some influence on the length of time devoted to a sale, his first step in a move toward termination is to decide when the bidding is completed. No decision is required in the Dutch system, for the one who bids, or bids first, is the high bidder. The questions in this type of auction then are: (1) Who is the first bidder? (2) Is the price bid at or above the reserve level, if

3 Sanka Knox, " 'Idol's Eye' Gem Sold for $375,000," *New York Times* (Western ed.), Nov. 15, 1962, Sec. L, p. 9.

any? The Japanese (simultaneous-bidding) system also gives the auctioneer little opportunity for discrimination. The only question is: Which of the bidders who have their hands in the air is the highest bidder? As there is little or no cajoling of bidders into raising their bids, the task of the salesman is simply to act as a referee to determine who really made the highest bid.

The haphazard auction schemes, including the written-bid and the touch-of-hands methods, leave little room for decisions as to when to knock the goods down. In the written-bid system the high bidder is the one who has filed the highest bid by the end of the allotted time period. The same thing is true of the candle auction, except that in this instance the bids are audible. In touch-of-hands auctions, the award is made to the bidder who is highest when each of the assembled buyers has had a chance to indicate his bid by shaking the auctioneer's hand. In this method the auctioneer has leeway for discriminatory treatment of some bidders over others, but little if any control over the amount of time taken to arrive at a decision.

In the English trading system the transaction does not come to an end automatically, as it does, for example, in the Dutch system; rather, auction officials must decide when the bidding is completed. Of all the unorthodox schemes analyzed in an earlier chapter, only the whispered-bid method permits the same type of discretion. Bids come sporadically as well as haphazardly, and the auctioneer may award the goods promptly or may wait indefinitely. He has complete discretion, as in the English system.

Such an auctioneer is in an ambivalent position. He is trying to speed up sales operations in order to keep buyers alert and to avoid wasting their time, but at the same time he wants to get the highest possible prices. Some auction men attempt to keep the sale going at a fast pace; some, conversely, try to "milk" every nickel from the crowd. The employment of these contrasting techniques varies with the type of goods up for sale and the character of the purchasing group.

Role of the Auctioneer

8 THE KEY functionary in auction sales is the auctioneer. It is therefore necessary to define the nature of his office, the functions he performs, the characteristics required of an auctioneer, his rights and responsibilities, and the arrangements for his compensation.

What Is an Auctioneer?

In considering the role of the auctioneer, we must ask ourselves not only what the term "auctioneer" denotes, but what the rights and responsibilities of auctioneers actually are.

Definition.—An auctioneer has been defined as ". . . one who sells property, or offers it for sale, by a system of increasing or decreasing bids, or by any other competitive method, or who has on his premises any notice, or wording, indicating that he is an auctioneer." [1] The auctioneer, basically an agent of the vendor, acts for his principal in the sale of land or chattels or both. He possesses authority to pursue this task and has the responsibility of acting in his clients' interests. An auctioneer differs from a broker in that the latter buys or sells, whereas the former usually confines his activities to selling.

1 George Mercer, ed., *The Auctioneers' Manual* (11th ed.; London: Estates Gazette, 1961), p. 1.

Technically, then, the auctioneer is the agent of the vendor in the selling of goods, but he may or may not personally wield the hammer in the auctioning process. The definition given above therefore includes, in a broad sense, the auctioning firm as agent for the client; or, more narrowly, it designates only the salesman who knocks down the goods in a particular auction. More often than not, the law covering the agency relationship, and probably even the functions of the auctioneer, refers to the broader concept. Sometimes, in practice, the two are identical because the actual sale is conducted by the owner of the auction house, or, as at Sotheby's or Christie's, by individuals who have a part interest in the auction firm. If the individual who conducts the sale is merely an employee of an auction firm—salaried employee or commission salesman, or both—a dual agency relationship prevails: one between the vendor and the auction house and another between the auction firm and the auctioneer-salesman. If an auction firm acquires title to the goods it is selling, any employee conducting the sale becomes an auctioneer serving as agent of the firm that employs him.

Whether viewed broadly or narrowly, the auctioneer is expected to represent mainly the vendor in the disposal of the property consigned to him. He is a functional middleman, in other words, who typically does not take title to goods but merely represents the vendor. Although an auction firm occasionally takes title to goods in advance of the auction, usually the auctioneer sells goods that belong to others.

Rights and responsibilities of the auctioneer.—The auctioneer's rights and responsibilities, as related to vendors and buyers, may be outlined briefly.

1. Principal rights:
    a. The auctioneer has considerable freedom in organizing the sale and in prescribing some but not all of the conditions of the auction.
    b. He has the right to receive a fee for his services, or a partial fee if the sale is not consummated through no fault of his own.
    c. He has the right of indemnity for expenses incurred if his authority is revoked before the sale takes place.

d. He may withdraw goods from sale if the price is obviously depressed or unreasonably low.

e. He may refuse to accept bids from minors, insolvents, drunkards, mentally irresponsible individuals, and others.

f. He has a lien on the vendor's property that is up for sale for his commission and for the charges of the sale; the lien is satisfied on being paid, or relinquished by agreement, but it is dissolved after the property is delivered to the buyer.

g. The auctioneer, with the authorization of the vendor, may shift responsibility for quality and authenticity to the buyer by selling goods "as is" on a *caveat emptor* basis.

2. Key responsibilities:

a. The auctioneer is the agent of the seller and, to a limited extent, of the buyer (in recording the transaction, for example).

b. The auctioneer typically organizes the sales effort and must exert every legitimate effort toward gaining maximum prices for the goods offered.

c. He must obtain a license to do business in the state or community, if required, and adhere to any regulatory legislation, but he should challenge any legislation that is not for the protection of the public but is, rather, arbitrary and unreasonable.

d. The auctioneer is obligated to inform himself of market prices and values of the kind of merchandise he is selling, as well as of the particular goods that are up for sale.

e. He must knock down the goods to the highest bidder if there is no reserve price (and no buyer collusion), or, if there is a reserve price, after it has been reached; he must decide on the identity of the highest bidder and reconcile any contrary claims.

f. The auctioneer assumes personal responsibility for any express warranty made without authority from the vendor.

g. The auctioneer should strive to avoid any dealing with ring members, and should take whatever actions seem indicated (such as withdrawing merchandise from sale) if such activities are detected.

h. He may, however, permit small buyers to consult with one another for purposes of consolidating buying power, thus intensifying buyer competition.

i. He may be liable for any loss resulting from negligence if he fails to obey his principal's instructions.

j. He is obligated to accept payment for the property and to deliver it to the buyer when the conditions of the sale have been met.

Concomitant with the auctioneer's rights and obligations are the restrictions limiting his authority. The most important ones are as follows:

a. Generally speaking, the auctioneer may not purchase goods in an auction sale for his own account, unless there is no conflict of interest and provision has been made for such purchases in the conditions of sale.

b. The auctioneer is a special agent who may not bind the seller by a warranty, unless specially instructed to do so or authorized by specific statute.

c. Usually the auctioneer may not sell goods that are up for auction on the basis of individual negotiation, although he may do so before the auction sale if proper notice has been given or if all efforts to dispose of the property have proved abortive.

d. The auctioneer is not entitled to compensation when no sale results because he has improperly conducted the auction.

e. If the sale is made on an "as is" basis, the auctioneer cannot avoid the implied warranty for sale of goods in the form and substance as advertised.

Functions of the Auctioneer

From a broad viewpoint, the functions of an auctioneer include many activities that are performed behind the scenes in organizing and preparing for the sale. If a narrow viewpoint is taken, the job of the auctioneer is largely selling, or at least arranging for transfer of title to goods that are sold. Although this is an important function, which is discussed in detail below, the concept of the auctioneer as merely a salesman is too narrow for the purposes of this treatise.

Regardless of the auction system employed, a firm attempting to organize a successful auction has much planning to do. Planning may be required before every sales session, as in the occasional sales of antiques, but in other instances, such as daily or weekly auctions, it may be needed mainly to get sales under way. In either event, presale planning by auction firm personnel is requisite for successful auction sales. The behind-the-scenes activities include assembling the property to be sold; appraising or evaluating the property if necessary; preparing a catalogue, if required; selecting the time and place of the sale (or devising a plan that would obviate congregating [2]); publicizing the sale and otherwise encouraging patronage; determining the conditions of sale acceptable to seller and buyers; and displaying the merchandise or the property to potential buyers in advance of the sale.

These behind-the-scene functions are not of equal importance in all auctions. For example, the assembling of goods is not important in a fish auction, as it is in an antique auction, at least after the auction company has arranged with the fishermen to handle their fish on a continuing basis. Appraisal of property, which is so necessary in some merchandise fields as a guide to intelligent sales effort, is in other fields more a matter of having up-to-the-minute market information. Finally, when buying groups are made up mainly of dealers, the task of inducing patronage is not difficult, for such buyers are eager to attend auctions.

It is crucial to the success of an auction firm to get the vendor's goods and the would-be buyers together at a convenient time and place. It is also the auctioneer's function to effectively represent the vendor in the presentation and sale of the property to would-be buyers. Certain minimal terms of sale must be established relating to who may bid, conditions under which title passes, payment for the goods purchased, delivery of purchases, and so forth.

Presale activities apply to auctions generally, regardless of the type. The nature and extent of on-stage activities, however, depend to a large degree on the type of auction system employed. They are particularly important in the English auction system, where buyer-competitors are stimulated by the promotional tactics of the auc-

2 See the discussion of telegraphic and similar types of auctions, pp. 198–204.

tioneer and by one another's bidding. The scheme that offers the least opportunity for auctioneer sales activities is the Dutch clock system,[3] in which the auctioneer is mainly a referee. Other methods possess varying opportunities for demand-manipulative efforts by the auctioneer.

Procurement of Consignments

In any auction, the first step is to obtain the goods to be sold from owners or from those having legal control over the property. The procurement problem has three aspects: (1) providing owner-vendors with a distribution channel for property they want to sell; (2) supplying the auction firm with needed stocks of goods; and (3) providing buyers with an opportunity to acquire difficult-to-purchase items.

Although an owner sometimes seeks out an auctioneer as the first step in the selling process, an auction company cannot sit and wait for business. To continue functioning, it must have property to sell, and must actively pursue consignments for its sales operations. Sometimes a company acquires the property locally, as when it auctions off household goods in a small community. On the other hand, some auction firms, like Sotheby's and Christie's, gather antiques literally from all over the world. A London auction firm may obtain goods in the United States, ship them to London for auctioning, and then ship them back to the United States for an American buyer. A Phoenix, Arizona, livestock auction with which I am acquainted attracts customers from as far away as north Texas, perhaps even farther. But regardless of the area from which goods are collected, the auction firm must play an aggressive role in acquiring the goods. One type of persuasive effort is to send a newsletter to prospective consignors, reporting by name the important buyers who attended recent auction sessions.

The problem of acquiring consignments varies widely. In some commodity fields, such as fish and tobacco, the auction company seeks out clients among limited numbers of known producers, and usually has to compete with other auctioneer-brokers. Such competition, which may involve rivalry from dealers as well as from

3 For a discussion of this auction method, see pp. 193–197.

other auction companies, may take the form of cash advances, pickup services, friendly persuasion, and even more advantageous financial arrangements.

Auctioneers who conduct sales of household furnishings are often sought out by owners of property who are moving away or by executors of estates that have to be liquidated. The fact that an auctioneer is an established resident of the community and is well and favorably known is helpful. Even so, promotional efforts may be necessary, especially if several auctioneers are competing for business. Advertisement of auction services, especially in the classified pages, is probably a minimal requirement. Acquaintance with attorneys who are in a position to recommend an auctioneer is an advantage. A reputation for successful sales is one of the best ways of attracting business.

The competition among auction firms for antiques is particularly keen. A crucial factor is the estimated prices the various lots will bring at auction. Owners of property or executors of estates are apt to be influenced by these estimates. The auctioneer therefore tends to put his best foot forward in order to obtain a commission. An unscrupulous auction house may even inflate the valuation with the expectation that the figure can be amended after the property is obtained. An honest, far-sighted appraiser is, however, more apt to arrive at a realistic figure and stick with it.

The reputation of an auction company is very important in long-run terms, for most property owners prefer to deal with a firm in which they have confidence. A large auction company with high overhead costs requires aggressive effort in obtaining commissions for the sale of property. Usually such firms—one that comes to mind sells industrial equipment and even entire factories in far-flung locations—are old, established enterprises whose owners are well known; some business naturally comes in from those acquainted with the reputation of the company. Firms with the finest reputation obtain unsolicited business from attorneys or from courts. Nevertheless, aggressive effort is still required to obtain the amount of merchandise necessary for efficient operations; in fact, some firms employ "bird dogs" to ferret out auctioning opportunities.

The auctioning of antiques requires especially aggressive procurement activity. A western United States firm that conducts auctions in Oregon, California, Arizona, and Texas on a kind of circuit basis requires large quantities of goods. Most of the goods are acquired in Europe by agents who consign the property to the company for sale by auction. The company does not purchase goods outright, but does provide advances to consignors against receipts from auction sales, and thus maintains a close working relationship with its sources of supply.

World-renowned auction houses, like Sotheby's, Christie's, and Parke-Bernet, cannot rely entirely on being sought out by those wishing to sell art treasures. In fact, such individuals may elect not to use an auction house at all, but may prefer to approach a dealer who will purchase the goods directly. The chairman of the board of one of the world's largest auction houses reportedly reads the obituary columns of the London *Times* each day in the hope of obtaining leads to auction materials. Leads may also come from "runners" who either are regularly employed by auction houses or sell their tips on a free-lance basis.[4] Any such lead has to be given at least a preliminary follow-up in order to determine whether the estate or property in question is a likely source of auction goods. The most promising opportunities are then given further personal attention, which often brings the auction house representative into head-on competition with other auction companies and with dealers who hope to purchase the property outright. The auctioneer may use certain arguments to counter a dealer's offer to provide the seller with immediate cash. He might, for example, point out that competitive selling may provide the owner with more revenue than outright selling to a dealer who is not competitively motivated.[5]

That the foregoing discussion oversimplifies an auction firm's task of acquiring commissions may be seen in the following analysis:

> One must understand the proprieties of the auction business. Neither [Peter] Wilson nor anyone else can walk into a man's library and say, "Well, sir, why don't you let us sell some of this stuff? You could probably use the cash." Even when a spy, some local man-about-the-art-world, has tipped Wilson off that So-and-So *might* be thinking of getting rid of his old armor, it is important not to risk offending him with an overt

4 See S. N. Behrman, *Duveen* (New York: Random House, 1951), p. 123.
5 John Carter, "The Auction Room," in Milton Grundy, *Money at Work* (London: Sweet & Maxwell, 1960), p. 168.

approach. In instances where the collector is obviously on his last legs, one may contrive to pay a social call and take a surreptitious look around (an expert can make a surprisingly accurate appraisal over the rim of a tea-cup), but obviously the visitor doesn't say, "What's going to happen to all this Louis Quinze furniture after you're dead?" Besides, it will end up in the hands of his executors and the auction house is going to have to negotiate with them in the end. So auction houses, and dealers too, for that matter, do have to sit and wait, avidly, for owners to come to them. What was vital, therefore, Wilson deduced, was to get word around that *his* auction house, owing to its energy, resourcefulness, and past record, would attract the biggest crowd to a sale, thus guaranteeing brisk bidding and the highest possible prices.[6]

The competition among auction houses for the right to sell the art treasures of an owner or his estate involves not only the estimated amount the property will bring in the market but the fee to be charged vendors for the auctioning service. As we shall see below, auction houses have scales of charges for their services, but transactions that promise immediate profit and at least long-run prestige give the bargaining power to the owner of the property. In such instances, undoubtedly, the auctioneer makes concessions to the vendor in the matter of the fee; it is conceivable that he would even offer to handle a sale without any charge whatsoever, if the assignment carries very high prestige.

The Auctioneer as Salesman

It is obvious that much indirect sales effort is required in an auction operation before direct selling can be practiced. Behind-the-scenes operations help to ensure the success of an auction sale, but the actual response of buyers on the day of the sale is the *sine qua non* of auctioning. To attain that response is the job of the auctioneer.

Sales efforts in different auction systems.—In an ascending-price system the auctioneer has considerable opportunity to promote the sale of the property he is handling. He may describe the item as he puts it up for sale, and may even pause in the midst of the bidding to point out any outstanding qualities he believes the buyers may have overlooked. Some auctioneers have assistants turn the item

6 Duncan Norton-Taylor, "The World's Fastest Art Market," *Fortune,* LXXIV (Sept., 1966), 138.

around during the soliciting of bids as its virtues are extolled, or show the audience, for example, how the drawer of a commode works.

In the Japanese simultaneous-bidding scheme, where all bids are made at the same time, the auctioneer has only one opportunity for salesmanship—in the brief interim between the time he puts up the goods and the time he recognizes the high bidder among the sea of hands. In a high-speed auction at the primary distribution level there is relatively little opportunity for promotional effort on the part of the auctioneer.

The Dutch system affords almost no chance for salesmanship. Only before the goods are put up for sale can the auctioneer describe them, for during the auction he calls out quotations in a descending order and is not apt to interrupt the rhythm of this operation. The high-speed Dutch clock system presents no opportunity at all for promotional efforts during the auctioning of an individual item, if only because of the short time interval during the running of the clock.

Direct sales promotional efforts have no place in the haphazard schemes in which buyers bid in complete secrecy, for they cannot influence prospective buyers who do not know how much competitors are bidding. In some auctions (for example, written-bid systems) even the auctioneer may be in the dark regarding the amounts bid during the bidding period.

Table 3 summarizes the sales promotional opportunities available to the auctioneer under different auction systems. It reveals that direct sales efforts are pertinent in some systems but not in others.

The type of product also has an important bearing on the opportunities for sales promotional efforts. Such efforts would have little validity, for example, in the sale of fresh fish, whose market values can be readily determined and are usually known to buyers. On the other hand, the sale of nonstandard items, such as antique porcelain vases, provides an excellent opportunity for persuasive tactics, both at the start and during the bidding process, especially if the bidders are mostly consumer-buyers rather than dealers. The same thing is true of auctions where subjective considerations may affect the bidding, as in the sale of horses. Even when promotional efforts have dubious value, the auctioneer may use them to stimulate lagging interest. Such an attempt could take the form of levity; I know one auctioneer who occasionally knocks down an item by saying, "Stole for *x* dollars."

TABLE 3

OPPORTUNITIES FOR SALES PROMOTIONAL EFFORTS IN AUCTIONS

TYPE OF AUCTION SYSTEM	OPPORTUNITY FOR SALES EFFORTS
English (ascending) Without time limit	Maximum opportunity, but application depends on speed of selling [a] and type of buyer [b]
With time limit (e.g., candle auction)	Some
Dutch (descending) Oral	Very little, if any
Electronic clock	None
Japanese (simultaneous)	Some possible, if opportunity given buyers to raise bids
Haphazard	
Whispered bid	None
Written bid	None
Handshake	None

[a] Tobacco auctions are too rapid to permit sales pressure, although in practice some promotion is exerted by the bid starter, mainly to impress farmer-vendors.

[b] In Seattle halibut auctions the English system is used and the fish are sold by the boatload, allowing plenty of time for promotional effort; knowledgeable buyers, however, are not usually amenable to persuasion.

Variations in sales skill.—Not only do auctioneers possess varying natural abilities and sales skills, but they also differ in their approach to the use of promotional sales efforts. Ideally, the qualities needed by an auctioneer include a good voice, a pleasing personality, good character, the ability to hold and interest an audience, confidence in himself, the ability to judge the value of the items being auctioned, honesty, poise, enthusiasm, and vitality. These qualities may be categorized as (1) physical and personal traits, including good voice, pleasing personality, vigor and vitality, honesty, good character, enthusiasm, good health, and imperturb-ability; and (2) skill in generating interest, seen in the ability to judge the mood of the gathering and hold its interest and confidence, an effective sales pitch before and during the sale of an item, good tempo, knowledge of values, and alertness in recognizing bids. Thus an effective auctioneer may induce some people to bid who might otherwise not have done so.

The effectiveness of a skillful auctioneer may be illustrated by the tale of a wallpaper salesman who, while driving down the main street of a New England town, found his way blocked by a large gathering. Parking his car and pushing his way through the crowd, he saw an auction being conducted on the lawn of a nearby house by an auctioneer named O. Rundle Gilbert. At first only casually interested, he soon became attentive: "So sweet is Mr. Gilbert's siren song when he is on the selling platform that it is almost impossible to resist. An incisive student of crowd psychology, he knows when to pour it on and when to break the tension." Within a few minutes the wallpaper salesman purchased a boat for which he had no use.[7]

It has been argued that an auctioneer should forget the crowd and concentrate primarily on the competition of two individuals who are bidding against each other. If, however, he adopts this tactic and then one of the two bidders drops out, he is left without buyer competition. Ideally, an auctioneer knows many buyers personally and literally looks to those who he expects will bid on certain items. He may even—as an auctioneer with whom I am acquainted occasionally does—drop a bargain into the lap of a likely prospect in order to get him started. Instead of paying attention to only two bidders, then, an auctioneer is simultaneously selling one person, attempting to interest three or four others, and entertaining an audience of hundreds.

A really good auctioneer may be quite influential in getting patrons to increase their bids. Peter Wilson, of Sotheby's, is said to be outstanding:

The acknowledged star of the world's great auction galleries, Peter Wilson, . . . has totted up for Messrs. Sotheby & Co. of London at least

7 James Stewart-Gordon, "Auctions," *Christian Science Monitor*, July 25, 1962, p. 9.

three world records in the last four years: £781,000 for seven paintings from the Jacob Goldschmidt collection, the largest sum ever paid [up to this time] at a single sale by auction of works of art; £130,000 for a Gainsborough portrait, the highest auction price ever fetched by an English picture; and most recently, £80,000 for Somerset Maugham's "Death of Harlequin" by Picasso, peak price for a painting by a living artist. Wilson—a remarkably tall man, pink-skinned and impeccably turned out—is himself something of a masterpiece, illustrating the special cool attractiveness generally described as "English"—correct in an imperceptible sort of way, sometimes amused, eminently convincing, perpetually exuding the silent suggestion that other people ought to be *doing* something. Mostly, other people can't resist, and what they do in Wilson's case is bid unheard-of bids for art.[8]

The skill of an auctioneer-salesman thus depends to some extent on his ability to elicit bids from hesitant bidders. An outstanding industrial goods auctioneer, while selling 25,000 gallons of insecticide at Pearl Harbor a few years ago, feared at one point that the bidding might die at $2,500. He therefore, behind his hand, urged one bidder to "scare him out for $3,000." The bidder responded, active bidding was resumed, and the closing price was $28,500.[9]

Good auction salesmen differ tremendously from one another, except perhaps in the magical ability of establishing rapport with would-be buyers. Different talents are required by different types of auctions. Many auctioneer-salesmen who do not possess all or nearly all the characteristics considered ideal for topflight practitioners are nevertheless successful, especially if direct selling efforts are not practicable. Even when the opportunity exists for reliance on promotional work, an absence of strength in one characteristic may be offset by unusual effectiveness in another, or an auctioneer's inadequacy may be counterbalanced by the quality of the goods. In the latter situation an auctioneer may attract a following and obtain top prices even if he does little to influence buyers directly.

Of incidental interest is the fact that auctioneers in the United States are often called "Colonel," because, it is said, army colonels mustered out after the Civil War were ordered to sell surplus prop-

8 "Peter Wilson, Sotheby's Sublime Auctioneer," *Vogue* (June, 1962), p. 118.

9 Russell Chappell, "The Auctioneer's Big Bid," *Newsweek*, Feb. 3, 1958, p. 78.

erty to the highest bidder.[10] The use of the title has persisted, and auction schools even confer it on their graduates.

Tactical use of seller bids.—It may come as a surprise to some readers that the auctioneer often bids for the seller, at least in the English auction system. The tactic is quite legitimate if a reserve price has been set, particularly when the right to bid for a vendor has been included among the conditions of sale, but it is undoubtedly employed illegitimately when there is no reserve price.

The right to bid for the principal is particularly important at the moment an item is put up for sale. It is a principle of sound auctioning procedure that the auctioneer not linger too long for the critical opening bid; he may have to "fish" for a bid by reducing the suggested starting price until a firm offer is received. If he does not obtain a genuine bid from the floor, he may start the ball rolling by making an opening bid in behalf of the vendor. The alternative, in the absence of bidding, is to withdraw the lot from sale.

In bidding for the vendor, the auctioneer's purpose is simply to prime the pump. He hopes that his opening bid (for the seller) will stimulate a genuine buyer to enter the bidding and that counterbids will follow until a satisfactory price is reached. I know of one outstanding auctioneer-owner of a fine European house who opens the bidding at a reasonable price, and then without retreating moves upward rapidly by actual or phantom bids until the reserve price is reached. At this point he either sells the item, if he has a genuine bidder, or bids it in for the owner's account.

The tactic of bidding for the vendor is also useful when there is only one bidder among the buyers.[11] It provides competition for the lone bidder, forcing him to a level closer to his highest demand price, and possibly enabling the auctioneer to pick up additional bidders along the way. The danger is that the auctioneer may be left with the goods if the would-be buyer drops out of the competition before a satisfactory price level is attained. If the auctioneer cannot then attract other genuine bidders, he may withdraw the lot from sale or announce that it is "sold."

When in actual practice this kind of maneuvering does not

10 Bula Lemert, "School for Auctioneers: How To Sell Out—for the Right Price," *Coronet* (Aug., 1966), p. 132.

11 See pp. 212–214.

work—that is, when there are no bids at all, or when the bidder or bidders drop out before the reserve price is reached—an abortive sale results. The auctioneer may withdraw the item from sale at the point of the highest bid, or, by bidding for the vendor, may try to get the price up to a level just below the reserve price. He may then withdraw the item from sale because it has not reached the reserve price, or he may knock it down to a "phantom" bidder at a higher price. This course of action protects the vendor from the publicity of a low bid which might adversely affect the value of the item. Such an unsold item may be returned to the owner-vendor, offered for sale on a private-treaty basis, or put up at auction again at a later session.

Closing the sale.—The salesman-auctioneer in an English-type auction could conceivably get a higher price for an item if he attempted to "milk" the crowd by intensively promoting each item to the fullest extent. But by so doing he might only string the sale out, with an attendant cost in buyers' time and an adverse effect on the rhythm of the sale, possibly resulting in loss of buyer interest and ultimately in lower prices.

There are two schools of thought on this matter. Some auctioneers, at least under certain conditions, like to make sales quickly; they detect bids rapidly, decide who is the highest, and knock the goods down promptly. Some auctioneers, on the other hand, move slowly in the hope of getting the highest demand price from the high bidder. The course chosen depends not only on the auctioneer's personality characteristics, but on the type of property being sold and the type of individuals who make up the market. Louis Marion, long an outstanding salesman at Parke-Bernet, explained that an auctioneer cannot simply say, " 'I have sixty thousand pounds; any more?' then down with the hammer," because the consignor would feel that there were bids "left in the room." The auctioneer must try to extract offers from reluctant bidders in order to satisfy the vendor, and he must have patience. In fact, Mr. Marion says that waiting calls for great auctioneering.[12]

An auctioneer who attempts to maintain a fast pace may, in a sense, be educating his buyers, and may even use a quick hammer to encourage them to respond quickly. He realizes that he may oc-

12 James Brough, *Auction!* (Indianapolis and New York: Bobbs-Merrill, 1963), p. 149.

casionally miss a bid by running an auction through fast, but he expects subsequent transactions to make up for any losses. The application of this tactic, should, however, be limited to auctions of goods that belong to one owner, for otherwise the price of one owner's goods may be sacrificed in order to enhance the price of another's.

The auctioneer is not only constantly looking for bids, but also for signs that some bidders have withdrawn from competition. His awareness of withdrawals helps him to complete a transaction promptly. If one of only two competing bidders shakes his head just as his opponent advances the bid, the auctioneer may knock the item down to the remaining bidder. On the contrary, he can wait to terminate the sale until he is sure no further bids are forthcoming.

The nature of the commodity being sold is related to the promptness with which a transaction is completed. In the sale of tobacco, for example, with an average of perhaps 350–400 transactions per hour, the auctioneer may not dillydally. Nor can he waste time while selling livestock, wool, produce, and other commodities, although they do not move so rapidly as tobacco.

In the auctioning of certain commodities, such as antiques under the English system, circumstances permit some choice in the speed of completing transactions. I believe that the fast-paced auction has advantages over the more leisurely type. It tends to keep would-be buyers alert and responsive to the selling effort of the auctioneer, and more vigorous bidding is likely to follow. Some auctioneers believe that while hard-to-get bids are not squeezed out of reluctant bidders by this method, live bidders tend to bid more promptly and the quickened pace may yield higher prices. In fact, one auctioneer told me he often ignores bidders who come in late in the bidding so as to get them in the habit of coming in early rather than waiting to see what is going to happen. He concentrates on the live wires and discourages the laggards. Another authority feels it is good policy to impart a sense of urgency to the bidders, to impress them with the need to file bids quickly or else risk the loss of opportunity to purchase the property.

When the auctioneer does decide to knock the goods down he may do so promptly, or he may warn the bidders: "Any further advance?" or "Fair warning!" and finally "Going once! Twice! and third and last time—Sold!!" Then he indicates clearly the price at which the lot was sold and the buyer to whom the property was awarded. In designating the high bidder, he may specifically name a firm or an individual—"Sold to Marine Fish Company" or "Sold to Mr. Abercrombie"—or he may announce a number or a location in the auction room—"Sold to number 362" or "Sold to you, sir, on the center aisle."

Compensation

An auctioneer, as agent for a vendor, is compensated for the services he performs, services whose value depends on his knowledge of the market and of the auctioning process. As a marketing institution, an auction firm must have revenue with which to operate; such revenue is usually derived from fees charged clients for services rendered. These services include ferreting out owners who desire or can be persuaded to sell goods; appraisal of items by experts; cleaning or otherwise refurbishing the goods; preparing catalogs; publicizing and displaying the goods; scheduling sales; supplying sales and display space; providing auctioneers for conducting sales; and receiving payment for the goods for the account of the owner-vendor. Not the least of an auction firm's functions is to be available if and when a vendor wants to make use of its services.

Auction fees vary considerably both as to form and amount, from one trade to another and from one community to another. The amount depends both on the extent of the service performed and on the competition among those who offer such services; the competition, in turn, depends on the amount of revenue that can be generated per unit of time expended. The rather large differentials may be explained by the high volume sales in some fields, in contrast with the infrequent sales in others, in relation to fixed overhead expense. In addition, there is likely to be a substantial difference in handling and other types of costs.

According to one authority, auctioneers in ancient Rome charged a fee of from 1 to 2 percent, which seems low in comparison with present-day rates. However, we do not know precisely what services the Roman *argentarius* (organizer of the auction) performed, or whether they were more or less than those of his modern counterpart. Therefore, we do not know whether the Roman charges were high or low.

Antiques.—The fee charged for auctioning antiques is a percentage of the sale price of the property. In some countries there are different charges for different types of items; percentage fees for selling paintings and other works of art differ somewhat from those for selling books. In London, for example, a leading antique auction company charges (*a*) 10 percent for pictures and drawings, furniture, rugs, silver, ceramics, and so forth, for lots totaling more than £100; (*b*) 10 percent for jewels and jewelry in any lot size; (*c*) 12.5 percent for any items listed in (*a*) selling in lots totaling less than £100; (*d*) 12.5 percent for old coins and medals, regardless of quantity purchased; and (*e*) 15 percent for books and magazines.

It is noteworthy that substantial differences in auction fees prevail among different antique markets. For example, it is reported that the fees charged in London range from 10 to 15 percent, whereas those in New York range from 12 to 20 percent. There are, indeed, differences within the United States which are just as striking; antique auction houses in southern California charge as high as 30 percent, which may be the result of unfavorable cost to volume relationships, which in turn are the product of high specialization and a thin market for this type of auction service.

Generally, an auction house charges about half its normal rate for lots failing to reach their reserve price. One English auction house sets its fee at 5 percent on a basis of the last genuine bid up to £100, and at 2.5 percent, above £100.

Livestock.—The auction fees paid by vendors of livestock are basically different from those in most other auctions, at least in southern California, where livestock is sold primarily by the head. For example, in one auction the fee for cattle weighing up to 400 pounds is $2.25 per head, the charge increasing to $3.75 or $3.50 on heavier stock, depending on whether the lot contains a single animal or two or more. The larger fee per unit of heavier stock, a reflection of the increased sales volume, would presumably mean a lower fee in percentage-of-sales terms.

For selling purebred stock, interestingly enough, the auctioneer is not paid by the head, but receives 5 percent of the sales price. The argument in favor of the per-head fee, which prevails generally in livestock, is that the auction company can count on a more stable income when prices fluctuate. On the other hand, the vendor is disadvantaged because of the relatively high fee he must pay when prices received are low.

Tobacco.—The fee structure in tobacco auctions in the southern United States is neither a pure percentage system nor a straight per-unit arrangement, but a combination of the two. Tobacco growers pay warehouse companies that sell their crop a percentage-of-sales fee, plus additional charges for warehouse and other services rendered. The basic commission is 2.5 percent of gross sales; the additional fees are an auction charge of 15 to 25 cents per pile and a weighing and handling charge of 10 cents per 100 pounds.[13] Offhand, the auction fees paid in the sale of tobacco seem low relative to the percentage fees charged in other fields, such as antiques.

Fish (halibut).—The fees charged for auctioning halibut in Seattle, Washington, are paid in part by the sellers and in part by the buyers. It may be that the buyers pay some of the fee because the product is in high demand and the sellers have a bargaining advantage over them. Whatever the cause of this atypical situation, dealer-buyers in the Seattle fishermen's exchange who have been "accepted as bidders" are required to pay $10 a month to the exchanges, for which they receive before the sale (*a*) names and catches of all vessels listing fish for sale, and after the sale (*b*) the names of buyers and the prices paid for fish purchased. This token charge is supplemented by a fee of $2 (the minimum charge) per $1,000 worth of fish or fish products purchased through the exchange. Half of this fee may be deducted by the buyer from payments to the seller.

Other fields.—Commissions in Los Angeles automobile auctions are on a sliding scale, running recently from a $25 minimum fee for the sale of cars at prices ranging from $500 to $995 to a maximum of $50 for cars selling for $5,000 and above. Although increasing in monetary terms, the fees decline on a percentage basis as the sale prices increase. A standard fee of $5 is exacted on all no-sale transactions, as when a reserve price is not reached and the car is unsold.

13 U.S. Department of Agriculture, *Tobacco Market Review* (Washington: Consumer and Marketing Service, March, 1965), p. 11.

Auction charges for the sale of stamps by a large London firm are on a variable percentage basis of the realized prices of the goods sold. Standard charges of 17.5 percent are in effect for lots selling for less than £100; 15 percent, for lots realizing from £100 to £250; and 12.5 percent, for lots amounting to £250 or more. Charges for unsold lots when reserves have been agreed on are set at a nominal 5s. per lot, but when goods are unsold and no reserve has been set, a commission is exacted on a basis of the "bought-in" price.

Fees charged for auctioning real property are usually a percentage of the sale price, with rates differing for improved property as compared with unimproved land. In southern California, for example, the typical fee for the former ranges from 5 to 6 percent, whereas for the latter it is 10 percent. Some firms, however, require an additional 5 percent of the estimated selling price for advertising the auction. Moreover, real estate transactions of this type may hinge on the vendor's specification of a realistic reserve price.

Selling charges at Aalsmeer, Holland, for the auctioning of agricultural and floral goods are on a percentage basis, but the charges vary not only by type of item but by status of client. Charges made by the auction institutions are 7 percent for members of the cooperative, and 10 percent for nonmembers.

The reasons for the differences in fees found in various fields are, first, the variations in services performed by auction firms in different commodity or product areas; second, the difference in the volume of sales over which the costs must be spread; and third, differences in the competitive conditions that exert varying amounts of pressures on standard as well as special fee structures.

The charges mentioned above are published fees and, like prices in any other segment of the business world, may be subject to negotiation. There is no doubt that concessions would be made on a percentage figure in the antiques field, and perhaps in others, especially if the consignment sought is particularly desirable.[14]

14 See pp. 52–53.

Bid Calling

9 THE CALLING of bids is an extremely important function in the English auction system. Indeed, auctioning would be impossible in an ascending-bid system without bid calling, since buyer competition is dependent on communicating the amounts actually offered to those who may be willing to raise the bids. Bid calling may be done by rhythmic or repetitive chanting or by the use of ordinary words and voice tones.

Initiating and Calling Bids

In ascending-bid auctions, there are two key requisites to successful sales operations. The first is the initiation of the bidding. Whoever starts the bidding must have knowledge of the approximate value of the goods that are up for sale, either of the type of goods being sold (as in an auction of livestock) or of the specific item that is up for sale (for example, antiques). The second requisite to a successful English-type auction operation is bid calling. Its purpose is to provide a basis for advances by rival bidders.

Bid calling is really necessary only in ascending-bid auction systems. In Dutch-type auctions the numbers enunciated are solicitations, not bids. In Japanese simultaneous bidding, individual bids are purposely not enunciated, for the system is based on maximum offers of bidders in the first instance, rather than on enhanced bids. In haphazard auctions, where the bidders are not informed of the bids of others and thus bid blindly, bid calling has no place.

Bid Calling without Use of the Chant

In starting the bidding, the auctioneer may permit the bidders to place the opening bid without any suggestion from him. In order to save time and to establish a fast pace, however, the auctioneer usually tries a figure (of $100, say) and then retreats (perhaps to $80) if he finds no one willing to bid at his proposed starting price. Once he gets an opening bid at least in the English system it is his job to call the bids, keep the audience interested, and stimulate further bidding.

The informing function.—If bids were always made audibly, bid calling would be less crucial than it is, but the communication of bids by signal in most English-type auctions makes bid calling indispensable. The signal may be by a wink or a movement of pencil, or the bidder may indicate simply by meeting the auctioneer's eye that he is topping the preceding bid. Signs are also used at times to indicate the amount of an advance; or a bidder may show, perhaps by moving his hand away from his body, palm down, that he is bidding only half the advance sought. He can accomplish the same purpose by using finger signals, such as showing five fingers to raise a bid by only $5 when the auctioneer is asking $10. When signals of any kind are used, the auctioneer must communicate the amount of the bid to the assemblage.

Often, but not always, the auctioneer announces not only the amount of the various bids as they are made, but also the amount he hopes to obtain. For example, he may say, "I have an offer of $500, ladies and gentlemen," thus indicating the present level of the bidding, and then follow with, "Who will increase the bid to $525?" In this type of bid calling the auctioneer overtly establishes the amount of the increase he wants. When bidding is lively, and it appears that he has started too low, he may lead the bidder up by larger advances than he asked for at first. Under reverse circumstances, he may choose to accept a smaller increase. Indeed, as the price approaches maximum levels, the auctioneer often decreases the normal advance in order to get the high bidder's maximum demand price without discouraging his participation.

In some English-type auctions, however, the auctioneer does not overtly indicate the amount of the bid that he is seeking. Escalations are standard in American tobacco auctions, and all buyers are familiar with them. At London antique auctions, the bidders are supposed to be sophisticated enough to know what the amount of the advance will be at various price levels. For example, if a bid is £100, the buyer assumes that the next bid should be £105; a bid of £1,000 will presumably be followed by one of £1,050. In other words, auctioneers seek intervals of roughly 5 percent, the amount of the escalation increasing as the price goes up. When buyers infer the amount of the rise from the level of the bidding, the auctioneer must fill in dead spots with some sort of verbalizing. It is hardly practicable, when sales transactions are expected to move at the rate of fifty an hour, say, simply to communicate the amount of the current bid to the audience and then wait silently for further bids. Buyer apathy would almost certainly result, except when the auctioneer-salesman is highly skilled.

When only the last bid is announced, bid calling is more complex than has been suggested, because the advance sought by the auctioneer may change in amount, although possibly not in percentage terms, as the bidding reaches higher levels. Whereas in the sale of antiques the step-up usually increases as the bids increase, in auctions of livestock in the United States the advances remain constant until the estimated selling price is approached, at which time the differential is reduced. The reason for the latter is that in such situations there is a retail market price limiting the maximum price that can be obtained in the primary market, and as this figure is approximated buyers can be induced to bid only if they are permitted to advance their offers by smaller increments.

The auctioneer who does not employ the chant must turn to another kind of verbalizing, if only to bridge the gap between the bids and thus keep buyer interest from dwindling. Sometimes he repeats the amount bid and, where applicable, the price he hopes to get, without resorting to direct sales promotional efforts. More often he points out the merits of the merchandise and cajoles, persuades, exhorts, and otherwise promotes sales in an attempt to elicit a higher bid. Thus the auctioneer utilizes the time interval between bids to influence directly the trend of the bidding.

Sales promotional function.—The auctioneer does more, then, than simply call out bids; he also, directly and indirectly, promotes bidding by potential buyers. One successful auctioneer I know interjects such remarks as: "Ladies and gentlemen, this is the best example of a French Provincial desk I have ever seen." Later, if the bids seem to bog down a bit, he adds: "This is *no money* for such a fine example of French Provincial furniture, ladies and gentlemen," or "You will be interested in knowing that an ordinary one went at Sotheby's only last week for twice the amount you are bidding now," or "Remember this is an original, ladies and gentlemen—you would pay more than this for a reproduction." Whatever the stratagem employed, it is designed to maintain, or enhance the interest of would-be buyers and thus enliven the bidding activity.

Much of the sales promotional effort would be unnecessary if sales were very brisk, with numerous individuals bidding rapidly. Then there would be no dead spots to cover, the bids would come spontaneously without promotional prodding, and the bid caller would simply recognize bidders in proper order and announce their bids, sometimes interjecting the amount of proposed advances and filling any silences with appropriate remarks designed to elicit further bids.

The effective auctioneer must be a kind of actor with the personality and the ability to play varying roles, depending on the circumstances of the particular transaction. An actor, however, has fixed lines composed by others to which he must adhere, whereas the auctioneer-salesman relies on lines of his own creation in his relations with different buyers. He may, for example, say to a bidder he knows, "This should be in your collection." [1] But he must always remember that it is easy to offend people and ruin a sale, and perhaps adversely affect future sales.

The auctioneer may use humor, where suitable, but he must avoid becoming a comic in the eyes of prospective buyers. On one occasion, Louis Marion of Parke-Bernet carried the day splendidly to break the $100,000 level when the highest bid for a Bonnard

[1] James Brough, *Auction!* (Indianapolis and New York: Bobbs-Merrill, 1963), p. 149.

painting seemed fated to be $98,000. He appealed to the prestige factor by saying: "Now wouldn't it sound a whole lot better . . . if when your friends come into your house, you could say 'I paid $100,000 for this painting'?" The price then jumped to $110,000 amid the hearty laughter of the auction crowd.[2]

Bid calling by American auctioneers is often characterized by considerable noise and confusion, a kind of carnival atmosphere, some of which arises from the auctioneer's sales promotional efforts. Many auctions, of course, are conducted in a dignified way. The type of performance put on by the auctioneer depends in large part on the nature of the buying group he is facing. In general, one would expect nondealers to be more amenable than dealers to the wiles of auctioneer-salesmen. Auctions frequented largely by consumer-buyers, as in the sale of antiques in the United States, would thus seem to offer more fertile ground for auctioneers' antics than those patronized by dealers. Yet even when dealers constitute a significant segment of the assemblage, there may be an opportunity for sales promotional efforts, especially if the property, like antiques, has no precisely determinable market value. When the market price can be easily determined, as it can be for large-sized, top-quality fresh halibut, it would be a waste of time for the auctioneer to exhort buyers to raise their bids. They alone know the price they can afford to pay in the light of market conditions and individual supply needs.

The English are quite sedate in some of their auctions (for example, antiques), while in others (such as fish) they are perhaps just as disorderly as their counterparts in the United States. Decorum in bid calling is at its maximum during the auctioning of antiques and art objects in the fine salesrooms of Christie's and Sotheby's, although evidently it has not always been so. "In the days when Sotheby's was founded—in 1744—it was customary for the man with the gavel to keep a stream of extravagant praises flowing around whatever was up for bidding, like a present-day peddler of watches hypnotizing a carnival crowd."[3] English auctions of antiques are, at worst, quite dreary, but at their best they resemble a fine stage production, with its quiet but subtle dramatic impact. As a member of an esteemed British auction firm wrote

2 Quoted in *ibid.*
3 *Ibid.*, p. 25.

me, "The British auctioneer . . . repeat[s] in a leisurely fashion
the bids as he is dealing with people who are regular attenders at
auctions." In contrast, some American auctions remind him "of
evangelical meetings with the congregation being worked up into a
frenzy." But the general principle is the same, whether the auction
is formal or informal: bids come slowly, and must be extracted pa-
tiently without losing the interest of the crowd. Just as much sales
promotional effort may be exerted in a dignified atmosphere as in
more informal surroundings.

Some of the most effective auctioneers of antiques ply their trade
at Sotheby's and Christie's in London and at Parke-Bernet in New
York. At sales conducted by these venerable London auction firms,
only the price actually bid is announced by the auctioneer; he
makes no overt indication of the amount of the advance he is seeking. This procedure is made possible by the prevalence of standard
escalations and the fact that most of the buyers are dealers, fully
aware of customary trading practices. Peter Wilson, the famous
auctioneer at Sotheby's, follows the soft-sell approach suited to the
clientele of the house he represents. There is little direct selling of
any item put up for sale; in view of the type of clientele, little is
needed. When the bids are coming in promptly, as they may well
be when Peter Wilson is on the rostrum, one might hear him announce, "Sixty-five thousand, the bid is in the front," or "Yours, sir,
in the fourth row." [4] When the bidding is slower he might say, "At
eight thousand, eight thousand then . . . ," or more pointedly, "It's
against you now, sir, the gentleman on the aisle," or, with a kind of
aggrieved air, "Will *nobody* offer more?" [5]

Bid Calling by Use of the Chant

A chant, according to Webster, is a "singing or speaking in
monotone often with strongly marked rhythmic stresses." It is utilized in auction selling in certain fields for a number of reasons.
Most important, chanting makes less obvious the sometimes long,
quiet intervals between bids, thus obscuring the fact that the bidding is anything but lively. Moreover, the rhythm of a chant, delivered in a monotone or very nearly so, may intrigue, and thus hold

4 *Ibid.*, p. 33.
5 Quoted in *ibid.*, p. 25.

the attention of, an audience. The chant is also considered a voice saver by those employing it, for, as in singing, the sounds come largely from the diaphragm, thus easing the strain on the vocal cords. The inherent fascination of a rhythmic beat, combined with the personality of the auctioneer, may bring into the bidding listeners who lack a fundamental interest in the item up for sale.

Sales to nonprofessional buyers.—The chant is often used in auctions patronized mainly by private buyers. It must then be understandable to a nonprofessional audience, at least insofar as the enunciation of prices is concerned. Without such comprehension, would-be buyers would have no basis for bidding, and few if any bids would be forthcoming.

The type of chant employed in the auctioning of property to nonprofessional buyers should contain five elements: (1) the starting price the auctioneer wants to get, whether or not he suggests it; (2) the actual bids received, which the auctioneer repeats for the information of competing bidders; (3) the bid he is attempting to obtain, which may be expressed either as (*a*) the amount of the advance or as (*b*) the total amount sought; (4) filler words and phrases, many of which are useful as tactical devices, even though they are meaningless in the sense of direct communication; and (5) the announcement of the sale to the high bidder. These elements really fall into only two categories: (1) monetary quotations that are essential to the bidder qua bidder and must be understood if the bidder is to act intelligently; and (2) nonsense filler and rhythmic words and phrases that are not necessarily understandable and are not required for intelligent bidder action. The first of these may be thought of as informational, and the second, as sales promotional.

Generally speaking, in auctions that employ the chant and are patronized mainly by nondealers, both the actual bid in hand and the higher bid that the auctioneer is seeking are announced. Otherwise the prospective purchasers would not know the customary escalations at various price levels, and would have no guidance in their bidding. As the chant is practiced in such auctions, buyers can easily detect the bid being sought and thus advance the bid intelligently.

The key characteristic of a chant designed for nonprofessional bidders is a pleasing rhythm, combined with clear enunciation of the prices bid and sought. The rhythmic beat may be provided by filler or nonsense words that are completely unintelligible to bidders, just so long as the prices uttered in the chant are clearly understood. For tactical purposes, filler words are often used between the amount actually bid and the amount the auctioneer is seeking. The word "now" is perhaps the most common filler word; after announcement of an actual bid, say $20, it means "Now who will make it 25?" Perhaps it should not be called a "filler" word, for it has the important function of indicating the meaning of the second price figure.

Filler words are employed in the auctioneer's chant to bridge silent gaps between bids and to give his spiel a rhythmic quality. There are two basic types: (1) phrases specifically designed to lead from the bid already in hand to the bid that is being sought, and (2) phrases used simply as gap fillers. Examples of these two types of filler material, collected in direct observation of English-type auctions, are shown in table 4. Although some filler material is designed as time-consuming noisemaking, much of it is utilized for lead-in purposes. Particularly in American sales, the auctioneer repeatedly requests a specific bid one step higher than the one prevailing, or concentrates on the advance he is seeking.

A competent auctioneer does not repeat the same words and phrases over and over again in his chant; he introduces variety into the pattern. For example, "Want to make it four. Now four. Who will give me four? Who will make it four? Will you give me four? I have four. Will you give me five? Will you make it five? Do you want it at five? Will you take it at five? All in? All done? . . ." In themselves, filler words do not create a rhythmic pattern; they merely supply the basis for such a pattern. The auctioneer must provide the rhythm, but his efforts are likely to be fruitless without lines designed to enhance rhythm. Thus: "I have a bid of twenty dollars. Who will make an offer of twenty-five dollars?" becomes "Twenty dollars bid, Ladies and Gentlemen. Who will give a five dollar bill to make it twenty-five?" The following sales pitch is potentially rhythmical: "How much will you give for it? I am bid twenty-five. Who will make it thirty? How to make it thirty? Where to get thirty? Will you give thirty? Thirty is bid. And now five. Will you give five? Make it thirty-five. Thirty-five is bid. Now forty. Make it forty. Give me forty. Where to get forty. Put 'em at forty. . . ." An auctioneer trained in the use of the chant can deliver these words with a rhythmical beat that is very pleasing to the ear.

In order to reduce excess verbiage, an auctioneer employing a chant may at times leave off "the handle" (as he calls it), thus

TABLE 4

FILLER WORDS AND PHRASES USED IN THE AUCTIONEER'S CHANT

CONNECTIVES BETWEEN ACTUAL BID AND AMOUNT SOUGHT	GAP FILLERS
1. Fifteen dollars bid. Now seventeen-fifty.	1. What will you give for it?
2. Ten dollars. Who will give me twelve-fifty?	2. Hey, hey, what do you say?
3. Six dollars. Anybody give me six-fifty?	3. How much am I bid?
4. It will take a twenty-dollar bill to buy it.	4. Are you all through?
5. Five dollars. Who will make it seven-fifty?	5. Thank you, ma'am.
6. Who will buy it at eight dollars?	6. Are you all done?
7. Eighty dollars. Now ninety dollars. Will you give me ninety dollars?	7. Where will you find another like it?
8. Who will take it at eight dollars.	8. How much am I bid?
9. Who will make it five dollars apiece for the mattress and springs?	9. What will it be—yes or no?
10. I've got a one dollar bill on it. Will you make it two?	10. Thank you, sir.

shortening the price quotation. He may, as an illustration, have a bid of $225 but be attempting to get a $25 increase. So he asks, "Who will give me $25 to make it $50?" or "Who will make it fifty?" Thus he leaves out part of the $250 he is attempting to get; he simply suggests a $25 advance to $50, when actually it is a $25 advance to $250. This device enables the auctioneer to maintain rhythm in his chant, but he must supply the handle occasionally lest the bidders be misled, to the embarrassment of all concerned.

An auctioneer who uses the chant sometimes employs "explosive" bid calling; that is, he momentarily departs from his usual rhythm and tone and shouts the bid he has just received, or the one he is seeking, in order to create the impression that the bids are coming in fast and furiously. Thus, "I have 200 dollars, will you make it 250? Do I hear 50? Thank you, sir. The bid is 50. YES, 50!!! Now will you make it 75 . . . 75!" The purpose of explosive bid calling is to stimulate lively bidding. It is used most effectively when considerable buyer interest already exists and the auctioneer wants to intensify that interest. The tactic holds much less promise as a means of developing interest from a standing start.

Chants cannot be fully understood simply through analysis of their verbal components, because delivery is a very important factor. No chant is precisely the same as another, even when delivered by the same person, because of quality variations in the item that is up for sale, the level of the starting price, the intensity of competition in the bidding, the type of buying group, and so forth. Just as each transaction in an auction is separate and distinct, so different combinations of words and phrases are brought into use in different circumstances. The skilled auctioneer has a reservoir of filler materials, inflections, stories, word combinations, changes of pace and tricks, which are called into play without conscious thought to meet the particular conditions of the moment. He has trained himself to open his mouth and speak rapidly, using a rhythmical delivery and the proper proportions of filler words and information in order to effectively woo bidders. His purpose is to extract bids from those not yet competing and to elicit higher bids from those already participating.

Sales to professional buyers.—In auctioning goods to dealers and other professional buyers who are constantly in the market, it is not important to make the chant intelligible. The esoteric chant sounds like gibberish to the uninitiated, even though it may be as fascinating to the ear as a child's nursery rhyme. It cannot actually be nonsense, however, because even professional buyers must have a basis for their bids, at least in English-type auctions, and the seemingly unintelligible words in a chant are actually quite intelligible to the trained ear. The experienced auction buyer mentally cuts through the gibberish and gleans the price information he needs.

Livestock auctions.—The chant used in livestock auctions in the United States is based on two premises: (1) the buyers are professionals who are sophisticated in bidding procedures and can understand the chant; and (2) the auctioneer announces the price actually bid and the increase he is trying to obtain. In livestock auctions bids are typically made by signals, and bidders who are new to a particular auction should inform the auctioneer in advance what signals they employ. A newcomer might explain, for example, that he always bids by looking directly into the auctioneer's eyes and that he is not bidding if his eyes are averted, or that he is bidding only when his hat is off or when he wipes his brow.

Because he is dealing with professionals, the livestock auctioneer does not need to make the chant intelligible to the layman. Even a layman, however, by listening to the ringman's starting price (in livestock auctions it is the man in the ring who usually acts as bid starter) and knowing the amount bid as well as the next higher bid the auctioneer is trying for, can follow the proceedings with at least a modicum of comprehension. In order to participate, of course, he must understand every nuance.

Livestock auctions are usually characterized by slow, deliberate bidding. If the auctioneer announced only the bids, and said nothing else, there would be dead spots that might adversely affect the price results. If he said, for example, "I am bid twenty-eight cents," and after a twenty- or thirty-second interval recognized a counterbid of twenty-nine, and then again waited in silence for a considerable period, he would undoubtedly lose his audience. He therefore bridges the gaps between bids with rhythmic and high-speed verbalizing.

In western United States livestock auctions, the animals typically are sold individually or in groups at so much per pound. When the poundage basis is used for price quotations, the standard escalation is 1 cent a pound. If the animals are sold by the head, as calves are, or by the lot, each lot including several animals, there is no standard escalation. Even in sales by the pound, however, the standard escalation is not adhered to as the price approaches the market quotation; at this point the auctioneer, sensing that he cannot get the full 1-cent advance, may ask for a fractional increase. The livestock auctioneer, like other practitioners of his trade, leads bidders to some extent by calling out the bid sought as well as the bid already in hand. He has three ways of covering silent intervals between bids: (1) repeating the amount of the bid he has in hand; (2) announcing and repeating the amount of the bid he wants to hear next; and (3) utilizing filler words.

The amount the auctioneer receives as a starting bid is important to the success of the sale. In livestock auctions the decision as to a reasonable starting price is the responsibility of the bid starter. The particular figure he chooses is not as crucial as one might think, however, because it is subject to adjustment. Let us say that the bid starter indicates a starting price of 25 cents, and the auctioneer tries to get a bid at this figure and cannot do so. The auctioneer then drops the suggested opening bid to 24 cents and, if necessary, to 23, in rhythmic delivery just as if he were advancing instead of retreating. If he gets a bid of 23, he may have to go into fractional bids at once, say 23.5 rather than back to 25 or even 24 cents. He may even try for a fractional amount of, say, 24.5 cents after failing to get 25 cents, depending upon his judgment of the market. If he gets the 24.5 cents, he may try to move up fractionally, first to 24.6 cents, then to 24.7 cents, in order to get the highest bid possible under prevailing market conditions.

Sound judgment on the part of both ringman and auctioneer is of importance in any transaction, not only in starting the bid but in deciding when to reduce the advance. Let us say a bid caller decides early in the bidding to reduce the amount of the advance to 0.1 cent. Almost certainly, as a result, (1) it will take too long to get to the top bid level, because the progression is by tenth-of-a-cent instead of full-cent intervals; or (2) the price will never get to the high level because bidder interest will be lost before the bidding reaches its normal climax. If, however, the bidding starts at 25 cents, moves to 26 cents, advances to 27 cents, and then—because the auctioneer knows that the market price is between 27 and 28 cents—to 27.1 cents and finally to 27.3 cents, top money has probably been squeezed from the assembled bidders. This practice of reducing the amount of the advance as the bids approach the prospective selling price achieves a better "fit" to the existing market price situation without seriously slowing up the sale. Thus the essential elements of a livestock chant are starting the bidding, obtaining the customary advances from bidders, and reducing the size of the advances as the price rises to higher levels.

Tobacco auctions.—The tobacco chant, long familiar to American radio listeners, is somewhat different from those used in the sale of goods to professional buyers in other commodity fields. For one thing, it is more melodious. For another, in tobacco auctioning only actual bids are enunciated; there is no reference to the amount of the next bid the auctioneer is seeking or even to the increase sought. The reason is that escalations in the tobacco trade are standard at 1 cent a pound, or 1 dollar per 100 pounds, except that quarter-cent advances apply on prices below 15 cents and half-cent advances prevail between 15 cents and 25 cents.

Furthermore, tobacco auctioneers usually employ very little filler material. The tobacco chant is made up almost entirely of price quotations rapidly enunciated, although the terms "dollah" or "mamma" are sometimes utilized. Extensive filler material is not needed because tobacco buyers make their bids in rapid succession. The selling of four hundred lots an hour—that is, one every nine seconds—is common in this field.[6]

Perhaps the most important reason for the uniqueness of the tobacco chant is that price quotations are called in a code that is understood by professional buyers. Code words provide rhythm and permit rapid enunciation. For example, the word "one" becomes *mun* or *mun-a;* the word "two" becomes *doo,* extended for filler purposes to *doodle oodle oo;* and "three" becomes *ree,* or *ree-nee* when further filler material is required. An extension is provided when the initial digit, or handle, is needed at the tens level: "sixty-three," for example, might become *singny-ree.*

The code words for quarter- and half-cent quotations at the lower price levels are also standard. A quarter cent becomes *wah,* or *wah-ta* if extended; a half cent is *hah,* or *hah-ta* if extended; and three-quarters of a cent becomes *ree,* or *ree-nee* if extended. These longer phrases enhance the rhythmic quality of the chant. A fractional figure is always given without the whole number preceding

6 L. A. "Speed" Riggs, famous as the Lucky Strike tobacco auctioneer, holds the world record with a chant at the rate of 784 words per minute for forty-two seconds. His normal chanting speed is 460 words per minute, while that of the average tobacco auctioneer is 340. In contrast, the usual tempo of an informal discussion is 70 to 90 words per minute.

it, which is understood inferentially by the buyers. For a bid of six and three-quarters, the auctioneer would say *ree-nee* until he got a bid of seven, which he would announce, in code terms, as *see-mon*. If the bidding goes above seven, he would again use only the fractional part of the figure.

At the beginning of a sale of a new lot of tobacco, the auctioneer suggests a starting price (given him by the warehouseman, or bid starter, who serves as evaluator). If the auctioneer gets a bid at the starting price, he chants that bid and then subsequent offers in ascending order until he is satisfied that he has the highest bid, at which time he knocks the lot down. If he does not get a bid at the suggested price, he reduces it 1 cent at a time (in rhythmic cadence, as if he were calling ascending bids) until he does get a bid, at which point he can start moving upward. Tobacco buyers usually make their bids surreptitiously by means of well-concealed signals.

While recognizing the fascination of the chant, one wonders why it is used in a rational sales operation such as tobacco auctions. There is little doubt that its use is traditional, but how it originated remains a puzzle. Regardless of its origin, the chant is now so ingrained in the set of behavior patterns that characterize tobacco auctioning at the primary level that it is unlikely to be replaced by another system.

Other Methods of Bid Calling

Bid calling is an ascending-bid phenomenon, and is requisite to the operation of English-type auctions. Other auctioning systems either do not require it (the Dutch and Japanese methods, for example, and auctions where bidding is blind), or provide for the bid-calling function in other ways.

Even when bid calling is used, bids are not always communicated to traders by means of the voice. In the variation of the English-type auction employed in the sale of halibut in Seattle, the auctioneer posts the bids on a blackboard, usually without any verbalizing. This procedure has the same effect as audible repetition of the bids.

The bid-calling function in a silent auction is performed by the bidder himself, who registers the amount of his bid, or advance, on a card that is displayed with the item that is up for sale. In effect, each bidder "calls" his bid for the benefit of other would-be buyers. As we shall see later, bid calling in ascending-bid electronic auctions is performed by a clocklike device whose hands continuously indicate the level of the bidding. Bids are registered by the pushing of a button that stops the hand of the clock. Thus, even in the absence of an auctioneer, the bid-calling function may be an integral part of the sales transaction.

Conditions of Sale

10 BECAUSE AUCTION firms act as agents of vendors, the latter should know what an auction firm professes to do for them in connection with transfer of title and what it intends to charge for its services. These matters are often individually negotiated between vendor and agent. The auction firm also has dealings, or prospective dealings, with buyers of the type of merchandise sold by the auction firm. The rules under which auction firms conduct their selling operations are known as the conditions of sale.

General Conditions of Sale

Before examining specific conditions of sale applicable to particular auction firms, students of auctions should understand their general characteristics. In discussing conditions of sale as they apply to seller-buyer relations, the judge in a relevant case stated: " 'An auction is a form of competitive bargaining with the object of a contract of sale resulting carried out in accordance with certain rules. These rules are the conditions of sale. They are framed by the seller [or his agent] to represent the terms upon which he is prepared to submit his property to competition. They are, so to speak, the rules of the game and they bind all the players.' " In commenting on this view of conditions of sale, a legal writer added: "When goods are offered for sale pursuant to them, they form the basis of the bargaining carried on between the auctioneer and the bidders [i.e., the players]." [1]

Conditions of sale may be characterized as follows:

1. Conditions of sale by their very nature are the terms of contractual agreement between the sales agent and the auction buyer under which the latter bids and the former accepts the offer by the fall of the hammer, thus consummating the transaction.

2. The owner of the goods may prescribe the conditions of sale but he may waive them; in the absence of such prescription, the auctioneer has considerable discretion as to the terms and manner of sale.

3. A recognized auction company typically has its own conditions of sale applicable to the type of operation it conducts, which the seller may accept in place of any he might set down.

4. Printed conditions are binding on the parties to the sale and the auctioneer is not permitted to vary them, at least verbally, without approval of his principal and without full notice to buyers, although he may explain them at the sale.

5. Conditions of sale announced or referred to by the auctioneer are binding on the purchaser whether he understands them or not, if proper legal notice has been given.

6. Advertisements of the sale have been held to be no part of the conditions thereof unless especially made such, but they may specifically mention some conditions and refer to the fact that those under which the auction operates are available for examination at the site of the sale.

7. Conditions of sale that conflict with a law of the jurisdiction in which the auction operates are not legally enforceable.

In some jurisdictions the auctioneer is required to refer to the conditions of sale at the beginning of each auction session, and to announce that they are available to prospective bidders. The conditions of sale under which an auction operates may be likened to the rules of a game in that they reflect the desire of an auction firm to regulate itself. The regulations are presumably within the laws of the municipality, state, or country in which the business is con-

1 Edward F. George, "Auctioneer's Refusal To Accept Highest Bid," *Law Quarterly Review*, LXV (July, 1949), 311.

ducted. Conditions of sale may not transcend the law of the land, but must be in accord with relevant legislative restrictions. For example, the law permitting withdrawal of a bid by a bidder in an auction before the hammer falls may not be superseded by conditions of sale purporting to circumscribe such a right.[2]

It goes without saying that would-be buyers at an auction should familiarize themselves with the rules within which they are expected to operate. The auction company is expected to cooperate in the informing process. There has been a trend over the years toward improved notification of participants:

1. Conditions of sale appear to have been an integral part of ancient auction operations; they were indicated in the *proscriptio*, or notice of sale, as well as expressed in brief form by the *praeco*, or auctioneer, at the time of the sale itself.[3]

2. In earlier days in England it was the practice to have the conditions of sale read amid the "confusion and hubbub of the auction," with a resulting impairment of communication and perhaps even with the intention of misleading would-be buyers.

3. In the course of time the conditions of sale began to be exhibited in auction rooms. This notice was considered fairly adequate for those wishing to participate, assuming that they were able to read.

4. The most effective method of communicating sales conditions, however, is to include them as an integral part of the catalog.

Today the conditions of sale are usually printed in the inside front cover of the catalog of the auction company that is conducting the sale. If there is no catalog, the salient provisions are posted on the walls of the auction room. When, as in some auctions, the posting of conditions is dispensed with, the purchasing group is composed of professional buyers who are expected to be well informed about the trading rules.

Conditions of sale cover all kinds of contingencies, such as the rights of the auctioneer in recognizing or not recognizing bidders; the proper disposition of tie bids; and the size of deposits, if any, re-

---

2 See *Becker* v. *Crabb*, 223 Ky. 549, 4 S.W.2d 370, 371 (1928).

3 J. A. C. Thomas, "The Auction Sale in Roman Law," *Juridical Review*, Pt. I (April, 1957), p. 43.

quired from successful bidders. The rules prescribe precisely how traders must behave, and in some instances make provision for handling disputes.

Specific Conditions of Sale

The importance of distinguishing between particulars of the property to be sold and the terms or conditions governing the sales transactions has been stressed by a legal writer: "The distinction between particulars [of property] and conditions [of sale] has been stated as follows: 'The proper office of the particulars is to describe the subject matter of the contract [i.e., the property]; that of the conditions to state the terms on which it is sold.' Accordingly, it follows that the particulars [and, indeed, conditions] form an essential part of the contract between the vendor and the purchaser, and [thus] must be prepared with [special] caution, clarity and accuracy; except in the simplest of cases the prudent auctioneer is well advised to obtain the assistance of a solicitor [i.e., attorney], not merely to draw the conditions but to advise in relation to the particulars." [4]

There is no question that descriptions of the property and the terms of sale are intermixed in auctions where such information is given orally, as in the sale of real property. No such confusion arises, however, if a catalog of items up for sale is provided by the auction firm. The catalog contains written descriptions of the property to be sold which correspond to the particulars that are often provided orally when real property is being sold. Particulars contained in catalog descriptions thus are distinguished from conditions of sale, the latter indicating the terms on which the property described in the particulars is to be sold.

The conditions of sale applying to auction selling fall into a number of categories. [5]

The purchase and sale transaction.—The bidding provisions in terms of sale may indicate that (*a*) the highest bidder shall be the purchaser, subject to certain reservations; (*b*) bidders may not ad-

4 David Napley, *Bateman's Law of Auctions* (11th ed.; London: Estates Gazette, 1954), p. 34.

5 For the ensuing discussion, heavy reliance has been placed on *ibid.,* esp. pp. 69–117.

vance by less than a specified amount; (*c*) no bid shall be retracted (even though such a provision may be legally unenforceable); and (*d*) when a dispute arises as to the highest bidder, the property may be put up again or the auctioneer may be given full power to decide to whom the award is to be made.

The right of the vendor to bid in an auction should be expressly stated in the conditions of sale. The conditions may also stipulate how many times this right may be exercised. They may specify, further, whether the property is being sold with or without a reserve price. The goods may be sold either way if the sale is not represented as one without a reserve price.

The conditions of sale may specify that immediately upon the fall of the hammer the purchaser shall make a deposit of a specified amount (10 percent of the purchase price, say). Typically it is made payable to the auctioneer, as the vendor's agent, or in some instances it may be paid to the vendor's attorney. If a deposit is a substantial amount, provision may be made for its investment until the completion of the sale, and for interest to be paid on the sum deposited.

Title to the property.—Some conditions of sale specify that title passes with the fall of the hammer; others provide that title does not pass until final payment is made. In the sale of chattels, it is assumed that the vendor has title and can convey it to the buyer. The conditions assume further that title to property sold at auction passes from vendor to purchaser. If, however, there is a defect in the title to the property, the particulars should (*a*) point out the defect and state that the merchandise is being sold "as is"; (*b*) refer the purchaser to the documents of title and require that he accept the title they disclose; or (*c*) indicate that the property is for sale with only such title as the vendor may possess.

Conditions of sale may also provide that if the purchaser makes any objections as to proper title or conveyance and if the vendor is unable or unwilling to rectify the defect objected to, the vendor shall have power to annul the sale. "Sometimes the condition is made to apply only to requisitions which the vendor shall be unable or unwilling to comply with on the ground of expense or difficulty; such a qualification prevents a vendor from being able to rescind the contract in order to accept a better offer." [6]

6 *Ibid.*, p. 91.

Completion of the purchase.—Conditions of sale usually specify the circumstances under which the purchase of property is to be completed, including any limitation for satisfying the requirements. In the absence of a provision to the contrary, the buyer must be ready and willing to pay the price in exchange for the goods, and the seller must be ready and willing to relinquish possession of the goods to the buyer in exchange for the price agreed upon.

Provision is commonly made for delivery of the property within a specified time. It is not always done, however, for a sales contract, by its very nature, implies that delivery is to be made and accepted within a reasonable time. Provision may also be made that the time may be extended by negotiation, or that the completion time specified is absolute.

Conditions of sale usually provide for the payment of the full purchase price before delivery of the goods. It may be stipulated that interest shall be paid on the balance of the purchase money if not paid by the time fixed for the completion of the purchase. It may also be specified that the seller pay the buyer interest on the deposit money in an aborted auction.

Misdescriptions of the goods.—The maxim *caveat emptor* is generally applicable to the sale of goods at auction, unless an express warranty is made. Vendors or their agents often specifically disclaim warranties of quality of goods. In the absence of fraud, the buyer purchases at his own risk unless the seller has given him an express warranty or unless a warranty is implied from the circumstances of the sale. Legally, the buyer purchases on the basis of his own judgment if he *selects* the specific merchandise he requires; he buys on the judgment of the seller if the latter agrees to supply goods that the buyer has no opportunity to inspect.

Some conditions of sale make provision for a warranty that the goods are "equal to sample." Presumably vendors can be held to such a provision, although buyers would be on sounder ground if it were contained in a contract. When goods are sold by description rather than by inspection, there is an implied condition that the goods shall correspond with the description, for which the vendor, again, is presumably responsible.

Conditions of sale relating to errors in description of a piece of property, which may or may not provide remedies, are intended to guard against errors that are unintentional. The vendor may not protect himself against misrepresentations calculated to mislead the purchaser, because fraudulent behavior is proscribed by law.

Although conditions of sale seldom so specify, the statement that goods are sold "with all faults" means all faults consistent with what the item is supposed to be, and it must be interpreted in the light of the context in which it is used. For example, a fishing boat sold "with all faults" but described as "copper-fastened" was so constructed only in part, and was not what is called a copper-fastened vessel in the trade; the purchaser was therefore entitled to recover damages for breach of warranty. A sale made subject to the reservation "with all faults" is voidable if the vendor is aware of latent defects and uses surreptitious means to conceal them.

Forfeiture of deposit and resale of property.—Conditions of sale usually specify that goods be removed from the sales premises at the purchaser's expense within a certain time, and that they be paid for prior to removal. The goods are the buyer's responsibility after the hammer falls, although the seller is expected to take reasonable care of the buyer's property after the passage of title. Conditions of sale sometimes specifically deny the right to demand delivery during the sale.

The conditions often contain a provision that upon the purchaser's failure to comply with specifications the property is to be resold; this provision may be legally redundant if the purchaser's conduct amounts to repudiation of the contract. Such provision may include the vendor's right to retain the deposit; it may even specify the right of resale and action for damages resulting from monetary deficiencies as compared with the contractual agreement. There is usually no provision for the reimbursement of purchasers if revenues acquired from reselling the lot exceed the contractual auction price less the deposit.

Disputes between buyer and seller.—Auction selling is carried on within the framework of certain terms of sale, but all transactions must be in accord with relevant legislation in the jurisdiction where the auction operates. Disputes between seller and buyer may therefore be settled by court action instituted by an aggrieved trader. Court records over the years abound with actions developing out of alleged failure of one party or another to perform properly.

Despite preventive measures, disputes do occasionally arise in auction operations. They may develop from a complaint by a would-be buyer who thought he was the highest bidder, or from complaints by those who thought the goods were misrepresented. Many such differences are resolved by negotiation; some conditions of sale, in fact, contain a provision for arbitration of disputes. Such provisions are much more likely to be found in auction operations patronized by profit-motivated dealer-buyers than those attended by consumer-buyers. In the auctioning of tea in London, for example, the conditions of sale provide not only for arbitration, but for the method of selecting arbitrators and the fees to be paid them. Arbitration is also provided for in the conditions of sale for wool auctions in Australia, in cases of nonperformance developing from strike conditions, if the problem cannot be effectively solved by a joint committee of buyers and sellers.

The conditions of sale for an auction, although similar to the rules of an athletic contest in their self-regulating aspect, do not tell how to operate an auction. They do not explain in precise terms the auction system that is to be employed in the sale. The only exception of which I am aware is Article 6 of the selling rules for auctions of horticultural and agricultural products in the Netherlands, which reads: "Auctioning takes place on a descending scale and in a way announced beforehand by the auctioneer." Perhaps such a provision is considered unnecessary in most auctions, but, regardless of the reason, the method of determining the highest bidder is not usually specified.

Another important difference between the rules of a game and those governing an auction is that the former are very detailed; they cover every possible move that can be made by a player on offense or defense. In contrast, the conditions of sale applying to an auction are usually very general, and cover only the rules that are thought by the vendor or his agent to be of importance in the particular sale. It follows that unamplified terms of sale are inadequate as guides to the playing of the "auction game."

Variations in Conditions of Sale

Again unlike the rules for an athletic contest, which are fairly standard for a certain geographical area, such as Canada or the United States, the conditions of sale for auction operations differ substantially from one another, even within the same political jurisdiction. Because they are subject to the discretion of the individual operating the auction, they are not standardized. Table 5 lists different conditions of sale applicable to auctions. This list, compiled from the printed conditions governing auctions of many different products—antiques, furs, wool, tea, stamps, fish, timber, to name only a few—reveals that the rules vary from auction to auction. Such differences result from variations in the problems of selling different types of merchandise, and from individual preferences among auction firms as to the manner in which they wish to do business.

TABLE 5

CONDITIONS OF SALE FOR AUCTIONS OF VARIOUS TYPES OF GOODS

1. Prescribing who may trade at auction.[a]

2. Specifying time of auction sale or sales.

3. Reserving the right to combine sales of individual items into lots.

4. All bids for single article, even if more than one is included in a lot.

5. Defining official grade standards, e.g., fish.

6. Buyer may inspect items prior to bidding.[b]

7. Goods sold on a reserve basis in absence of statements to the contrary.

8. Lots may be withdrawn before the fall of the hammer without explanation.

9. Bids may be executed for buyers by auctioneer.[c]

10. Auctioneer has right to advance bids at his discretion.

11. Auctioneer may refuse a bid if bidder is not responsible.

12. Bid may be rejected when the advance is fractional.

13. The high bidder is the buyer; any disputes to be decided by auctioneer.

14. Auctioneer may make bids on behalf of the vendor one or more times.

15. Auction company has right to sell its own goods as well as those of client-vendor.

16. Title passes at the fall of the hammer.[d]

17. Terms cash—no credit.

18. All sales final—no recourse.

19. Successful buyer must make deposit and provide purchase money for the goods before delivery.

20. Goods sold "as is" with all defects therein and with all errors of description,[e] and all measurements are approximate.

21. Claims for variation from samples must be submitted within x days.

22. Delivery of property purchased made after specified time and after payment of balance due.

23. Government taxes in connection with sale to be paid by buyers, when appropriate.

24. Auctioneer fee shared with licensed brokers representing buyers (of real estate).

TABLE 5 (continued)

25. No article may be removed from the premises until presentation by buyer of receipted bill.

26. Lots to be taken away at buyer's expense within *x* days.

27. Buyer assumes all risk in connection with the goods purchased upon the fall of the hammer.

28. Failure of buyers to comply with conditions may result in resale of property in default and liability for any loss incurred.

29. Any vendor liability for goods damaged or stolen after sale limited to amount of bid.

30. Buyer liable for interest on unpaid balance after a time limit given for the payment of an account.

31. Auctioneers are agents only and are not responsible for correct descriptions, authenticity, and warranties.

32. Provision made for arbitration of disputes between buyers and sellers.

33. Every buyer subject to a levy for use in publicity campaign for commodity sold.

34. Conditions of sale cannot be altered, except in writing, by auction house.

35. The auctioneer disclaims any liability for default of the purchaser or the vendor.

36. Each buyer shall sign a copy of the conditions of sale which will be considered as part of a contract between buyer and seller.

---

a An auction may be open to all sellers without discrimination, as is the Seattle halibut exchange, or it may be restricted to clients who are required to meet certain specifications.

b In some instances, however (e.g., in the sale of fish by the boatload), inspection of the goods does not take place until after the sale, at the time of grading and weighing.

c One auction firm disclaims liability for errors in executing such bids.

d At least one important auction operation explicitly provides in the conditions of sale that title does not pass until goods are paid for.

e In some auctions, however, goods are specifically warranted. The relevent provision in the London stamp auction reads as follows: "Unless otherwise indicated each lot is sold as genuine and properly described."

There are, however, some provisions which, though not absolutely standard, appear in the terms of sale of many auctions. These include:

1. Highest bidder becomes the purchaser; no bid will be accepted after the fall of the hammer.

2. Any dispute arising during the sale of a lot results in putting the property up for sale again at the last undisputed price level, or in having the auctioneer determine, at his discretion, the identity of the successful bidder.

3. The purchaser must give his name and address to the auctioneer after the goods have been bought and must make a deposit

of a prescribed percentage of the purchase price, if requested to do so.

4. Failure to pay for goods results in a resale, and any difference between the price at the first sale and that at the resale is to be borne by the first purchaser.

5. No compensation is to be paid by sellers or their agents for faults or defects in or misdescriptions of the goods, assuming no fraudulent misrepresentation by the sellers.

6. The sale of each lot is to be at buyer's risk from the fall of the hammer, and removal is to be at the buyer's expense.

Some differences in the conditions of sale for different auctions are more apparent than real. The absence of a certain rule among the published conditions of sale does not necessarily mean that the sale is not conducted in accordance with that rule. As an example, an auction may operate under the condition that a trivial advance by a bidder will not be accepted without specific inclusion of this provision among the conditions of sale, although it may in some instances be included. Some conditions are expressly enunciated and some are only implied, suggesting that two auctions with different specified conditions may operate in much the same manner.

Among the genuine and very important differences that do exist in conditions of sale, based either on differences in commodities or on variations among the executive decisions of auction houses, are the following:

1. In certain auctions anyone can trade—these are genuine public auction sales—while in others prospective purchasers must produce satisfactory evidence of their qualifications to bid.

2. In some, perhaps most, auctions title passes from seller to buyer at the fall of the hammer (although such a provision may not be contained in the firm's conditions of sale), while in others title does not pass until after payment for the goods by the purchaser (for example, Hudson's Bay Company fur auctions in London).

3. In some auctions where sales are made before unloading the cargo (for example, fish), provision must be made for "weighing out" the cargo, while in other auctions this rule would be meaningless.

4. Some auctions provide that sales are to be made on a reserve

basis, and some clearly provide that the goods are to be sold without reserve.

5. Most auctions do not contain a provision for the payment of the auction fee by the buyer, because such a fee is ordinarily paid by the vendor, but in the conditions of sale governing two auctions with which I am familiar there is a clause requiring the buyer to pay part of the auction fee.

6. In some auctions book bids are accepted from "responsible parties," usually accompanied by a specified minimum deposit, while in other auctions bids must be executed either personally or through a broker.

7. In certain auctions conditions specify that delivery may not be made during the sale, while the conditions governing other auctions specifically permit such delivery.

8. In some auctions the conditions of sale provide that responsibility for the good after the hammer falls belongs to the buyer, whereas in others the conditions provide that the risk of the goods in storage shall be borne by the auction company or the vendor.

One of the most important differences in conditions of sale is in the warranties given the buyer by the vendor or his agent.[7] For example, when books are sold at auction, in England and perhaps elsewhere, the conditions usually state that they are in "perfect condition" unless otherwise expressly stated, and that they may be returned by the purchaser without liability within ten days of the date of sale. But periodical publications, interestingly enough, are sold "with all faults and errors of description." In selling paintings at auction, a clause often states that the names of the artists given in the catalog are those to whom the works are attributed, and that care was taken in the preparation of the descriptions, but the auctioneer does not hold himself responsible for correct descriptions or for the authenticity of any lot.

In the timber trade, because of the nature of the commodity, the goods are usually to be delivered "as and where they lie" at the buyer's expense with all faults and defects and without any allowance for errors in description. Stamps, on the contrary, are commonly sold with a money-back warranty. Horses may be sold with

7 The examples given below were taken from E. R. H. Ivamy, "Conditions of Sale at Auctions and Their Exclusion," *The Solicitor*, XVIII (Sept., 1951), 200–201.

or without a warranty; but if there is a warranty, the conditions of sale sometimes provide that an animal may be returned within a specified time, providing the purchaser brings a certificate from a competent veterinary attesting to the defect.

Importance to Buyers of Understanding Conditions of Sale

Although conditions of sale are rules applying to the vendor's selling operation, their impact is largely on the buyers. The vendors or their agents are giving notice to buyers that these are the rules under which they must purchase in a particular auction. It is therefore very important that buyers—particularly lay buyers—apprise themselves of the rules of an auction they intend to patronize. By this means they inform themselves about auctioning methods in general and also gain valuable information about the operation of a specific auction. If they were to learn nothing more than that a preview of goods is provided prior to the sale, that a 25 percent deposit is required of all successful bidders, and that the goods are sold strictly on a *caveat emptor* basis, the effort of studying the conditions of sale would be eminently worthwhile.

The individual who is contemplating bidding should know precisely what his rights, responsibilities, and obligations are. If the conditions are not incorporated in a catalog available at the sale, the buyer should inquire about them from the auctioneer or one of the associates, and then familiarize himself with them. He must understand any representations that may be made by the vendor, and what his specific responsibilities are in connection with the purchase. Such knowledge is essential to intelligent purchasing; it complements knowledge of the merchandise itself gleaned from catalog descriptions and supplemented by preauction inspection.

Strategy and Tactics
of Purchasing

11 THE PHRASE "strategy of auctioning" usually brings to mind the selling side of the market. It implies the planning of sales procedures in such a way as to create a favorable bidding situation from the point of view of the vendor. Buying strategy—that is, how the buyer at auction behaves or should behave in order to acquire the goods most advantageously—also merits consideration.

Buyer's Preauction Preparations

Since the vendor and his agent, the auctioneer, in attempting to get as much as they can for the goods that are up for sale, will employ various schemes designed to involve buyers emotionally, the buyer's best defense is to avoid such involvement. His first step is to prepare the way for rational behavior by carefully examining the merchandise in advance of the sale and seeking to discover its worth, in both general and specific terms. A necessary substep is occasional checking of manufacturers' or distributors' catalogs for prices of comparable new items. The buyer should then be able to set a ceiling above which he will not go, no matter what the extent of his emotional responses. By establishing his own maximum demand price, he faces the buying task rationally rather than emotionally.

Routine preparations.—The preauction preparation task is often relatively simple. The prospective purchaser of a secondhand refrigerator at a storage company auction, for example, should first examine the property during the preauction display period. Then he should determine the point beyond which he would not wish to go in his bidding, based on the existence of better alternative opportunities, either other secondhand goods or new items. His maximum price is, of course, only a maximum; he would hope to purchase the item for less if possible. Even uncomplicated preauction preparations require time and effort for actual examination of goods, for checking the prices of alternative supplies, and for arriving at the maximum bid to be offered.[1]

On the other hand, the problem of preparing to purchase at an auction sometimes is quite complex. Buyers who do not know precisely what type of item they require must attend the preview primarily to determine the specific items or lots on which they might bid. Next, they must inform themselves about the values of the several items. Only then are they in a position to decide what each item is likely to be worth in the market as well as to them.

The complexity of preauction operations may result from the expertise required in the evaluation of an item, particularly a fine-quality antique or a masterwork. While some auction houses can be relied on to properly represent the authenticity of their goods, others may not even undertake such an evaluation. The prospective bidder may therefore have to enlist the aid of a qualified expert in order to determine the provenance, or "pedigree," of an item; a dealer in paintings, for example, might consult with a specialist on Dutch masters or with a Rembrandt expert. Such authentication may be necessary either because (1) the auction firm has evaluated the article but sells on a *caveat emptor* basis, thus making it necessary for the buyer to check the value himself, or because (2) the buyer suspects that the firm's evaluation is too low and believes that he must determine whether the item is worth more than its estimated value. Each auction firm has its own way of rating the authenticity of a particular work of art. Sotheby's, for example, might rate a painting attributed to Sir Joshua Reynolds as *Sir Joshua Rey-*

1 See "What To Know If You Buy at Auctions," *Good Housekeeping*, CLVI (Jan., 1963), 122.

nolds, P.R.A. (highly confident of its authenticity), *Sir J. Reynolds* (probably authentic but not positive), or simply *Reynolds* (caution indicated).[2]

Sometimes the problem may be even more complex, as in the purchase of secondhand machinery. For example, the buyer may need one unit of a certain type of machine of which three are available. He may prefer item 16 if he can get it at or below his highest demand price; if unsuccessful, he will bid on item 17 up to his maximum demand price. If he fails again, he will bid on item 18, but then he may be forced to go beyond the maximum demand price he determined earlier. This would be particularly true if his need for the equipment was urgent and delivery of new machinery could not be obtained immediately.

The situation is further complicated if the preferred item is put up last instead of first. In that instance the would-be purchaser may decide that it is advisable to hedge against failure to acquire the preferred unit by bidding first on less desirable items. He may choose to bid casually on the alternative item or items and intensively on the preferred item. If this strategy proves completely successful, he will acquire the item he wants but not the alternative one. If partial success takes the form of obtaining both items, he can sell the one he does not need on a private-treaty basis. If, however, he acquires the alternative item rather than the preferred one, he can get along, at least minimally.[3] Success obviously may hinge on chance rather than on strategic planning.

Bidding on alternative choices may complicate the would-be buyer's preauction preparation, not only because of the added investigatory effort required, but because of the iffy character of the decision. Often, however, evaluation is simply a matter of gathering

2 John Carter, "The Auction Room," in Milton Grundy, *Money at Work* (London: Sweet & Maxwell, 1960), p. 152 n. 2.

3 In a written- or sealed-bid sale, the buyer would not know whether he had been successful in his bid for the first item before bidding on others. Consequently he might choose to bid on only one item, taking the chance of not acquiring any of the items, or he might hedge and bid on two or more with the expectation of disposing of the surplus later by private-treaty sale. For a discussion of the strategy of bidding in sealed-bid situations, see Alfred R. Oxenfeldt, *Pricing for Marketing Executives* (San Francisco: Wadsworth Publishing Co., 1961), pp. 47–52.

proper market knowledge, rather than of making judgments about the value of a particular item.

Planning the bidding.—Sometimes, as when a reputable owner sells a famous painting, there is really no problem of determining authenticity of the masterwork. In that event the prospective buyer can concentrate on deciding how high he wants to bid or will have to bid to acquire the item. He must also decide who will do the actual bidding and whether any tactical tricks should be employed, such as taking a giant step upward at some point in the bidding in an effort to shake off the opposition. His judgment must be based, in part at least, on the identity of the competitors and their probable reactions.

Because evaluation is essential to intelligent purchasing at auction, the preparation for bidding on a masterwork is a formidable task. For example, among the prospective buyers of Rembrandt's "Aristotle Contemplating the Bust of Homer" at Parke-Bernet Galleries in 1961 were the Metropolitan Museum of Art and the Cleveland Art Museum.[4] They held preauction strategy conferences for the purpose of determining (1) how important its acquisition was to their collection; (2) how high they were willing to go in attempting to obtain the painting; and (3) what would the likely selling price be. In the preauction preparations for the "Aristotle" sale, the director of one art museum correctly predicted the exact price this famous painting would bring.

The crucial questions here are the strength of the desire for a particular item and the translation of that desire into monetary terms. The judgment may depend, of course, on the reputation the bidder is attempting to build for the institution he represents. He may decide that it would be better to fight a losing battle to obtain the item than to avoid the conflict altogether. One astute trader I know, when he wants something so badly that his judgment is warped, withdraws from the competition as a protection against overbidding.

After evaluation, two strategic decisions remain for the would-be purchaser of a desired item: (1) what the amount of his top demand price will be, and (2) who is best equipped to bid on it for

4 James Brough, *Auction!* (Indianapolis and New York: Bobbs-Merrill, 1963), p. 15.

him. The former depends to some extent on what he will have to bid in order to buy the item, which, in turn, requires some guessing as to what rivals might be bidding against him and what their top demand prices are likely to be.

The person who actually does the bidding for a multimillion dollar item must have certain qualifications, particularly coolness under fire. He may be someone outside the buying group whose experience in and aptitude for handling purchases of this magnitude peculiarly fit him for the task of acquiring an item of high and uncertain value.

In some auctions (for example, the sale of halibut in Seattle and of tuna in San Diego) the goods are purchased sight unseen, and preauction examination of the property is impossible. However, the buyer knows the reputation of the fishing boat's master as well as the general nature of the cargo, and he may base his judgment of how high to go in his bidding on such information. Moreover, as he usually exercises some control over the grading of the fish at the time they are unloaded, his bidding is not entirely blind. Yet not all risks are eliminated. I know of one purchaser of what was supposed to be medium-sized and large-sized skipjack who found that he had purchased mostly small fish; he incurred considerable loss because of the lower meat yield and the added labor costs of processing smaller fish. In this instance the vendor may have misrepresented his wares, but the buyer may have been equally culpable in not being alert to the possibility of misrepresentation.

In some auction sales of household goods, the prospective purchaser has no opportunity for prior inspection. For example, auction sales of sealed containers—so-called mystery auctions—are commonly conducted by storage companies in southern California. The risk involved in buying such containers, with no sound basis for determining the value of the contents, suggests that the bidder who participates likes to engage in gambling. He may find that he has paid $20 or $25, or even more, for some carefully packed cracked dishes or other worthless items, or, on the contrary, that he has acquired priceless recordings for a relatively small sum. I know of one buyer of a mystery package who, after opening the carton, left it in the parking lot of the storage company because its contents were not worth taking away, but I also know of bidders who obtained valuable goods in exchange for small expenditures.

Bidding Strategy

"A bid is an offer by an intending purchaser to pay a designated price for property which is to be sold at auction."[5] Thus the individual bidder who is considering the purchase at auction of an item or lot should have three things in mind: (1) the quality of the item on which he is bidding and the extent to which it fits his individual requirements; (2) the highest demand price that he can afford, especially if he is a dealer or a broker who hopes to resell at a profit or who is buying for someone else, possibly with specific limitations on how high he can go; and (3) the possibility that he will be able to obtain the item for less than his top demand price.

A prerequisite of sound strategy in auction bidding is to know as much as possible about the property on which one intends to bid. An individual bidder must also understand merchandise or commodity values in the relevant field, so that he has at least a fair idea of what an item is likely to bring in a current market transaction. But even then he must decide what the goods are worth to him. In the absence of such an estimate, the buyer is likely to be the victim of emotional crosscurrents in his striving toward sound purchases.

In considering his strategic and tactical behavior in auction operations, the buyer should understand his role in the price-making process. It is the buyers who, by bidding and counterbidding, actually make the prices in an auction operation. All bidders, underbidders as well as actual bidders, thus participate in the price-making process, for the underbidders force the successful bidder to enhanced price levels.

One facet of bidding strategy is the knowledge that those who attend auctions are usually interested only in certain items. Thus a buyer should concentrate his attention on items of interest to him, and not become embroiled in the emotional atmosphere of an auction. He may, however, bid on a lot in order to force a competitor to pay a higher price. Or he may decide to become a speculator and bid on an item he does not want for himself, if it seems to be going for a lower price than is justified by general market conditions. The intelligent bidder, however, will avoid tumbleweed tactics.

5 "Auctions and Auctioneers," in *Corpus Juris Secundum* (Brooklyn: American Law Book Co., 1937), VII, 1240.

It is not usually sound strategy for a buyer to decide to purchase an item regardless of its price, for then his demand price is limited only by what he will be forced to pay. Such a policy is hazardous in that the buyer is especially vulnerable to upward pricing pressure. An auctioneer in the English system, aware of a buyer's determination, could "take" the buyer "for all he is worth." I know of an auctioneer who was ordered to buy an item for a customer whatever the price. Presumably the price actually paid was determined by the amount of the highest floor bid, but an unscrupulous auctioneer could have had a field day by using the technique of phantom bids.

It appears at first glance that a would-be buyer determined to acquire a particular item can do so simply by outbidding others. This course of action is practicable in the English system, because a bidder always knows what he must offer in order to top a competitor's bid. In some auction systems, however, the bidder has little or no knowledge of competitors' bids, and can top them only by estimating the bidding levels of likely opponents.

In any auction system, a prospective buyer should establish a maximum price which he will not exceed. When he is in the dark regarding competitive moves, he does not know how high he must go in order to acquire the item. If a bidder in such a system badly needs an item, he may have to bid at or near his high demand price, although even that may not be enough. Again, the successful bidder in an English-type auction has an advantage over those who compete in "blind" systems.

A would-be buyer in the English system, though able to see his fellow bidders and to hear their bids, cannot always identify his adversaries. They may bid by signal rather than audibly, or they may represent anonymous principals. And some individuals who are in attendance may not be bidding at all. Nor does reliance on observation of actual bidders recognize the likelihood that the auctioneer may have book bids from buyers who are not present at the auction.

The would-be buyer who does not know the identity of his opponents can resort to making intelligent guesses based on the nature of the offering. A collector of antiques, if reasonably sure that an opponent is a dealer who must allow for a retail markup in his bidding, may consider himself safe in raising the latter's bid, although he must always keep in mind the basic value of the item in order to avoid a trap. A potential purchaser is also helped by knowing whether his opponent is a small or a large buyer. In fish auctions, for example, a large buyer may allow a small buyer to prevail in the bidding, knowing that the small buyer will take only a few boxes, leaving the balance of the lot for him. In this way he is likely to pay a lower price than if he had entered the competition initially.

Another issue related to bidding strategy is whether to be bold or cautious in initial bidding. The man who strongly desires an item will jump in with both feet, as it were, or try to rout the enemy by starting out with a high, possibly loud, bid intended to "knock out" his opponents. Sometimes he even tops his own bid. This approach may discourage competitors at the outset and prevent them from ever getting caught up in the spirit of the bidding. In a very different strategy, a prospective buyer, even though determined to purchase an item, bids tentatively and cautiously in order to feel out the opposition. He hopes that by indicating a low regard for the offering he will lull opponents into a false sense of security. Simulating lack of interest is particularly effective when the would-be buyer is known to be a specialist who purchases both high-quality and medium-quality merchandise. An even better approach for an outstanding collector or dealer is to stay away from the auction altogether. A buyer can also adopt the strategy of staying out of the bidding at first with the idea of entering later in order to confound his competitors, but this course would have quite different implications.

Another element of bidding strategy is to decide whether one should execute bids himself or employ an agent to do so. A buyer who is known as an outstanding figure in an important field frequently chooses the latter approach, for his own bidding, if detected, suggests that the item is highly desirable and therefore arouses strong competition, or it causes opponents to bid the price up to make him pay more for it.

On the contrary, Paul Getty in June, 1938, departed from his usual practice and not only went to an auction but actually did his own bidding. In Mr. Getty's words: "The dealers, sensing my determination to secure certain objects, had little interest in bidding prices up in vain, so resigned themselves to the inevitable." [6] Although Mr. Getty did not say so, it is possible that dealers were more cautious in the depression years than they would have been in normal times.

Another reason for having a deputy do the actual bidding is the principal's lack of experience in bidding tactics, of aptitude to handle the job skillfully, or of competence in a particular market. He could easily become rattled at a crucial point in the bidding, or prove not to be a match for his opponents. A knowledgeable collector is not always a skilled trader. The assignment of a proper deputy is an important matter, as is shown by the Metropolitan Museum's acquisition of Rembrandt's "Aristotle." In most instances a would-be buyer can enlist the aid of a reputable dealer and thus draw off one of his potential competitors, thereby "killing two birds with one stone." He may, on the other hand, employ the services of the auctioneer by leaving with him a book bid to be executed at his discretion. In this instance the auctioneer must be completely trustworthy.

In the English system, as the price ascends to a level near its market value, the would-be buyer should be particularly alert to potential opportunities for moneysaving tactics. As the price approaches higher levels, if bidding activity declines substantially, as is quite possible, the auctioneer may accept a buyer's advance that is smaller than the one he is attempting to obtain. The canny bidder offers half the proposed advance, usually communicating his offer by hand or finger signals to the auctioneer.

The successful bidder in a nonreserve auction has the right to expect that he has been opposed by bona fide bidders, rather than by phantom bidders who exist only in the mind of an auctioneer acting for the vendor. A suspicious buyer may with propriety request assurance that the bidders are in fact actual competitors, though, on the other hand, underbidders may wish to remain anonymous lest their identification impede the progress of the sale. Exactly how far it is practicable for a buyer to go in determining whether his competition is bona fide is a moot question.

Thus far the discussion of bidding strategy has been limited to

6 J. Paul Getty and Ethel Le Vane, *Collector's Choice* (London: W. H. Allen, 1955), pp. 75–76.

transactions concerning a single lot or item. In bidding on certain commodities—livestock, for example—for himself or for a principal, a buyer may want to purchase several lots. In so doing he would still purchase on an individual lot basis, but he would be influencing the price of his purchases as he acquired additional lots. Such buying calls for a special type of strategy designed to keep the average cost of one's purchases down. It is possible to improve the end result at any time during the session by buying at favorable prices and increasing one's purchases at such prices.[7]

Executing the Bid

Buyers do their bidding at an auction in various ways: "A bid may be made in any mode by which the bidder signifies his willingness and intention to give a particular sum or price for the property . . . [up] for sale; thus, it may be made orally, as by words uttered aloud in the hearing of the by-standers, or spoken privately to the auctioneer, or by a wink or a nod, or by writing in words or figures, or by letter."[8] I have even seen bidders use an abacus to indicate the amount of a bid.

Floor bids.—Typically, but not always, bids are executed by those who are present at the auction, yet audible bids are relatively unusual. In certain types of auctions the voice is not employed at all. The Dutch clock system is an example of inaudible bidding.[9] The Oriental handshake system does rely on the voice but only secondarily; the vital information is transmitted by the bidder's squeezing of the auctioneer's fingers. The whispered-bid system depends on the voice of the bidder (or, alternatively, on an abacus), but the communication of the offer is audible only to the auctioneer.

In the English system bids may be communicated by the bidder to the auctioneer by voice, but for various reasons they are usually transmitted by signal. Such signals may be in the form of a wink, a nod, scratching an ear, lifting a pencil, tugging at the coat of the auctioneer, or even staring into the auctioneer's eyes—all of them

7 See, for example, Stephen H. Sosnick, "Bidding Strategy at Ordinary Auctions," *Journal of Farm Economics*, XLV (Feb., 1963), 163–182.

8 *Corpus Juris Secundum*, VII 1253–1254.

9 See pp. 193–197.

perfectly legal. This method of communicating bids gives the process of bidding an aura of secrecy.

For a number of reasons, buyers prefer surreptitious to overt bidding. The most important of these are as follows:

1. To avoid the noise and confusion resulting from audible bidding, especially when numerous spirited bidders are present.

2. To provide a more accurate way of communicating bids.

3. To prevent private collectors from following the lead of knowledgeable dealers who thus may be forced to pay higher prices and might even lose out in the bidding.

4. To protect buyers who bid on a low-quality item from the ridicule of colleagues.

5. To prevent dealers from detecting the interest of competitors and thus forcing them to pay higher prices than might otherwise be necessary.

6. To protect a professional who overbids on an item from loss of face with rival bidders.

7. To hold confidential the actions of traders who want to keep their business to themselves.

8. To prevent detection of a dealer's interest in what appears to be a "find," so that he will not lose his advantage.

Bidding covertly usually develops, not from auction regulations, but simply because individuals are following their own best interests. Complete secrecy in bidding probably evolved from buyers who desired anonymity arranging with the auctioneer to substitute signals for audible bidding. Signals would hardly protect a famous collector or dealer, for his presence at an auction would almost certainly be a giveaway.

The auctioneer's task is more difficult when bidders transmit their bids so as to avoid detection by others. Many surreptitious bidding arrangements are designed for exclusive use by certain bidders. Sometimes a bidder's peculiar bidding signal may be well known in the trade; at other times the auctioneer may have to be informed before the sale of a bidder's particular signal. A certain type of special arrangement (for example, "I am bidding until I signal that I am no longer bidding") gives the auctioneer flexibility in the execution of the bids.

Bidding signals may be extremely complicated, as were those used by Norton Simon in his successful bidding for Rembrandt's

"Titus" in Christie's London auction rooms in 1965. A preauction agreement in writing stipulated that when "Mr. Simon is sitting down, he is bidding. If he bids openly, he is also bidding. When he stands up, he has stopped bidding. If he sits down again, he is not bidding unless he raises his finger. Having raised his finger, he is bidding, until he stands up again." [10] Not surprisingly, the auctioneer lost track of the procedure and mistakenly awarded the painting to another individual before being challenged by Mr. Simon, who was, in fact, the high bidder. The Simon-Christie arrangement was not unlike one used in an auction in the United States more than a hundred years ago. By the terms of this agreement, made in 1852, "during the bidding he [the bidder] would put his thumb in the button-hole of his coat, and *while it remained there* the auctioneer should continue bidding for him, advancing each bid in the ratio or proportion of the immediate[ly] preceding competitor's bid" [11] (emphasis added). In each instance, communication failure led to a dispute between would-be buyer and vendor's agent.

Bidding difficulties sometimes result from lapses by the bidder. The former president of Parke-Bernet reports that a dealer attending a sale of eighteenth-century French furniture had arranged to unbutton his overcoat whenever he wished to bid; buttoning the overcoat again would signal that he had ceased bidding. The dealer, coat unbuttoned, was in the midst of bidding for a Louis XVI sofa when he saw someone outside to whom he wished to speak and suddenly left the room. The auctioneer continued to bid for the dealer who, when he returned to the room, found that he had become the owner of the sofa at an unexpectedly high price. An argument then followed as to whether an unbuttoned coat not in the auction room is the same as an unbuttoned coat in the auction room. [12]

The rules of one large auction operation—the wool trade in Australia—specifically prohibit the use of signals in bidding. The reason for insisting on audible bidding is difficult to discover, unless it is a fear that covert bids would enhance opportunities for buyer

10 "Son of Rembrandt," *Time*, March 26, 1965, p. 70.

11 *Conover* v. *Walling*, 15 N.J. Eq. 173, 179 (1852).

12 Leslie A. Hyam, "Manners and Morals of the Auction Room," *Atlantic Monthly* (March, 1962), p. 117.

collusion. In the London fur auction, where signals are employed, it is considered unethical for anyone to turn his head and spy, intentionally or otherwise, on his neighbor. Bids are announced but the identity of the bidders is kept secret until the goods are knocked down, at which time the high bidder is usually identified.

It should be emphasized that secrecy in transmitting bids, at least in the English system, merely prevents the identification of bidders; it does not affect publicizing of the amounts of the bids. Knowledge of the bidding level is an integral part of the English auction system, and it is the auctioneer's function to announce each bid so that the assembled buyers can proceed from that point. In some auction systems both the bidder and the amount of his bid are kept secret, and occasionally even the amount of the successful bid is withheld.

Book bids.—In some auctions, it is common practice for those not having an opportunity to attend in person, or for those wishing to remain anonymous, to file their bids with the auctioneer before the sale. These book bids are very important in certain fields, particularly in the auctioning of postage stamps. For the buyer, book bidding opens up supply sources that would otherwise not be available to him; for the seller, it broadens the geographical market. In handling book bids, the auctioneer acts as agent for the buyer, but because he is primarily the vendor's agent, there arises the possibility of conflict of interest.

Book bids may be submitted by mail, as in the London stamp auction, or may be given to the auctioneer orally, as in some English primary fish markets. Bids registered in advance are maximum offers only; the amount the book bidder pays for an item he wants is determined by competition from bidders in the auction room, from the book, or from both. Let us suppose that a single book bid of $20 has been registered with the auctioneer for a certain stamp, and that, as the auction gets under way, a bid of $10 is called from the floor. If the standard advance at this price level is $1, the auctioneer comes in with a bid of $11 for the book bidder. If this bid is countered from the floor, it is immediately advanced again by the auctioneer in behalf of the book bidder. And so the auctioneer will always have a counterbid on behalf of the book bidder until the latter's maximum is reached.

In book bidding, the award is made at one level, or price

interval, above the floor bid or the second-highest book bid, whichever is larger. If there is more than one book bid, the auctioneer
starts the bidding at one price interval above the second-highest
book offer. The second-highest book bidder (along with any others
below him) is thus automatically eliminated, and the auctioneer
looks to the floor for bids. If he gets no bid from the floor, the
goods are knocked down to the highest book bidder at a price just
above the offer of the second-highest bidder.

The situation is more complicated when a reserve, or upset,
price is placed on the goods. Such a price serves very much the
same function as a book bid, although the two are by no means
identical. Suppose there is a reserve of $50 and no book bids; the
auctioneer may start at $35, take a bid of $40 from the room, make
a bid of $45 himself in behalf of the vendor, and then get a
climactic bid of $50 in the room. At this figure he sells the lot
because the reserve price has been reached, unless he receives more
bids from the floor. Any bidding by the auctioneer in behalf of the
vendor must place the floor bidder "in step" with the reserve price,
that is, so that the auctioneer's bid for the vendor is not at the
reserve price. Assuming next a book bid of $60, everything else
remaining the same, the auctioneer might start at the reserve price
of $50, bidding for the book bidder against the room. If he gets no
floor bids, the item goes to the book bidder at $50. The assembled
buyers are at a disadvantage in not knowing the amount of the
reserve (if any), or whether a lot is actually sold to a genuine
buyer. The integrity of the auctioneer is a singularly important
ingredient in book bidding.

Because a book bid is available for use at any moment that the
auctioneer chooses to employ it, he is given a certain degree of
flexibility. He can time his use of the book bid so as to increase the
tempo of the sale. If bids from the floor are coming in slowly, the
auctioneer can achieve dramatic emphasis by throwing in a book
bid at a critical moment. Should floor bidders fail to react quickly,
however, the gesture loses much of its effectiveness. On the other
hand, when a skilled auctioneer does succeed in quickening the
responses of laggards, the book bidder may suffer in the end by
being forced to pay more for the goods he acquires.

A peculiar situation obtains when there is only one book bid
and no bid from the floor. The book bidder, as the high, and only,

bidder, may be awarded the goods on the basis of his bid. The weak spot is that there would have been no competition, which might well have reduced the book bidder's price. If he had bid $20, for example, and a floor bidder had offered $15 and then withdrawn, the book bidder would have obtained the goods for $16, assuming a step-up of $1. Without competition, he would theoretically have paid the full $20. The lower the final floor bid, the lower the price the book bidder pays, if there is no reserve price.

In this situation, the book bidder should be protected by his buying agent, the auctioneer, in some manner, in accordance with the auction principle that prices are based on competitive bidding. The goods should perhaps be withdrawn, at the buyer's option, and held for sale at a later session when floor bids might be forthcoming to provide competition for the book bidder. The selling price would then more closely reflect market conditions.

Quantity Options

In most auctions, bidding is for a lot, and the quantity in the lot is understood to constitute the quantity purchased. When the unit of purchase is inflexible, the chosen size of lots may not fit the requirements of all buyers, some of whom are therefore unable to participate in the bidding. For this reason, buyer options are sometimes provided by the vendor or his agent. These options also accelerate auction operations through the sale of large lots to buyers who can conveniently handle them.

In the simplest type of quantity option, a lot consisting of two or more items is put up on a per unit price basis, the buyer deciding whether he wants one or more units. Since the decision regarding quantity is made after the unit price has been established, the buyer may be influenced in his judgment by the price at which the item is knocked down. If the successful bidder does not take the entire lot, others are usually permitted to buy the balance at the same price. The auctioneer may, however, have to grant a price concession to buyers in order to move the remaining units. Alternatively, he could reauction them, either immediately or at a later time.

The problem is more complex in commodity sales when lots are large and options cover wide ranges of quantities. The goods are typically sold by the unit, the buyer deciding how much he wants after the price has been determined. A would-be buyer has to decide whether to participate in the bidding or wait in the hope that he can obtain part of a lot which a successful bidder did not take. By choosing the latter course he may satisfy his requirements at a lower price than if he had participated in the bidding, although he runs the risk of having to pay more.

In the sale of produce by the clock method in auctions in the Netherlands, the successful bidder must indicate the portion of the lot he wishes; otherwise it is understood that he is taking the entire lot. If the high bidder does not purchase the total quantity, either competitors are given an opportunity to buy at the same price or the balance is reauctioned. The latter course is better for the vendor, because the former could encourage buyer agreement to abstain from bidding.

In other instances (for example, fish in English port markets), the high bidder must indicate whether he wants the entire lot or only a part of it immediately after establishment of the price. If the balance is sold either at the price established by the high bidder or at a discount, other bidders must consider the strategy of refraining from bidding and thus taking a chance of filling their requirements from unclaimed portions of lots. Their success in getting what they need in this way depends largely on the circumstances of the market.

A device called "lowers," or a quantity discount, is used in the auctioning of fish in certain English primary markets. The unit price is established without reference to the number of units the bidder intends to take. The buyer must then decide how much he wants to purchase. If he is a small buyer who only wants ten boxes, say, he purchases at the established price. A large buyer, however, may offer to take the whole square, consisting of some two hundred boxes, if he is granted a quantity discount. He has to choose between bidding for a lot or refraining from bidding in the hope of acquiring at a discount the balance of a lot purchased by a small buyer. As all buyers know, some auctioneers use standard lowers figures. Others vary the amount depending upon the state of the market. In either event, the amount of the lowers is not mentioned during the sale. A buyer I know asks at the outset if the auctioneer is "in a good mood"—that is, can he expect a favorable deal. If the response is in the affirmative, he takes the lot and later learns the

amount of the discount. The quantity discount is frequently criti-
cized because it gives an advantage to large buyers. Smaller buyers,
however, can offset that advantage to some extent by pooling their
purchases in order to qualify for lowers.

An interesting type of option arrangement is practiced in fur
auctions in both Leningrad and London. Known as "string selling," it gives the successful bidder for a particular lot the option of
buying other lots consisting of similar or identical skins at the same
price; he may continue until his wants are satisfied, until the string
is ended, or until challenged by a competitor. He simply bids on
related lots at the same price by telling the auctioneer he intends to
do so. The latter knocks each item down, at one- or two-second
intervals, as the bidder nods his head or otherwise signals his bid.
Sales by this method are obviously very rapid.

The auctioneer selling on a string basis stops only when the
buyer signals that he wants to reduce his bid, or when another
buyer indicates his intent to raise the bid by shouting "Up!" In the
former instance the auctioneer announces the amount of the new
bid. In the latter instance the original bidder may counter a competitive offer, but any challenger who takes over continues the
bidding for the lots in the string until he is finished or is, in turn,
challenged, or until the sale of the string is completed. The buyer
who is bidding on a string of lots can also relinquish his position by
notifying the auctioneer that he is through. Another bidder may
then come in at a slightly lower price. If he is successful in this
tactic, the sale of the string continues with little if any interruption,
but at the lower price. Such a bid may be countered, however, by a
rival buyer. If there are no bids at all for the remainder of the
string, it may be offered again, with a new price level established
through the conventional auctioning process.

Entirety Bidding

Entirety bids are feasible only when the items that are up for
sale possess a unifying characteristic. A good illustration is a sale of
numerous lots that together form a complete manufacturing plant,
including building, machinery, and land. When such property is
worth more to a buyer in its complete state than it would be if sold

in individual parts, a bidder is likely to make an offer for the goods in their entirety.

Conceptual analysis.—Obviously the vendor wants to obtain the highest possible price for his goods, and the auctioneer is equally desirous of getting the maximum price for the items he is selling. This is especially true if the auction is being conducted under court order. Hence it is sometimes the strategy of the vendor or his agent to announce at the beginning of the sale that bids will be entertained for the property *in toto,* in the expectation that resulting competition will yield a higher net return than if bidding were confined to piecemeal offers.

Either the auctioneer or a potential purchaser may take the initiative in proposing entirety bidding: the former asks if anyone desires to offer an entirety bid, or the latter inquires whether such a bid will be entertained. The acceptance of entirety bids depends on many imponderables, including the nature and condition of the property. The competition that develops depends not only on the total of the piecemeal offers made for individual items, but on the existence of other bids for the property as a whole.

The fundamental characteristics of entirety bidding are the same, although the process varies in different parts of the United States. These differences concern the point at which such bids are entertained. In one section of the country the entirety bid must be registered before bidding begins on individual lots. It is conditional on its exceeding the total of bids on individual lots; conversely, once an entirety bid has been registered, bids on individual lots are conditional upon their exceeding, in total, the amount of the entirety bid. In other areas of the country the auctioneer does not entertain an entirety bid until the bidding on the individual lots has been completed, though he does announce earlier that entirety bids will be accepted. Under such an arrangement the sale of individual lots is conditional until the entirety bidding has taken place.

In any event, entirety bidding cannot legitimately be introduced into a sale after bidding on individual lots has begun, unless proper notice has been given before the opening of the sale. Otherwise, those making offers on individual lots would be bidding in good faith with the reasonable expectation that each transaction was separate and distinct, and that the highest bid on each lot would take the goods, when, in fact, their efforts might be futile.

Entirety bidding in practice.—While the principles of entirety bidding are simple enough, the device becomes quite complex in practice. The following examples illustrate various facets of the strategy and tactics of entirety bidding.[13]

1. Some years ago the contents of a modern machine shop with an appraised value of some $45,000 were being offered for sale, with bids for separate lots to be entertained. On the morning of the sale the auctioneer was approached by a prospective buyer, Mr. A, seeking "advice." Mr. A, who hoped to open a machine shop, was willing to make a single bid "exceeding the probable total of the piecemeal bids." He asked the auctioneer to estimate the total of the individual bids. The latter, seemingly an honest man, first mentioned $45,000 as his appraisal of the total worth of the shop, but then cautioned that competition might force the total up by $10,000. He ended by suggesting, conservatively, that $60,000 might be a good entirety bid. The would-be buyer placed that bid, without competition, at the beginning of the sale, signed a contingent agreement, and made a deposit.

As the auctioning of the individual lots got under way—the sale of each lot being conditional on the total of all such offers topping the entirety bid—another individual, Mr. B, asked the auctioneer to reopen the entirety bidding so that he could enter a bid for the total property. This request was refused, presumably on the ground that the opportunity for entirety bidding had passed. Mr. B then instructed the auctioneer to bid for him on each of the 350 lots at prices that would ensure his being the top bidder on each lot and that the total of his bids would top Mr. A's entirety bid. He was told that if competition developed on individual lots the total might exceed the entirety bid by as much as $20,000, or even more. Mr. B accepted his obligation to "expect the unexpected" and posted his deposit. Eventually, as top bidder on every lot, he took the entire machine shop at a total of $95,150. His strategy had been to outbid all opposition on a piecemeal basis.

2. In a bankruptcy sale of a firm that made prefabricated houses there was an entirety bid of $275,000. A certain firm, for sentimental reasons, wanted to acquire one of the prefabs as a sample of

13 The first three examples are drawn from Louis McLean, "Auction Anecdotes," *Oklahoma Bar Association Journal,* XXVI (April 30, 1955), 683–686.

the early work of the bankrupt firm. In the meantime, the entirety bidder, to make certain that he would be awarded the property, raised his own bid, against no competitive entirety bid, to $325,000. The group that wanted one prefab very carefully recorded all bids on individual lots; when the house it wanted finally came up for sale, it found that a bid of $21,500 would be sufficient to raise the total of the piecemeal bids to an amount that would top the entirety bid and therefore that the property would be awarded to the individual bidders.

As a result, the entirety bidder was confounded by the determination of those willing to pay whatever was necessary to acquire a single house. In fact, they paid $21,500 for a prefabricated house that sold originally for $9,000, including erection charges. It should be noted that the stratagem employed would be practicable only if (*a*) the desired item was scheduled to be put up for sale last, and (*b*) the referee in a bankruptcy proceeding would not permit the entirety bidder to raise his bid at the court hearing.

3. A bankruptcy sale of the machinery and equipment of a large plant in the eastern United States was initiated by an entirety bid of $260,000. Shortly thereafter, a bidder who had thought he was in the entirety-bid group found that he had been "dealt out" by the syndicate. His pride hurt, this individual evidently decided to get revenge by bidding piecemeal on the property. As a result, the total amount bid for the machinery and equipment was $279,000.

At the subsequent court hearing, the syndicate countered with a $285,000 entirety bid, whereupon the bankruptcy referee postponed the decision until the next day. During the interim, the individual bidder had cocktails and dinner with a bright young attorney, whom he finally engaged to represent him in the balance of the proceedings for a fee of $500. When the hearing resumed the next day, the newly engaged attorney argued vigorously against acceptance of the second entirety bid on the ground that it would be costly to "the piecemeal buyers who had spent their time and money in establishing values in excess of the original entirety bid." He pleaded with the court not to reopen the bidding.

At this point the syndicate, evidently realizing the danger to its position, decided to compromise. Syndicate members invited the individual bidder into the corridor and "eagerly reasoned" with him to accept a full partnership, to which he "reluctantly" agreed after successfully demanding $2,500 for his attorney's fee, five times what he had promised. The plea on behalf of the small bidders was therefore withdrawn, and the one "wronged" found that "revenge is sometimes sweet, and profitable."

4. Prior to an auction of five buildings owned by a southern California public utility firm,[14] it was announced that three of the buildings constituted a complex and would be auctioned first separately and then as a package, subject to a raise of no less than 5 percent over the top individual bids on each building. If no entirety bid was forthcoming, the individual bids would stand, subject to acceptance by the city council. When asked if individual bidders could make counteroffers after an effective entirety bid, the auctioneer replied that he would entertain any bid or combination of bids until the fall of the hammer, in order to obtain the highest possible price for the city.

In the first stage of the auction, the top individual bids on the three buildings were $180,000, $180,000, and $100,000, respectively, or a total of $460,000. The sale was then open for an entirety bid, the minimum offer to be $460,000 plus 5 percent, or a total of $483,000. The first entirety bid was for precisely that amount. Then came a bid of 7.5 percent over the $460,000 total, followed by others of 10 percent and 15 percent over the total of the individual bids. The three buildings finally went, tentatively, to the entirety bidder offering a premium of 15 percent over the individual bids, or a total of $529,000.

The auctioneer then announced that the individual bids could be increased. Two of the individual high bidders raised their offers by 20 percent each, but the third shook his head. The new total of the individual bids was $516,000, still less than the entirety bid. The one who had not raised then asked how much was needed to top the entirety bid, and was told the figure was $14,000. When he agreed to raise his bid by that amount, the individual bids totaled $530,000, or $1,000 more than the entirety bid.

The entirety bidder countered this move by raising his bid by 5 percent, and again bidding resumed on the individual buildings. After spirited competition over the first of the three buildings, which just minutes before had received a top individual bid of only $180,000, it was finally awarded to a man who had not entered the

14 This account is based on observation by a field assistant.

bidding during the first round but now made the top offer of $345,000. The individual bidders on the other two buildings stood firm, since the total of the bids already exceeded the entirety bid. Again the entirety bidder raised his bid for the three buildings 5 percent, to a total of $691,950. At this stage, one of the individual bidders argued at great length against the proceedings, but the auctioneer reminded him that the terms had been clearly announced in advance and that, as auctioneer, his job was to get the highest price and he intended "to do just that so long as no subterfuge is involved."

Because of the intensive competition of entirety and piecemeal bidders, the individual bids eventually totaled $807,240. The entirety bidder, angrily protesting, walked out of the room to confer with his advisers. When he returned, he announced that he was now shifting to a piecemeal basis and would increase the bid on one building by $10,000 and those on the other two by $5,000 each. The auctioneer reminded him that by placing individual bids he faced the possibility of not getting all three buildings. He indicated that he understood his position. The original individual bidders, realizing they had been defeated, withdrew from competition. The strategy of knocking out opponents by switching to an individual-bid basis was thus successful. The buyer secured all three buildings with a raise of $20,000 ($10,000 plus $5,000 plus $5,000), rather than one of $40,362 (5 percent of $807,240). The final price for the three buildings was $827,200, substantially more than the $460,000 bid on an individual basis before the entirety bidding began.

The procedure of entirety bidding should, however, be used with caution. An attempt by the owner and his agent, or by a court representative, to maximize returns from a sale by entertaining entirety bids can result in losses in subsequent auctions. Professional buyers may consider themselves too busy to patronize abortive auction sales in which lots of goods are knocked down conditionally and not confirmed until after entirety bids have been entertained. Entirety bidding, while practicable and even advisable in some instances, should be resorted to only to serve special purposes.

Price-Influencing Activities
of Sellers and Buyers

12 THE DISCUSSION in earlier chapters has stressed the actual working of various auction systems. Now we turn to an inquiry about the factors that influence the prices made by this mechanism.

The Problem Examined in Broad Perspective

In auction selling prices are determined by the supply of and the demand for the particular type of merchandise offered, assuming that there is competition among buyers and that buyers and sellers are well informed and behave rationally. This statement, while true enough, conceals more than it reveals. We must, therefore, examine the matter in more detail by first asking: "What are the factors that affect auction-made prices?"

Procuring adequate supplies.—The supply of wanted goods is a basic price-determining factor in auction selling. The quantity and the quality of goods may substantially influence the price results, not only because of the inherent value of the goods, but because of the effect of such offerings on attendance at an auction. Hence the successful seeking out of attractive goods is a key factor in an auction's favorable outcome. Long before the goods are put up for sale, auction officials must interest sellers in consigning goods to them for sale or in selling them the goods outright for resale at auction.

There is a saying in the merchandise field, "Goods well bought are one-half sold." While the auction firm does not ordinarily purchase goods for resale, the type of goods it handles has an important bearing on the success of the auction. The quality of the goods may attract or repel attendance, and thus potentially affects the prices developing out of the auction process. It follows that an equally important supply factor is the reputation the auction company possesses for putting up merchandise that conforms to market requirements.

The location of the auction and the time of the sale are also important supply factors, as far as bidders are concerned. The availability of the goods at a convenient place and time is an integral part of the supply of goods.

Activating the potential demand.—Since demand is a function of the desires and incomes of human beings, the first factor in a consideration of demand is the size and composition of a group of buyers at an auction. If only a handful of curiosity seekers are present, bidding will be anything but spirited and prices will be low. Conversely, if there are numerous would-be buyers who are interested in the offerings, one may expect active bidding resulting in good prices.

But the number and the type of individuals attending an auction hinge on other factors as well. For example, the location of the sale, the time of the year, and even the time of day the sale is held, not to mention weather conditions, all have a bearing on convenience and hence influence attendance. Another important factor is communication, for would-be bidders cannot attend an auction if they do not know that it is being held. It is important to inform potentially interested buyers, through published advertisements or direct-mail announcements, not only that the event is to take place but that certain items will be auctioned—items that would obviously interest those to whom the advertising effort is directed.

Announcements that list numerous items employ the "shotgun" technique, the strategy of which is to attract numerous individuals with varying interests. Among those attracted there will probably be two or more persons with sufficient interest in each item to compete for it. Even though some of those attending the auction have no initial intention of bidding, the attractiveness of the goods combined with the reaction of the crowd may cause them to participate in the bidding.

Advertising cannot by itself convey the quality of the merchandise; at best one can hope to induce interested individuals to examine the goods at first hand when they are given an opportunity to do so. Descriptions of the goods that are up for sale, plus the reputation of the auction company, should attract interested individuals who may remain to make purchases.

Influencing the competitive climate.—As to its effect on prices, competition in auction selling has two principal aspects:

1. Seller competition. Seller competition is a kind of extension of the supply factor. If two auctions are in direct competition with each other—selling the same type of merchandise at the same time in the same vicinity—the supply of goods is expanded. The impact on price results will depend on the effect of such an expansion of supply on the number and type of patrons attracted to the auctions. Two auctions held simultaneously may produce better overall results than two scheduled at different times. If patronage that was formerly concentrated in one auction is divided between two auctions, prices, at least of some items, would tend to be lower. If, however, total patronage increases in response to the expanded offerings, prices may be just as high or even higher. The key factor is the enhanced demand to match the expanded supply.

2. Buyer competition. Buyer competition is in a sense an extension of the demand function. An intensive demand on the part of one buyer is hardly enough to force him to pay his full demand price. Competition is required to elicit maximum bids from individuals with high demand prices. It is, however, probably just as natural to collude as it is to compete, and buyers will cooperate with one another, where practicable, reducing the upward pressure on prices.

Influence of Sellers

The seller and his agent will do everything in their power, within the law at least, to maximize the returns from an auction sale. The auctioneer has at his disposal various price-enhancing tactics. Some of these can be individually implemented; some require the cooperation of others.

Individual activities.—Seller activities of this type may be set forth as follows:

1. Promotion of bidder interest. Some auctioneers are more skilled than others in eliciting and detecting bids from buyers at an auction. Almost any means may be employed in auction selling in order to (*a*) interest buyers in entering into competition and (*b*) induce them to compete with one another for the purchase of an item. Unprincipled auctioneers even employ conscious product misrepresentation, despite the fact that it is fraudulent.

2. The personality of the auctioneer. The auctioneer's appearance, voice, rhythm of patter, good nature, imperturbability, and storytelling ability may have an effect on bidding activity, thus enhancing prices. Knowledge of the type of item offered is of significance, too, in lending authority to any representations made concerning the goods that are being sold. Knowledge of practical psychology is another valuable factor; successful auctioneers have flexible minds and are constantly on the lookout for opportunities to practice their art.

3. Accelerating the pace of the auction. Since a brisk market depends basically on the presence of alert buyers, a skilled auctioneer has various methods of keeping bidders on their toes. He may put up for sale particularly interesting items at the outset of the auction and knock them down rapidly, thus setting the pace for a fast sale. If interest lags in the midst of a sale, an astute auctioneer knocks the wanted item down to the first bidder to shock potentially interested buyers out of their lethargy. One successful auctioneer even drops a breakable item occasionally in order to wake up the audience and at the same time put them in a jolly mood. In some auctions, when lack of interest manifests itself, the auctioneer may switch to a different line of goods in an attempt to stimulate bidders who have not as yet participated.

4. Use of book bids. Bids deposited with the auctioneer in advance can be utilized to stimulate the activity of floor bidders. Because of their flexibility, book bids, sometimes known as proxy bids, can be employed by the auctioneer at appropriate levels precisely as

though they were floor bids. A skillful auctioneer can quicken the pace of the bidding by coming in fast with a book bid, thus stimulating floor bidding.

5. Use of a reserve price. A reserve price, which is in a sense the seller's own bid, can be used to enhance the selling price in somewhat the same way as a proxy bid. That is, the auctioneer, who may not let the item go below the reserve figure, may enter a bid himself at any point below the reserve price in an attempt to stimulate the bidding. Should the seller be the high bidder, however, the item remains unsold. Such a tactic may force the price above the reserve figure; if it does not, the item may be offered on a private-treaty basis or in another auction session in the hope of then getting a higher price.

6. Use of "running" (or trotting) by an auctioneer. In the absence of book bids or reserve prices, the auctioneer can provide "competition" for a single authentic bidder by "recognizing" phantom bids. He pretends that he has received a counterbid in order to push the would-be buyer to a higher level. He may also pretend that a well-known buyer who is present is actually a bidder when, in fact, the latter is unaware of his role in this transaction. The running tactic may be employed even when the auctioneer has no bids; that is, he merely pretends that he has a bidder and a counterbidder. Unless one or more genuine bidders can be induced to enter the "competition," however, the scheme is doomed to failure.

An auctioneer may be able to increase prices by this means, but alternatively he may discover that he has bid the merchandise in himself, with the result that it remains unsold. He must be able to appraise the market accurately in order to make a sound judgment as to the possible success of the trotting tactic. A knowledgeable auctioneer is not likely to run the prices up so high that no one will bid against him.

7. Attempting to isolate those with intensive interest. If buyers reveal a special interest in a particular item, the auctioneer has a potential advantage over them. He may be able to detect the special interest of individuals in certain items during a preview period. Also, some auctioneers encourage would-be buyers to indicate the items they would like to have put up next in order to discover their

vulnerability to special sales promotional effort, and even to running prices up.

8. Uses of the "planting" device. Planting is a tactic that involves the mixing of nonauthentic, or substandard, items with those that are obviously valuable, for the purpose of enhancing the value of the nonauthentic items. This tactic is occasionally used in art auctions by unscrupulous sellers, or their auctioneer agents, in collaboration with one another or on their own.[1] A planting of paintings by unknown artists among genuine art treasures may make it possible to sell the former at prices greatly in excess of their value. If the intent is to mislead buyers rather than simply to combine items for efficient sales purposes, such action is a form of fraud and therefore illegal. Antique auction firms no doubt do at times mingle items from various sources with those from well-known collections without fraudulent intent, and achieve price-enhancing results.

Cooperative activities.—Auctioneers may also engage in various types of cooperative price-enhancing activities:

1. Trotting with the cooperation of a confederate. One of the weaknesses of the running or trotting device, as described above, is that the auctioneer may have to knock the lot down to a nonexistent bidder, and that, because buyers are often known to one another, he may get caught red-handed. Once the auctioneer has "accepted" a phantom bid, he cannot very well retreat and make the award to the last bona fide bidder, although this is done at times. An auctioneer I know got caught "running" and admitted embarrassedly, "I guess I own it," much to the delight of his audience, and without further ado he reauctioned the goods to the assembled buyers.

One way of avoiding embarrassment is to have a prior agreement with an attendant at the auction to stand by and "accept" the goods if the auctioneer finds it necessary to knock them down to him. As the cooperator is a potential buyer, the situation is more advantageous to the auctioneer, not only for the sake of appearances

---

1 A recent example of this tactic was the apparent planting of two imitation abstract paintings at a Larchmont, New York, auction of otherwise authentic art pieces (Ethel Beckwith, "Friends Shocked at Auctioneers Fraud Indictment," *Sunday Herald* [Bridgeport, Conn.], Sept. 19, 1965, p. N 27).

but because the confederate may actually purchase the goods. The price the latter pays, however, is likely to vary considerably from that at which the goods were ostensibly sold. For example, fish may be sold to an ostensible buyer at an adjusted price (as a *quid pro quo* for the service rendered), or the auctioneer may negotiate by telephone for the sale of the fish at whatever price he can get from one or more of his buying contacts. The perishability of such a commodity rules out the possibility of selling it at a later auction session. Hence the auctioneer would hope that the phantom-bid stratagem would attract genuine bids at a higher level, thus precluding postmarket sales arrangements.

2. Bids by confederates. In some auctions, the auctioneer seeks to enhance prices by arranging for fictitious bids. A confederate is employed to counter bona fide bids, not with the idea of buying the item but simply for the purpose of pushing the bona fide bidder to a higher level. Success cannot be guaranteed because the genuine bidder does not always react to the stooge's bid, and then there is no sale. The effectiveness of the tactic may, however, be enhanced by the confederate's speedy reaction to genuine bids, which quickens the tempo of the sale. When bidding is by public outcry rather than by signal, bids by confederates are more effectual than phantom bids; it would be rather difficult to make a convincing pretense of accepting a nonexistent outcry bid.

3. Touting by auctioneer's agents. Sometimes auction merchandise is touted by ostensibly disinterested parties employed by auctioneers to stimulate bidding activity.[2] Confederates may tout the goods either during a preauction inspection period or while the auction is in progress. A well-aimed word or two within the hearing of apparently interested buyers—"Look, there is a genuine Chippendale piece!"—can do wonders to perk up flagging attention. Closely related to by-bidding or puffing, touting borders on fraud and is likely to be used only by dishonest auctioneers.

4. Fraudulent use of auction technique. A perversion of the auction system, used in some areas, is characterized by a sham auctioneer and dummy bidders. The latter act as come-ons who "sell" and "buy" merchandise of good quality at bargain prices in order to attract bona fide buyers, who thus become involved in purchas-

2 See Mrs. H. Montague Broaddus, "How To Behave at an Auction," *American Home,* XVIII (Nov., 1937), 110.

ing the shoddy merchandise that is actually on sale. These mock auctions are traps set for the unwary by perpetrators of fraudulent selling who employ the auction form for illicit purposes. This subject, treated in more detail elsewhere,[3] is mentioned here to reveal the extremes to which vendors sometimes go in their efforts to obtain higher prices.

Influence of Buyers

It is clear that vendors selling at auction derive advantages from the employment of price-enhancing tactics. On the other hand, buyers have at their command devices that will tend to depress prices.

Individual activities.—It may be difficult to believe that a buyer can single-handedly depress auction prices. Yet such an end can be accomplished by tactics designed to curtail the bidding of others.

1. Interrupting the rhythm of an auction. The introduction of a distracting influence into an auction may disrupt sales activity and thus depress prices. This maneuver is similar to that in a football game when the defense takes time out in an attempt to interrupt a successful offensive drive and thus slow down the opposition. Such tactics in auctioning, as in football, may or may not be successful. One auction official has related the circumstances surrounding the interjection of an impertinent question designed to interrupt the bidding when the price of a piece of property was rising fast.[4] A buyer in another auction actually succeeded in disrupting the sale by a "move for adjournment" when he became dissatisfied with the

---

3 See pp. 254–256.

4 "Many years ago John Q. Habendum, counsel for some of the city's [Philadelphia's] biggest real estate interests, was bidding for a client-purchaser at the sale of a central city property. Brisk action brought ascending prices, and to Mr. Habendum's astute mind a diversion was indicated. What could he do? He would call: 'Time out.' At loss for a more appropriate remark, he shouted: 'Mr. Auctioneer, did you ever sell a monkey?' The auctioneer, professionally never at a loss for a retort, replied with appropriate equanimity, 'No, Mr. Habendum, I never have, but if you care to step up in front I'm perfectly willing to try.' There was a by-play of chuckles and laughter but the rhythm of the sale was not lost. It was a fast play, but 'no sale' for the 'monkey'" (Louis McLean, "Auction Anecdotes," *Oklahoma Bar Association Journal*, XXVI [April 30, 1955], 683).

proceedings. Chilling or damping tactics, so called, are unacceptable at law, and a vendor thus victimized may be able to obtain damage judgments.

2. Discouraging other buyers. A dealer, noting the particular interest of a private collector in a certain item, may intentionally mislead him regarding its desirability, in an attempt to depress the bidding. Prior to the sale or while the bidding is in progress, he may make disparaging remarks about the quality or authenticity of the item. Indeed, it is not unheard of for a dealer to propose a joint buying arrangement in order to prevent the bidding up of the price, only to renege on the agreement after he has acquired the item.

Similarly, a private buyer desiring to purchase property at a bargain price may select as his proxy bidder someone toward whom others will be sympathetic and against whom they will be reluctant to bid, such as the widow of the testator in the sale of an estate. By so doing, he may discourage bidding by other potential buyers.

3. Evading the price-inflating activities of competitors. It is well known that buyers at auctions attempt to make competitors pay higher prices for goods purchased for resale by bidding up a desired item. According to an official of a company handling fish products, a certain buyer attended an auction only when he urgently needed supplies; his competitors, soon realizing this, bid up the prices to his disadvantage. He could have reduced, to some extent at least, the upward pressure simply by attending the auction regularly and participating in the bidding, whether or not he needed the goods. By so doing he would have avoided tipping his hand, and thus would have blunted the price-enhancing weapon of his competitors.

4. Deferring to a small but eager buyer. In order to raise prices, an auctioneer pits eager buyers against one another. An astute buyer, realizing that he can do better in his purchasing if he is not opposed, waits until some buyers have satisfied their needs before bidding in earnest. The tactic is difficult to implement in that he may not be able to identify the bidders to whom he should defer. A livestock buyer friend of mine, however, did precisely that; detecting an individual who was eager to buy, and learning that the man required only half a dozen animals, he simply waited until these

were purchased before resuming his bidding. Then, presumably, he was able to satisfy his own needs at a lower price.

5. Withholding competition in favor of small buyer. When quantity options prevail, the big buyer may find an advantage in not actively competing against a small buyer. He avoids increasing the prices by abstaining from bidding, but yet may obtain the merchandise he needs by purchasing the balance of the lot bought by the small buyer at the price paid by the latter. He may even be granted a quantity discount as part of the bargain.

This waiting tactic is practicable only if the large buyer can ascertain who is doing the bidding and decide whether he can withhold his bids and still obtain needed supplies. Other large buyers who also want to buy at bargain prices may be present, or the auctioneer may decide to reauction the balance of the lot in the hope of obtaining higher returns.

6. Absenting oneself from the market. When a buyer is known to be an important dealer in a particular field, his presence at an auction, especially if he bids, tends to stress the desirability of the goods and push up the prices. If he bids openly on a specific lot, suggesting his special knowledge about its value, others will probably try to outbid him and thus exert an upward pressure on prices. By the simple expedient of absenting himself from the market and leaving the buying to an unknown colleague, such a buyer can relieve the upward pressure and probably even depress prices.

It is conceivable, however, that a buyer wants to enhance rather than depress prices. For example, a dealer in possession of a stock of a certain artist's work might purposely attend an auction and bid vigorously in order to raise the prices of this artist's work. He would thus indirectly increase the value of the items in his own stock. Lord Duveen, one of the great dealers of yesteryear, occasionally employed this strategy.[5]

5 "It was a fixed policy of Duveen's to establish a high market value for anything he had a lot of. One thing he had a lot of, early in the century, was Houdon busts. He had fifteen. There was a happy time when you could get a Houdon bust for twenty-five thousand dollars. After buying several at that price, Duveen began to feel sorry for Houdon. Twenty-five thousand dollars was a stodgy and humiliating figure, and if Houdon was worth collecting at all he was worth more than that. Duveen set about correcting what he now realized was a scandalous state of affairs. At a public auction, he paid seventy-

7. Purloining an integral part of item to be sold. Some individuals resort to removing parts of an item that is up for sale in order to depress the price. One who is guilty of this nefarious practice then either buys the item as "faulty" at a low price, after pointing out the deficiency to auction officials, or purchases it at the market price and asks for an abatement on the basis of its imperfection after the sale is over. Or, to avoid direct involvement in the sales transaction, he approaches an interested party during the preauction display and offers to sell him the integral part (presumably at a substantial profit for his expenditure of time and effort) if he should by any chance purchase the item (at a bargain price, of course, because of its condition).⁶ A person associated with a firm about to go into bankruptcy may even remove key parts from equipment and then buy it back in a court-supervised auction at a fraction of its value.

Cooperative activities.—Buyers may seek the cooperation of others in their price-depressing activities.

1. Use of proxy bidder. Although the identity of the actual bidder at an auction may seem immaterial, it can have a significant effect on prices. Aside from a bidder's technical competence, his reputation may influence other bidders and hence affect the prices. Consider, for example, the impact that participation by a prominent collector or dealer like Lord Duveen could have on competitive bidding. The inferred interest of such an individual in the auctioning of a particular item could well enhance the desirability of the

five thousand dollars for a Houdon bust—an unprecedented figure. He then returned to his Fifth Avenue gallery and looked at his other Houdon busts more respectfully, and with a righteous feeling of having vindicated their honor. The world market in Houdons followed Duveen's lead; presently, you couldn't get one for less than a hundred and fifty thousand" (S. N. Behrman, *Duveen* [New York: Random House, 1951], pp. 228–229).

6 George Mercer, ed., *The Auctioneers' Manual* (11th ed.; London: Estates Gazette, 1961), p. 142, warns "auctioneers who have not been long in practice that keys and pendulums of clocks, and similar movable articles, should be removed before the commencement of the sale, or possibly they may not be forthcoming at the proper time, and the article will then have to be sold as 'faulty.' These appendages are frequently taken by the objectionable *habitués* of the sale . . . who, by watching the bidding when the lot in question is submitted, discover the purchaser, and subsequently make overtures to supply the missing parts for a consideration."

goods in the minds of competitors. Thus it would be to his advantage to employ a proxy bidder and stay away from the sale himself.

2. Joint buying. The purchase of goods jointly by two or more individuals is common practice in certain fields. One reason for this procedure is that one individual may find it financially burdensome to handle the transaction alone. Even though originating as a convenience, joint buying can have a depressing effect on market prices. Buyers may therefore collude specifically for price-depressing purposes. By entering into a joint buying arrangement, two aggressive competitors avoid bidding against each other.

3. Elimination of competition. There is no question about the potential effect of buyer collusion. The organization of buyer rings is characterized by an agreement among a group of buyers to refrain from bidding as individuals and to assign one of their number to bid for the group. Theoretically, the organization obtains the goods at a price considerably lower than the one that would have been established by the competitive process, and participants share in whatever gains accrue from the excess of the market value, as determined by genuine competitive bidding, over the noncompetitive price.[7]

Influence of Seller-Buyer Cooperation

In addition to separately influencing prices, sellers and buyers may engage in cooperative activities that will depress or enhance auction prices. While cooperation is probably rarer in actual practice than its theoretical potentiality might suggest, the matter is briefly examined here in order to complete the discussion of price-influencing activities.

1. Buyer's proposal to auctioneer. The most common type of seller-buyer cooperation is perhaps that in which the initiative is taken by the purchaser. For example, a would-be buyer who desires a particular item may approach the auctioneer with a preauction offer. This maneuver in itself does not necessarily affect the price, but it may develop into an agreement between auctioneer and buyer for the purchase of an entire lot at a discounted price. Collusive arrangements of this kind, which are certainly not legitimate, are

7 See chapter 13 for a full discussion of buyer collusion.

fortunately rare, possibly because it would be difficult to avoid detection.

2. By-bidding by another purchaser. By-bidding or puffing—that is, bidding for the purpose of artificially stimulating the market so that prices will go up—is usually practiced by a person who has no interest in purchasing. An actual buyer, however, may perform a by-bidding service for an auctioneer on items he does not intend to purchase in return for favored treatment on goods that do interest him. Auctioneers are approached from time to time by potential buyers with offers of this kind, although they are unethical and indeed illegal.[8] Such an arrangement is practicable only when the owner of the goods sold to the stooge is also the owner of the goods whose prices he helped to enhance, else one vendor gains at the expense of another.

3. Vendor's influence on buyer's broker. In some fields all bidding must be done by a broker representing the buyer rather than by the buyer himself. The broker obviously has less interest than the buyer himself in obtaining the property at a low price, especially if he is paid on a percentage basis. In the sale of apartments by auction in Paris, in which postauction counterbidding was permitted, the buyers' broker allegedly colluded with the vendor to raise the price, to the ultimate disadvantage of the buyers.[9] Whatever the particular situation, there is always a possibility of conflict of interest between the broker's role as representative of the buyer and his relationship with the vendor or his agent.

4. Silent by-bidding by large buyers. As noted earlier, a prominent buyer may avoid bidding or even appearing at an auction through which he hopes to acquire needed supplies at reasonable prices. Even if he does not actually engage in bidding, he may by simply putting in an appearance cause prices to move upward, for other traders would assume that he would not be there unless he was interested in the merchandise. Thus a well-known buyer for a large concern may be induced to attend an auction for precisely this purpose. The price-enhancing result may be even more marked in

8 For a brief discussion of this type of activity see O. C. Lightner, *Buying at Auction* (Chicago: Hobbies Publishing Co., 1942), pp. 19–20.

9 Carlton Lake, "For Sale at Auction," *New Yorker*, Nov. 5, 1955, pp. 139–141, 143–144, 146, 148–154, 157–161.

the long run because of stepped-up consignments to an auction patronized by important buying representatives, and the resulting increase in auction attendance occasioned by the better offerings.

5. Sweetening lots for favored buyers. Those who set up lots for sale are in a position to conceal an item of great value in one of them, and then apprise a favored individual of this fact. In return for such advantageous treatment, the buyer divides the spoils with auction officers or employees, or by-bids on other items for which the auctioneer hopes to obtain high prices.

Summary

The foregoing analysis of price-influencing tactics is merely an attempt to classify various activities employed by traders to influence prices one way or the other, not a judgment on the ethics, or lack of ethics, of those who may practice them. No implication of applicability is intended except in the sense that the techniques mentioned are workable under certain circumstances.

These techniques are available to both buyers and sellers who want to influence auction prices in one direction or the other. Some of them are perfectly legitimate sales promotional activities; others are unethical and perhaps illegal, for they at least border on fraudulent behavior.

The inference that these tactics are available to all auctioneers and are typically practiced by them is not correct. Some of the price-influencing tactics utilized by unprincipled auctioneers are special-purpose devices that are not applicable in all auction operations. For example, the practice of planting unauthentic items in an auction featuring authentic pieces is not always feasible. Also, some price-influencing devices are impracticable in certain auctions because the buying group is too sophisticated to tolerate promotional activities of a doubtful kind. Touting would hardly be effective, for example, at a preview session of a machinery auction. Finally, the use of one price-influencing device often obviates the need for another: an auctioneer who runs up the price with phantom bids does not also need a stooge.

Furthermore, the impression that price-influencing devices on the selling side will offset those on the buying side is also erroneous. Not only are the tactics inapplicable in certain circumstances, but if applicable they may not be employed by both sides, either because of ethical considerations or because of ignorance. When such tactics are used by both sides, the results are likely to vary with the relative effectiveness of the devices utilized and the skill with which they are employed.

One must also consider the ethical standards peculiar to those who conduct auctions. Whereas some people might run the price up by use of phantom bids, they would not mix fake with genuine items and thus perpetrate a fraud, or employ professional touters to conduct a whispering campaign during or preceding an auction session. It is thus very difficult to evaluate the impact of price-influencing tactics of sellers and buyers in auction operations.

From the consumer-buyer's point of view, caution should be the watchword. Auctioneers in general are doubtless honest within the ethical framework of their craft, but unquestionably some of them do occasionally practice price-enhancing tactics. Auctions should be approached on a *caveat emptor* basis, at least until buyers have satisfied themselves of the honesty of the operation.

Buyer Rings

13 BRIEF MENTION has already been made of buyer rings, particularly in connection with price-influencing behavior. Because the subject is so important to a complete understanding of auction pricing, it deserves a closer look.

Theory of Ring Operations

In auctions, would-be buyers compete with one another in their attempts to purchase the goods that are up for sale. But buyer competition may be materially reduced or eliminated by the existence of a ring of colluding buyers who have secretly agreed *not* to compete against one another. When all the buyers who are interested in the same merchandise are included in the ring, buyer competition gives way to monopsony, or buyer monopoly. The purpose of a ring is to eliminate buyer competition and thus gain an unfair advantage over vendors. The term "ring" apparently derives from the fact that in a settlement sale following the auction, members of the collusive arrangement form a circle or ring to facilitate observation of their trading behavior by the ring leader.

The aim of a ring operation is to reduce or eliminate competition among buyers and thus obtain substantial or complete control of the auction price. Some buyers who

would ordinarily be expected to bid for a particular item are induced not to bid. Usually participants divide the profits representing
the difference between the price bid in the rigged auction and the
returns derived from the sale at the market price, or receive their
share of needed goods at bargain prices. In other words, those operating the ring buy at a noncompetitive price and share out the gains
made by selling at a competitive price.

If there is only one buyer, there is no competitive bidding, and
the resulting price will be less than if competition among buyers
prevailed. But one must not assume that such a condition is easy to
achieve. Not only may identification of interested buyers be very
difficult (as in trades where the buyers are mainly collectors), but
agreements may be hard to effect, even assuming such identification. The chances of successfully organizing a ring are enhanced if
the market for the item is a narrow one, because then there are
fewer buyers to identify and to influence.

There are two general approaches to the problem of eliminating
or reducing buyer competition at a public auction:

1. An attempt is made to identify and make arrangements with
all buyers who are expected to be interested in a particular item
or a lot of goods. Once this task is accomplished, one buyer,
acting for all, is in a position to exert complete monopsonistic
power and thus depress prices drastically, assuming the vendor is
unaware of the value of a commodity.

2. Only those buyers who are expected to know that a particular
item possesses special characteristics (causing it to be more valuable
than the vendor thinks) are identified and approached. There
would then be a dual market situation: one market would include
all the interested buyers, uninformed as well as informed, and the
other would include only those who are informed. It is the informed segment that the ring leader attempts to control, leaving
those in the uninformed segment free to bid as they please. There
may be vigorous competition up to a certain point, representing the
unrestricted bidding of those who because of ignorance undervalue
the item. But after the highest bidder in the uninformed group has
registered his bid, the monopsonist can, in the absence of a reserve
price, purchase the item by exceeding the last uninformed bid by
only one price interval (in the English system, at least). Competition in the lower price ranges may even be advantageous to the

ring, since it would allay the suspicions of those conducting the auction. Controlled bidding is undoubtedly advantageous to the participants at the expense of the vendor.

Even if all would-be buyers are not included in the combine, the ring's activities do not necessarily come to nought. Its success depends to some extent on the behavior of competitors outside the ring. One might assume that ideally a successful ring operation eliminates from competition all but one bidder, who then bids the item in at rock-bottom prices. Even if this end can be achieved, it may not be desirable from the standpoint of the buyer. An obvious absence of competition would almost certainly alert the seller or his agent and lead to defensive action against the ring, and, in the longer run, would cut off or at least impair the source of supply.

In theory, the ring leader may choose not to eliminate all competitors in a given market situation. Instead, he may welcome competition from independent buyers, especially if it is not particularly vigorous and poses no serious threat to the success of the ring. In fact, the appearance of competition is so important that the head of the group may find it necessary, in the absence of actual competition, to provide simulated competitive activity by assigning bidding roles to certain ring members, who stop either at a prearranged cutoff point or at a signal from the leader.

Ring Operations in Practice

The practical application of the theory of buyer rings may be illustrated by examples drawn from representative commodity fields.

The antique trade.—There is considerable evidence that buyer rings exist in some English antique auctions. They may develop from the discovery by a specialist (in Meissen ware, for example) that an item soon to be sold is undervalued in the catalog description. Or they may develop because of the generally superior knowledge of ring leaders compared with the average audience at a certain type of sale, such as a country auction. The item or items may be much more valuable than either the owner or the auctioneer realizes.

It is conceivable, although not likely, that the person who makes the discovery of an underrated catalog item is the only one who knows its real value. If so, he possesses monopsonistic power which can be put to practical advantage. It is more likely, however, that other specialists with similar interests are also aware of the under-valuation. Probably the expert making the original discovery would be able to guess the identity of the knowledgeable individuals among the antique dealers known to him. If his guesswork is accurate, he can communicate with them and propose the organization of a ring as an alternative to bidding against one another.

A ring is more likely to be successful if its members are retail dealers seeking to purchase items in a narrow market, for then it is practicable to line up all would-be buyers. The organization of a buyer ring for the purchase of antiques—ceramics, furniture, paintings, silverware, and the like—is much more complex than a similar venture in other fields. Numerous dealers or even hangers-on may recognize the value of an unusually fine antique; even if they are in no position to acquire it, their possession of such knowledge is a constant threat. For instance, they could combine their knowledge with capital provided by a more affluent but less knowledgeable dealer. In any event, such individuals have to be compensated in some way for their willingness to withhold bids and to keep their knowledge to themselves.

An even more important reason for the complex nature of ring operations in the antique field is that the ring must not only bring all informed buyers under its control, but must devise a workable scheme for disposing of the goods at or near the actual market price. After acquiring the goods at monopsonistic prices at a public auction, the ring holds a private sale to liquidate them and divide the gains among ring members. When an item is not divisible, liquidation is the only means of realizing profits. This solution is not difficult if only one item has been jointly purchased and if several individuals have an equal stake in the enterprise. But when numerous items are bought in a joint operation, the settlement becomes more complicated, if only because there are many minor participants with whom arrangements must be made. The "little guys," incidentally, may act as "bird dogs" for large dealers in exchange for some kind of compensation.

A public sale in which a ring is operating is the same as it would be in the absence of such an arrangement, except that some or all of the interested buyers of some items have agreed to operate within the framework of the buying organization, or ring, and thus buyer competition is reduced or eliminated. Although collusive activities prevail in parts of the auction, unaffiliated buyers who are probably not even aware of the existence of a ring behave normally. Possibly the only outward evidence of a rigged auction is sluggishness of bidding, and even this is sometimes eliminated because a well-organized ring provides for simulated competition at lower price levels.

A fairly recent example of the purchase of an item at public auction and its subsequent clandestine liquidation was the sale of an antique mahogany Chippendale commode.[1] When it was put up for sale along with other items at an auction in a community a hundred or so miles northwest of London in late 1964, bidding was sluggish, and the commode fetched £750. The slow pace of the bidding might have been a tip-off on the operation of a ring. As discovered later, the auctioneer and the trustees of the estate of which the commode was a part had indeed been taken by ring operators. On the evening of the day of the auction, the commode was reauctioned in a private sale open only to members of the ring. At the so-called knockout sale, held in Leamington, several dozen dealers were present to bid in earnest on lots acquired earlier in the rigged sale. At least five of them knew the true value of the commode, had the resources to buy it, and believed a good profit could be made if it could be acquired for £4,000. Actually, the commode brought £4,350 at the private sale, when only a few hours earlier it had sold for £750 in the public auction. The tremendous profit was divided equally among the ring members who remained for the final sale.

The complicated settlement required when there are numerous minor participants in the ring is based on the principle of testing members in a series of reauctions of less important items. The ring leader, or whoever is in charge, "names out" those persons who are required to "defend themselves" by actively bidding on such items. Some of the impecunious and less able traders fail to meet the test and are paid off immediately. Additional participants are elimi-

1 "The Curious Case of the Chippendale Commode," *Sunday Times* (London), Nov. 8, 1964, pp. 8–9.

nated when more expensive items are reauctioned, and so forth. This process of selling monopsonistically acquired items at competitive prices and thus compensating minor traders clears the path for the climactic event—the selling of the major item acquired by the ring. At this point only a few astute and financially competent dealers are left to bid against one another for the grand prize. The bidding is likely to be spirited, not only because of the profit possibilities but because of the prestige accruing to the one who acquires the prize, and the price may be pushed to maximum levels. In the example given above, the commode, purchased for £4,350 by one of the ring members at the postauction sale, reportedly brought £10,000 in a subsequent transaction.

At a knockout sale,[2] the surviving ring members all have a stake in the net yield (or dividend). The bidders are therefore owners as well as would-be buyers, a situation that may lead to conflict. As a buyer, each member of the ring wants to obtain the property at as low a price as possible; as part owner who will share in the proceeds, he will benefit from a high price for the item. The reconciliation of such conflicts depends on the motivation of individual ring members. It has even been suggested that the buyer of an item in the final round may pay as much for it in the end as if he had bought it in open competition at the public auction, because he may use up his dividend in overbidding at the settlement.[3]

One art critic reveals that sometimes there are even inner rings.[4] That is, not only is there a ring whose purpose is to eliminate competition in the public auction, but a ring within the ring for the purpose of paying off unimportant members on the basis of a modest enhancement in price, thus leaving most of the advantage to those in the inner circle.

This system works as follows: A ring composed of five men, say, acquires a painting at a very low price and retires to a private

2 "Knockout," according to the *Oxford English Dictionary*, means "Characterized by 'knocking out' . . . of, or in connexion with, an auction sale. . . . 'Combinations, by a set of men who attend real sales, and drive, by various means, respectable purchasers away, purchase at their own price, and afterwards privately sell the same, under a form of public auction, termed "Knockout Sales." . . .' "

3 "The Ring and the Book," *The Economist*, Aug. 11, 1956, p. 468.

4 See Robert Wraight, *The Art Game* (New York: Simon and Schuster, 1965, 1966), pp. 110–111.

room to resell it on a competitive basis. Normally, one would expect competition to be all-out at this stage of the proceedings. But in this instance, three of the five ring members may agree to allow one of their number to bid for them. Thus there are only three bidders in the first knockout sale, and obviously the inner ring leader will bid only high enough to acquire the item. After the profit represented by the excess of the first knockout sale price over the monopsonistic price is distributed among the five ring members, the two who were victimized go their ways, leaving the other three to bid against one another for title to the item. The differential between the price established by the two competing ring members and the inner ring leader in the first knockout sale and the price established by the three inner ring members in the second knockout sale is divided among the inner ring members, including of course the actual purchaser who thus buys the item at a discount.

The fish trade.—Buyer rings are occasionally found in the sale of fish, at least in English primary markets. The principle here is exactly the same as it is in other fields: reduction or elimination of buyer competition with a resulting downward pressure on prices. The differences arise in application of the principle. Unlike rings in the antique field, those that operate in fish markets face no complicated system of settlement; the fish are simply divided among the ring members. Moreover, fish prices are not drastically influenced by joint purchasing activity, especially in modern markets where communication is highly developed.

The latter point requires further elaboration. Basically, fresh fish is no different from any other commodity in its susceptibility to price control by monopsonistic effort. For example, buyers in a primitive fish market located in an emerging country can conceivably act jointly and thus depress the price to any level they choose, even to zero. Primitive markets are particularly vulnerable to monopsonistic control because they lack pricing data from other sales which can be used for comparisons, and in emerging countries legislative proscription of such activity is unlikely. Those exerting price control would, however, hesitate to force prices to inordinately low levels, because fishermen would soon quit the trade and seek out another way of earning a living, and there would be no more fish.

But when bench marks are available for comparisons, and sales of a commodity are not yielding sufficiently high prices, vendors can assume the existence of buyer control. Sellers or their agents can then initiate countermoves to neutralize the monopsonistic efforts. Therefore the leader of a ring operation in the fish trade in England, say, does not usually attempt to purchase what he needs at sharply depressed prices, but tries for more modest gains. Nor does he seek to corner the market—though that is customarily a ring leader's real objective—because the commodity is in wide demand and concerns many traders. Rather, he chooses a variety of fish having a narrow market and a limited number of buyers. The latter is a key factor in any successful ring operation, for each buyer has to be identified and then enlisted in the joint buying effort. Recruitment of a small number of buyers of a not too popular variety of fish—jumbo haddock, for example—as members of a ring is not too difficult.

Nevertheless, the implementation of any scheme for joint buying is not easy. The first step is to organize dealers who would otherwise buy individually and thus compete against one another. Next, the necessary buying arrangements must be made, either with or without preauction contact with the auctioneer. A common form of preliminary negotiation, especially in the fish trade, is to approach the auctioneer with a book bid before the sale starts. Such a bid is merely an offer for an entire lot, which the auctioneer considers along with other book bids and with bids made from the floor. No suggestion of collusion necessarily accompanies this tactic, though it may in fact exist. The auctioneer, knowing that the floor bidder, even if his bid is high, may take only a few kits and leave the rest to be sold at possibly a lower price, may well be interested in a "deal." When the goods are actually put up at auction, the auctioneer may use a fictitious price in knocking the goods down to the book bidder, but he is more likely to use the flexible discount, or "lowers," device.

An auctioneer's amenability to participation in arrangements for joint buying may be the desire to grant a return favor to a ring leader who has helped him out by taking a supply of fish at a time when sales were badly needed. The auctioneer may also be keeping an eye on the possibility of future cooperation. More practically, he may find it advantageous from the standpoint of bookkeeping to knock the whole lot down to one bidder and save the time and effort required to sort out a number of transactions after the auction is over.

Although a ring leader may try to squeeze an auctioneer by informing him in preliminary negotiations that all the buyers are lined up, such an effort is not likely to succeed. Rather, according to a ring leader in a large English fishing port, it would ensure failure, because an auctioneer cannot afford to permit a buyer to exercise such extensive market control. Instead, he would knock the goods down to another buyer, possibly his own company, in order to confound the ring leader. If the latter does have all the buyers lined up, he may have some of them simulate genuine bidding in order to provide an appearance of normal conditions until a certain price is reached, at which time he takes over. If his operation is undetected, he may acquire the goods at slightly less than the competitive market price for merchandise of like quality. Since he is buying the whole lot, he is probably also able to obtain a quantity discount, or lowers. If the ring leader is not a merchant or a businessman whose purpose is to obtain his own fish at less than the market price, his compensation is the difference between the price he pays and the amount the ring members pay him.

In summary, the leader of a buying ring in the fish trade has followers who know from experience that they can gain an advantage by cooperating with him in acquiring their supplies. The ring leader gets the best price he can, including lowers, from the official auctioneer. He then prices the fish out to each buyer or ring member on a basis of (*a*) giving buyers an advantage—more to some than to others—but (*b*) retaining as much profit as he dares for himself. Thus modest gains, but no "killings," are possible in operating a fish-buying ring in advanced societies where market information is readily available.

Timber rights.—Much of the timberland in the United States is owned by the federal government, and from time to time the Forest Service announces the sale of timber rights connected with the land. Buyers, including lumber mill owners, veneer processing plants, logging firms, and the like, are invited to enter their bids in competition for these awards, either in sealed bids or in oral auction.

It is in the latter type of sale that collusive activities are particularly prevalent.[5] Those wanting to bid in the oral auction must first qualify by entering a preauction sealed bid at least equal to the government's appraised price, which serves as the minimum level for bidding in the oral sale. In the oral auction, which is based on the ascending-bid principle, bids are made by outcry, with advances varying from 5 cents to several dollars per thousand board feet at the discretion of buyers. Trivial advances may, however, be rejected by the auctioneer.

Buyers of timber rights in an auction are usually concerns operating in the vicinity of the timber that is to be sold. They may bid against one another or may enter into a collusive arrangement, a common practice in this field. A collusive agreement may take the form of a joint buying arrangement, usually secret, or of abstention from bidding by some potential purchasers, with or without a sharing arrangement.

An individual who wants to organize a collusive buying group for the purchase of timber rights invites all interested parties to convene at a certain time and place to discuss strategy. Alternatively, he approaches several individuals with a specific proposition, which can be either a sharing arrangement or a promise of reciprocation in future sales. To obtain cooperation, the initiator of the plan may have to threaten other potential buyers with exclusion from his future business.

Although theoretically all interested operators may be included in a collusive buying agreement, in actual practice it is difficult, if not impossible, to make a ring all-inclusive. Those joining a ring may or may not wish to qualify for oral bidding in the first, or sealed-bid, phase, but the individual selected to bid for the ring must qualify. Some of those who will not do the bidding may qualify so as to make oral bidding possible in an emergency (for example, if the one designated to act for the group withdraws), or to keep an outsider from getting the sale or make him pay a higher price. Not all those who do qualify are interested in buying; some of them qualify in order to provide a basis for bargaining at a later

5 See Walter J. Mead, *Competition and Oligopsony in the Douglas Fir Lumber Industry* (Berkeley and Los Angeles: University of California Press, 1966), esp. pp. 142–158.

time—"Although qualified I didn't bid against you last time, remember!"

The question as to whether the federal government is taken by collusive buyers of timber can be answered only in terms of the effect on prices, which is not even theoretically determinable in the absence of information about bidders who remain outside the ring. The effect of collusion on prices really depends on completeness of the collusive effort and the maximum demand prices of the outsiders. Although a joining together of two or more erstwhile competitors in an auction tends to lower prices, the effort is unavailing if a single would-be buyer with a high demand price remains independent. Because bidders in Forest Service timber auctions cannot go below the government appraised price, it follows that proper appraisals tend to preclude profit making based on collusive activities. They also protect the government, as seller of the timber, from loss of part of the value of its holdings.

The wool trade.—In the Australian wool trade, auction companies located in various areas act as agent-middlemen in transactions between growers of the commodity who wish to sell it and different types of functionaries who wish to buy it. There appears to be a strong tendency among buyers of wool to organize rings, or so-called pies. Why they prefer collusion to competition is a matter of conjecture, but a key factor is that the product is not homogeneous. There are hundreds of types and subtypes of wool, and the large total number of buyers in any one market shrinks to only a few when related to the purchase of a particular type and grade. Because the requirements of users of wool are also very specific, joint effort is necessary to fulfill those requirements.

Buyer collusion in the Australian wool trade is more complex than in any other trade with which I am familiar. Although it is easy to make joint buying arrangements with a small number of buyers of the same kind of goods, the large number of types and grades of wool complicates monopsonistic buying. No one buyer is likely to find others whose total requirements are precisely the same as his. Buyers who engage in ring operations are therefore apt to belong to a number of pies, each having a different combination of buyers. One buyer reported that he belonged to thirteen two-member and thirteen three-member rings. Undoubtedly pies are very widespread in the Australian wool trade, and are probably as common as they were before World War II.

Pies are organized by buyers of a certain grade and type of wool who join forces and agree to split joint purchases among themselves. The one who takes the initiative starts by asking other wool buyers, "Are you agreeable to splitting?" A typical ring may operate as follows:

> Although composition, size and method of operation of pies vary, a pie is essentially an informal agreement between two or more buyers not to bid against each other. . . . When a lot has been procured by a pie member, any other member of the pie can "claim" on the buyer who has procured the lot. . . . The pie member keeps a "split book" in which pie transfers are recorded. If there are two members in the pie and X does all the bidding for the pie Y is entitled to only half the wool which he claims from X. In a three-member pie Y would be entitled to only one-third of the wool he claims on. When a lot is transferred from X—the original buyer of the lot—to Y, X will instruct the selling broker to accept Y's directions regarding the shipment of the lot. The price Y pays for a transferred lot is identical with the price at which the lot was sold to X.[6]

Although the exact terms and conditions of joint buying arrangements differ in detail, "they all possess one common feature, namely, that in general, parties to such an arrangement refrain from outbidding each other in an effort to secure lots of wool which they are all desirous of acquiring, in return for which forbearance each member is entitled to claim some of such lots from the member who succeeds in obtaining them." [7]

One purpose in organizing a buying syndicate in the Australian wool trade is to reduce upward pressure on prices. But an equally important objective is to simplify the buying of wool. Buyers who belong to a pie share in the purchase of a needed type and quality of wool, instead of making all-out individual efforts to fill their requirements.

Agreements for joint purchasing of Australian wool presumably

6 F. H. Gruen, "Goulburn, Forward Prices and Pies," *Review of Marketing and Agricultural Economics,* XXVIII (June, 1960), 90–91.

7 R. Cecil Cook, *Further Report by The Honourable Mr. Justice Cook under Section 8 of the Monopolies Act, 1923, concerning the Trade in Wool,* Parliament of New South Wales, 2d sess., 1959, before the Industrial Commission of New South Wales, no. 305 of 1958 (Sydney: Victor C. N. Blight, Government Printer, 1959), p. 3.

cover (*a*) the particular type and quality of product desired; (*b*) the specific behavior of members during the bidding; and (*c*) the method of splitting the purchases. The second and third points require elaboration. Unless signals are used, which is not usual, a stratagem must be devised to control the bidding of ring members. Competition may be open to all until the leader comes in, or until he catches the auctioneer's eye, and then other pie members fade out. Competition among buyers is thus affected, but not necessarily eliminated, by the operation of a pie, unless it includes all would-be buyers. In splitting purchases of wool, the payoff is in kind; participants obtain a share of the goods acquired rather than of the profit earned by the joint operation, a figure that would be difficult to compute. Pie members, including the leaders, are all primarily wool buyers, not market manipulators; their only concern is to get needed supplies of goods at the lowest possible prices.

Buyer collusion in a pie operation tends to have a depressing effect on prices because some competitors are necessarily eliminated. The actual effect, however, may be negligible, or even nonexistent. The precise impact depends largely, if not entirely, on the structure of the buying side of the market after organization of the pie. The key question is: Has competition been eliminated or does it still exist? Assuming it remains, is it as effective as it was before the pie was formed in forcing the buyer with the highest demand price to maximum levels? The answer depends on whether all buyers of a certain type and grade of wool are included, or whether some are excluded, even inadvertently. Because most pies do not include all buyers, pie members and individuals operating independently would bid against one another. Furthermore, the existence of more than one syndicate would lead to competitive bidding. If, therefore, the collusive effort is not complete and unified, prices are likely to reach competitive levels. It is, however, impossible to predict the precise effect of pies on wool prices, because the effect on the demand prices of those who are eliminated cannot be calculated.

Combating Ring Operations

In practice, collusive buying in auctions is not very common. The organization of rings (sometimes known as "kippers") when the buyers are collectors is difficult, if not impossible. Even when potential purchasers are mainly dealers, alert vendors can often combat ring activity. To do so they must first recognize the existence of buyer rings; such recognition is based on knowledge of the value of the goods to be sold and therefore of the likelihood that attempts will be made to rig the market. Second, the vendor who would combat ring operations must select a weapon to use against the syndicate.

One approach is to invoke the law against perpetrators of a ring operation. The law recognizes the existence of buyer collusive activities and in general proscribes them if their purpose is to depress prices, although there is no special legislation directed against illegal ring operations in the United States. It has been broadly held in common law cases that prospective bidders at a public sale may not fraudulently agree to refrain from competitive bidding against one another, and that to do so renders void or voidable the sale to any one of the cooperating vendors.[8] If, however, a joint-buying agreement is entered into without any desire to commit fraud (i.e., to depress prices), but to enhance the purchasing convenience of the parties, or for any other honest purpose, the sale is considered valid.[9] For example, two persons, neither of whom is able to purchase the whole property because of financial limitations, may join together to make a bid.[10] In fact, one outstanding auctioneer occasionally suggests the impromptu organization of a syndicate of small buyers, and gives them time to get together before proceeding with the sale.

In England, the Auctions (Bidding Agreements) Act of 1927, sometimes called Lord Darling's Act, proscribes unlawful inducements for abstaining from bidding:

> "If any dealer agrees to give, or gives, or offers any gift or consideration to any other person as an inducement or reward for abstaining, or for having abstained, from bidding at a sale by auction either generally or for any particular lot, or if any person agrees to accept, or accepts, or attempts to obtain from any dealer any such gift or consideration as aforesaid, he shall be guilty of an offence under this Act." [11]

8 *Fulgham* v. *Burnett,* 151 Miss. 111, 117 So. 514 (1928).

9 *Kearney* v. *Taylor,* 15 Howard (56 U.S.) 494, 14 L. Ed. 787 (1853).

10 *Holmes* v. *Holmes,* 24 S.C. Eq. 61 (1850).

11 B. S. Yamey, "Bidding Agreements at Auctions," *Butterworth's South African Law Review* (1955), p. 76, quoting Auctions (Bidding Agreements) Act.

Recognizing the legitimacy of certain joint buying arrangements, the law further provides that " 'where it is proved that a dealer has previously to an auction entered into an agreement in writing with one or more persons to purchase goods at the auction *bona fide* on a joint account and has before the goods were purchased at the auction deposited a copy of the agreement with the auctioneer, such an agreement shall not be treated as an agreement made in contravention' of the Act." The Bidding Agreements Act is seldom invoked, and has had almost no effect on ring operations in England.[12]

Because recourse to law is at best a doubtful way of stamping out ring activities, vendors turn to extralegal activities in their efforts to combat rings. In some auctions, the most effective way of overcoming a buyers' ring is to set a reserve price, prohibiting sale of the item below its estimated value and thus impairing the profitability of a collusive operation. This practice is common in London antique auctions at Sotheby's and Christie's, but it is less frequent in country auctions because experts are not easily available and sales volume is too low to cover the costs of investigation. Of course, experts' evaluations are not needed in some fields, such as fish, where market reports are available prior to the auction.

Another possible weapon against rings is the auctioneer's refusal to award an item put up for sale, if the price situation is depressed. Upon recognizing the existence of a ring, the auctioneer not only can disregard the bids of the ring leader, but can actually make a sale to a friendly buyer; the latter may not even have bid, but arrangements with him can be made later. This kind of opposition to a ring, though causing a loss on individual transactions, may bring overall gains in the long run.

Perhaps the most effective defensive tactic is to run up the price of an article by the use of phantom bids, or bids from nonexistent traders. The ring leader would find it difficult to cope with this stratagem; he cannot admit that he has all the buyers tied up, and thus he can scarcely argue that the auctioneer is taking bids out of the air! An auctioneer who is aware of a ring operation can also withdraw a lot and hold it for sale at a later session (after the ring has been dissolved), or he can sell it by private treaty.

Buyers themselves sometimes try to eradicate the evil of ring operations. Associations of dealers, for example, agree not to engage

12 *Ibid.*, p. 77.

in collusive activities. In 1956 the Antiquarian Booksellers Association of England adopted a rule disqualifying firms that participated in rings and thus contravened the Auctions (Bidding Agreements) Act. More recently, the British Antique Dealers Association went on record as opposing knockout sales, an integral part of antique rings.[13] The attitude of these associations and the alleged difficulties of enforcing British laws against rings suggest that cooperation between dealers and the government would hold a promise of success.

Not all these anticollusion weapons are applicable in all circumstances. A tactic that is effecive in a certain market under one set of conditions may not work at all in another market under different conditions. A particular approach should be carefully examined in the light of special circumstances, and should be used only when appropriate and practicable.

13 "Antique Shops Make New By-Laws," *Times* (London), Dec. 18, 1964, p. 5.

Modern Communication Systems

14 TECHNOLOGICAL ADVANCEMENTS in the field of communication offer great potentials for increased efficiency in selling goods at auction. Application of such scientific developments has varied with particular types of auctions and among geographical areas.

Auctioning by Electronic Mechanism

Auction selling to assembled buyers by means of electronic devices is not a new phenomenon. Until recently, however, the use of such mechanisms has been largely confined to the Dutch (descending-price) system. Rapid developments in electronics during the past few years have created new opportunities for a more general application to the English (ascending-price) system and to the Japanese (simultaneous-bidding) system. In addition, the computer has become an integral part of auction selling.

The Dutch auction system.—Under the Dutch system, it will be recalled, an auctioneer announces suggested prices in rapid descending order until one of the buyers accepts an offer by calling "Mine!" A bidder must avoid waiting too long, lest he lose out to a competitor.

Some years ago an electrical clocklike mechanism was introduced into the Dutch auction system to replace the auctioneer's calling of offers. An indicator, or hand, moves counterclockwise through a series of numbers in descending order, stopping when a bidder presses a button to register the amount of his bid. The Dutch clock, designed and manufactured on special order for clients all over the world by van der Hoorn & Wouda, a firm in Utrecht, has gained wide popularity in Holland as well as in other countries. It is particularly effective in the sale of standardized or semistandardized items.

The clock is usually located in front of a deeply tiered amphitheater with a normal seating capacity of a hundred or more buyers, who sit at desks facing it. Each seat holder can stop the movement of the indicator by pressing a button when the quotation declines to the point at which he chooses to bid; simultaneously, the number assigned to the bidder flashes on a screen on the face of the clock. Thus the clock indicates the price bid and gives the number of the first, and hence the successful bidder. The auctioneer and his staff are located in a booth above the selling floor; having a good view of the clock, they can record each sale, arrange for buyer options, and transact other business related to the auction, such as feeding in special information required by the computing equipment.

One difficulty attendant upon an auction conducted in an amphitheater is that inspection of the product and the bidding sometimes have to be separated. In the sale of produce and flowers in the Netherlands, however, the auction area is so constructed that goods can be inspected during the sale. Loaded trucks and barges move into position in front of the buyers, and special attendants display samples of the goods. This advantage is offset by the costliness in manpower and time.

In each transaction in the Dutch clock system, a lot of goods is offered on a per kilo or a per unit basis. The indicator on the clock, in the interest of speed, moves continually rather than intermittently, but the auctioneer exercises control by allowing it to move only through the relevant price range. If the highest price expected for a certain item is 25 cents per kilo, he starts the indicator at that figure. In a second or two the item may be sold at, say, 21 cents, and then the auctioneer moves the pointer back to another starting position. The buyer usually has an option to purchase all or only a portion of the lot in which he is the successful bidder.

Auctioning by electronic clock is basically the same as oral descending-price auctioning. The mechanism simply replaces price calling by the auctioneer and voicing of bids by buyer. It also reduces to nil, once the bidding is under way, the auctioneer's influence on bidding activity, which in any event is less in the Dutch system than in the English system. The auctioneer's functions in the clock system are merely (*a*) to decide where to start the indicator in each sale; (*b*) to recognize the first bidder as the high bidder and officially accept his offer; and (*c*) to arrange for options, if they are being used.

The Dutch clock is a simple mechanism. If the decimal system is utilized, it has 100 price points around its rim. One difficulty is that in high price ranges the movement of the hand registers smaller percentage changes than it does in low price ranges. For example, a move from 100 to 99 is a change of only 1 percent, whereas a drop from 10 to 9 is a 10 percent change. The manufacturer of the clocks has attempted to overcome this difficulty by providing fractional numbers in lower price ranges; a price interval in the higher registers may be one cent, but only one-half or one-quarter cent in the lower ranges.

The Dutch clock makes auctioning a speedy process. It is possible to complete 600 transactions in one hour, or an average of one sale every six seconds. The speed is due to the rapidity with which the clock moves and the resulting need for instant response by bidders, to the absence of delays between transactions, and to the skill of the auctioneer in starting the bid high enough to obtain the highest demand price, but not so high as to waste time in scanning.

Another advantage of the electronic system is the virtual elimination of tie bids. The clock operates on a basis of milliseconds, so that individual bids are distinguished unless they occur within the same thousandth of a second. Ties occur only once or twice a week even in a very busy auction, like the one handling flowers at Aalsmeer, Holland. When two numbers show up simultaneously on the clock, indicating a tie, the goods are reauctioned.

When the clock mechanism was first introduced, its speed was set at about six complete turns a minute. The rate has since been increased to twelve turns a minute, except where the clock system has recently been installed and traders require time to become accustomed to its use. Bidding by the clock is very tricky, and without experience a participant in an auction tends to hit the key either too early or too late, thus either paying too much for a lot or losing out to other bidders. Some buyers, in fact, practice hitting the keys in order to achieve proficiency, or vie with one another during the off season in an attempt to improve their speed and accuracy.

The English auction system.—The experimental use of electronic bidding equipment in ascending-bid auctions is not new, but until lately practical difficulties have prevented full application of the idea. The main obstacle has been the problem of providing for bidding intervals. If one interval is provided after each bid, in several transactions there would be two or three, or even more, such intervals. As a result, the selling process was slowed down considerably.

A recent modification of the Dutch clock system is designed to overcome the weakness of earlier electronic equipment used in English auctions. In the new device, the price indicator moves clockwise on an ascending basis, in contrast with the counterclockwise movement on a descending basis in the Dutch system. Once the sale of an item has started, the clock moves constantly upward from zero until the transaction is completed. As long as two or more bidders are pressing the keys, the hand of the clock moves and prices advance. It continues to move until all bidders except one withdraw, at which time the clock stops and the number of the top bidder is flashed on the screen. He is the buyer, assuming that the reserve price level has been reached.

Instead of bidding by successive discrete bids and counterbids, as in nonelectronic auctions, bidders using the electronic clock bid simply by maintaining pressure on the bidding keys. They resemble a floor bidder in the orthodox system who has told the auctioneer that he is bidding continuously as long as he keeps his hand in his pocket, or a book bidder whose bid is constant so long as the level of floor bidding is below his maximum offer.

Among the advantages of the new system is the flexibility of the equipment. With only a minor adjustment, it is interchangeable with the mechanism used in Dutch-type auctions. The new system also eliminates the wasteful time intervals characteristic of earlier ascending-bid electronic systems. It has, however, one weakness: it does not inform potential buyers how many individuals are bidding, but indicates only that two or more bidders are in the running. The stimulating effect of knowing that lively interest exists among a number of competing bidders is therefore absent. This flaw is, however, by no means fatal, because the equipment could easily be adjusted to provide for the dissemination of such information.

The Japanese auction system.—One of the most interesting applications of electronic equipment to auctioning is a system designed for use in Japanese wholesale fruit and vegetable markets. The equipment was designed by the Fuji Electronic Communication Manufacturing Company of Tokyo. Before its development, bids were given simultaneously by hand signal. With the advent of electronic equipment, would-be buyers, after inspecting the goods to be sold, convene in a kind of amphitheater and take their places at desks. The key features of the new system are (1) an identifying plate inserted into an electronic slot on the bidder's desk; (2) a multiple-key board on the desk, to be used by the bidder in communicating the amount of his bid; and (3) an electronically operated board in front of the auction room.

When potential bidders are seated and ready to bid, the auctioneer requests bids for the first transaction, and the bidders push the dispatch buttons simultaneously, or approximately so. Each bidder registers the precise amount he wants to bid, and the board at the front of the room registers only the high bid and the high bidder's identification number. Sales transactions follow one another in rapid succession; operating rules stipulate a five-second period for bidding on each lot. In practice, however, the auctioneer may terminate the bidding within two or three seconds, thus precluding the raising of bids already made, even if bidders had a basis for changing their bids.

There are two reasons for using a short time interval in this type of auction operation. One is to encourage bidders to make their best offer at the outset—the distinguishing principle of a simultaneous-bidding system. Second, time is of the essence in this kind of auction, and an overallowance of time would be wasteful. Bidders have all they can do to register their high bids within the brief time allotted.

When the time permitted for bidding expires, the goods are knocked down to the highest bidder, the bidder whose price is registered on the electronic board. The auctioneer is then ready to invite bidding on the next lot. Thus the practice of strategic lagging, which is at least theoretically possible when hand signals are used, is almost nonexistent. This scheme not only possesses a high-speed potential, but provides a good opportunity for obtaining the highest demand price of the high bidder.

Computing equipment in electronic auctioning.—An outstanding feature of electronic auction selling is the use of automation to record the details of sales transactions. It simplifies the reporting of sales and prices to the vendors whose goods are sold, and the billing of customers who have purchased the goods.

The information required by the computer is gathered from two sources. First, the clock itself, which in the Dutch system is wired to the computer, supplies the price at which a lot was sold and the identifying number of the buyer. Second, supplementary information is fed into the machine by the auctioneer or one of the clerks at the time of the sale: for example, the vendor's number and the amount of goods sold to each buyer. The machine turns out punched cards which provide the raw data for the preparation of statements to buyers and sellers.

The potential manpower saving is enormous. Thousands, or tens of thousands, of sales transactions have to be accounted for to the vendors of the goods, and the same number of reports must be made to the buyers. Manual sorting out of all the sales transactions in any one week would be burdensome and time-consuming. Moreover, in a data processing system, information placed in the computer becomes part of the "memory" of the machine and can be retrieved whenever required. The production of printed statements by name of vendor or client is effected by feeding the punched cards into the printer and programming the machine for the task assigned it. In addition to its laborsaving aspects, this operation has the advantages of complete legibility and a high degree of accuracy. The goodwill of both seller and buyer is thus gained.

Auctioning by Teletype

Until fairly recently it was assumed that buyers, because they are the price makers in auctions, had to be assembled at the point of sale. Methods now available, however, permit buyers to bid from decentralized points through a two-way communication system which also describes the wares that are up for sale. Absentee bidding is feasible only when the goods possess a certain degree of standardization.

A system developed in the mid-1940's in the United States under the trade name Selevision made it possible to conduct auction sales by wire.[1] Under this plan, which operates on an ascending-bid basis, citrus fruit can be put up for sale at a Florida shipping point to buyers assembled in various distant cities. Potential buyers are supplied with specifications of the fruit before the start of the auction. The equipment includes teletype machines at both selling and buying points; apparatus for coordinating bids from the buying locations; a time clock for indicating the seven-second time interval within which bids in each transaction are to be made; and a screen, just below the clock, to show the offers made by bidders on a per crate basis. Bids must be registered within the time interval, otherwise the word "sold" replaces the amount of the bid on the screen. Counterbids made within the seven seconds may result in a higher price.

A variation of this method is used in Denmark for the auctioning of fruit.[2] On the day of the sale, sample boxes of the commodity are placed in front of auction halls in Copenhagen, Aarhus, and Odense. When the auction begins, an individual who wants to bid on a particular lot pushes a button in the auction hall where he happens to be. All bids so made are registered on a screen in front of the auctioneer in Copenhagen, who consolidates them as they are received from buyers located in the three cities. The name of the buyer and, presumably, the price at which the lot was sold are announced when the auctioneer determines that he has secured the highest price for a particular lot. Sales are made at an average rate of more than one a minute.

In the spring of 1961, after three years of experimental study, auction sales of livestock by wire were inaugurated in the province

1 "Auctions by Wire: Nine Large U.S. Cities and Florida Citrus Market Are Linked by Selevision," *Business Week*, Jan. 13, 1945, p. 85.

2 Frank Meissner, "Synchronized Fruit Auctions in Denmark," *Foreign Agriculture*, XVIII (April, 1954), 70–71.

of Ontario, Canada, by the Ontario Hog Producers' Cooperative.[3] The special teletype hookup includes a master teletype machine and an electronic broadcast repeater in the cooperative's central office in Toronto; buying machines in the seventeen principal packing company offices throughout the province; and a buying machine in the central office to handle the bids of the smaller packers. The equipment is integrated so as to permit communication between the central office broadcaster, which describes the lots that are for sale, and the buying machines, which receive descriptions and invite bids at various price points.

Hogs are sold every day between 9 A.M. and 5 P.M. The animals are offered in successive lots of seventy-five or more as they arrive at one of the forty-five marketing yards. All hogs in Canada are sold by grade and yield, and offers are made per hundredweight, dressed. Bids are registered by packers on the assumption that the animals, when inspected, will be grade A. Grade B carcasses automatically yield 1 dollar less per hundredweight than the bid price.[4]

The Ontario plan works as follows. When an offering is about to be made, the operator of the master teletype machine alerts the buyers in each packer's office by ringing a bell. He then gives the location of the hogs, the lot number, the quantity, and other pertinent information. As the Dutch system is employed, quotations must start at a point high enough to allow for obtaining the highest demand price for each lot. Quotations on numbered lots start about 50 cents higher per hundredweight than the price at which it is hoped the sale will be consummated. The quotations descend by intervals of 5 cents until a bid is received or until the reserve price, if any, or the dollar-drop limit is reached. The price is never permitted to drop more than 1 dollar during the sale of a particular lot; when that limit is reached the lot is withdrawn from sale. A red light flashes on the electronic broadcast repeater when a buyer,

3 For further information see Robert H. Kular, "Sales by 'Wire'—Teletype Hog Buying by Dutch Auction—Ontario Packers List Pluses, Drawbacks," *National Provisioner*, July 21, 1962, pp. 19, 22, 23, 43; Charles R. Koch, "Hogs on the Wire," *Farm Quarterly*, XVI (Winter, 1961–62), 70, 71, 84, 86, 88; and Harvard University Graduate School of Business Administration, "The Copaco Case" (mimeographed, *ca.* 1962).

4 Kular, *op. cit.*, p. 19.

having pushed his button at a specific price faster than his competitors have, becomes the successful bidder; all those participating in the sale thus know the price at which the lot was sold. The successful bidder, whose identity is known only to the operator of the master machine, is given confirmation of the sale.

An egg auction conducted by telephonic communication, which employs somewhat the same principle as the sale of hogs in Canada, was inaugurated in 1961 in Scarboro, Maine.[5] No information is available as to which auction system is used, but probably almost any type would be practicable for the sale of a standardized commodity with well-established grades, because buyers would know from the grade designation precisely what they were buying. Such auctions, however, permit no inspection of the goods or samples thereof, either before or during the sale. Buyers must rely completely on grade information and on the integrity of the vendor or his agent.

Use of Television in Auctioning

Television is used in auction sales (1) to accommodate overflow audiences, and (2) to permit distant buyers to participate.

Accommodation of overflow audiences.—In a recent conversation, an executive of a world-famous antique auction house told me that his company had used television in auctioning only to handle overflow audiences. In this simple application of television, people who cannot be accommodated in the main auction room observe the proceedings on closed-circuit television in other rooms. This gesture of goodwill to patrons encourages attendance at auction sales and may influence newcomers to develop enthusiasm for the auction game. Were publicity the only objective, television would serve auctioning better if the sale was telecast to home sets; this has indeed been done in England.

It is, however, practicable and perhaps desirable to go a step further and arrange for television viewers to participate in the trading. Bid spotters among the overflow audience who are in direct communication with the auctioneer in the main auditorium could relay to him any bids they receive. These bids might even

5 "Telephone Egg Auction," *Poultry Processing and Marketing*, LXVIII (Feb., 1962), 104.

stimulate the bidding of traders in the main room. It is possible, although perhaps unlikely, that the high bid would come from the overflow group. In any event, the participation of television viewers would be welcome, for all bids contribute to price making by auction method, under the English system at least.

In the famous Parke-Bernet sale of Rembrandt's "Aristotle" in November, 1961, only 500 of the 1,800 tickets distributed for the affair were white ones, permitting the holders to sit in the main gallery. The balance of 1,300 pink tickets were honored in lesser galleries equipped with television sets.[6] The bidding started at $1 million and moved up by $100,000 jumps until the high bid of $2.3 million was reached. Three of the bids came from observers in the overflow audience, whose contribution to the success of the sale was recognized by the auctioneer, who quipped: "In the future . . . they'll get tickets to the main salesroom." [7]

Participation of distant buyers.—The use of closed-circuit television in auctions can be extended so as to include not only bidders in another room, but those in distant cities as well. Major cities throughout the world can be hooked up in two-way communication systems, permitting television viewers to see what is being put up for sale and make offers through officials assigned to the various cities. Those wishing to participate in the bidding congregate at designated locations.

Use has actually been made of this scheme in the sale of several types of commodities, including government surplus supplies and fine art objects. A few years ago the United States Department of Defense auctioned off some $2 million worth of surplus army, navy, and air force equipment from three supply depots.[8] Bidders in New York, Chicago, Philadelphia, Boston, Columbus, and St. Louis observed the proceedings on giant television screens, and registered their bids with attendants who transmitted them to the auctioneer. More than the usual number of bidders—570 at the six locations—took part, and the sales volume was well above the average for this type of sale. The network cost of almost $100,000 may, however, be a deterrent to wide use of this system.

6 James Brough, *Auction!* (Indianapolis and New York: Bobbs-Merrill, 1963), pp. 18, 19.

7 Quoted in *ibid.*, p. 19.

8 "Now Closed-Circuit TV Makes a Direct Pitch to Customers," *Business Week*, Oct. 17, 1959, pp. 54–55, 57.

Closed-circuit television was also used in a benefit auction of collector's items in 1960. Art buyers in New York City were linked up electronically with those in Chicago, Dallas, and Los Angeles. At a gathering in each of these three cities was a spotter who relayed bids to the auctioneer in New York. The Museum of Modern Art garnered $871,750 for its building fund, as some 3,000 professionals and amateurs bid, city against city, collector against collector, for fifty-one donated modern paintings and pieces of sculpture.[9] In Los Angeles, admission to the auction was restricted to holders of catalogs, and before the auction colored slides of the items on sale were shown by appointment to prospective bidders.[10] The key auctioneer, Louis Marion of Parke-Bernet Galleries, where this first transcontinental art auction originated, implored attendants in the outlying cities to bid, and at times managed to arouse some intercity rivalry. Of the total, however, only $100,000 came from outside New York, suggesting that absentee bidders were reluctant to participate.

Auctions are sometimes conducted through the medium of home television sets, a method periodically utilized by an educational TV station in San Francisco to raise funds for its operating expenses. Provision is made for firsthand inspection of contributed items at a preview, after which the goods are offered for sale via television in groups of ten or more items. Bids are communicated by telephone, and from time to time the camera is focused on a blackboard which shows the name of the item and the highest bid made up to that point. Meanwhile other groups of items are presented in the same way. After three such views are given of the high bids on the items making up each group, the auctioneer goes down the list of items in order, knocking down each one to the individual registering the highest bid.

In the most recent use of television in decentralized auctioning, the Early Bird satellite telecast the first transatlantic art auction.[11] Assistants at Parke-Bernet in New York took bids and relayed them by transatlantic telephone to auctioneer Peter Wilson at Sotheby's

9 "TV Doubles as Art Auction Block," *Business Week,* May 7, 1960, pp. 30, 32.

10 Mary Matthew, "Angelenos To Buy Art via TV," *Los Angeles Times,* April 15, 1960, Pt. II, pp. 1, 4.

11 "Auction via Early Bird: Satellite Takes Bids in Transatlantic Art Sale," *Los Angeles Times,* May 25, 1965. Pt. I, p. 2.

in London, where the sale originated. The paintings were viewed in New York, and the New York audience was shown in London, via television transmission. A 1945 Italian landscape painted by Sir Winston Churchill was sold to a wealthy Texan, bidding from New York, for a record price. Millions of British television viewers were given the opportunity to watch the auction on the B.B.C. program "Panorama," a weekly news show. Thus the experiment served promotional, as well as price-stimulating, purposes.

Television auctioning possesses certain advantages over the orthodox method of assembling buyers at a single location. It saves time for buyers who would otherwise have to travel long distances. More important, it broadens the market to include bidders who without it would have been unable to participate. The use of television in selling real estate has been prognosticated by a man who has faith in the system: "Florida real estate, even low-cost developments, would be a natural for an auction playing all along the Eastern seaboard where a lot of people just can't run down and see the property." [12]

Modern Communication and Market Intelligence

Communication is a factor influencing auction prices, as well as part of the auction system itself. Without it, each market is independent of other markets and behaves accordingly; with communication, market behavior becomes to some extent interrelated through the transmittal of market information.

Communication between producers and markets.—In the absence of communication between a producer and markets, the former makes decisions as to how much to ship, and to what markets, without adequate intelligence. On the other hand, information from the markets provides him with a basis for deciding whether to ship at all at a particular time or, if he is going to ship, where to send the goods (see table 6). The producer has little if any option as to whether to ship perishable commodities, but he has considerable leeway in his choice of markets, assuming that alternative markets are available to him, as they usually are.

Modern-day communication systems thus make possible the shipping of goods to the most advantageous markets and, contrari-

12 Quoted in "TV Doubles as Art Auction Block," p. 32.

Peter Chance auctioning a van Gogh portrait at Christie's in London.
(Photograph, courtesy Christie, Manson and Woods, Ltd.)

Milton Wershow and Roger Ash auctioning a machine works in Los Angeles.
(Photograph, courtesy Milton J. Wershow Co.)

Auction of construction equipment in Gardena, California. (Photograph, courtesy Milton J. Wershow Co.)

Auction sale of tobacco in North Carolina. (Photograph, courtesy U.S. Department of Agriculture.)

Sale of cut flowers by Dutch clock in Aalsmeer, Holland. (Photograph, courtesy van der Hoorn & Wouda N.V.)

Clock used in Dutch (descending-price) auction, showing number of buyer (below) and price (above). (Photograph, courtesy van der Hoorn & Wouda N.V.)

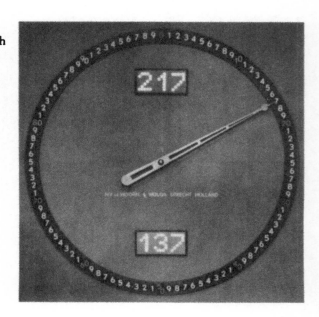

Japanese simultaneous-bidding auction. (Photograph, courtesy Toka Osaka Tobu Seika K.K.)

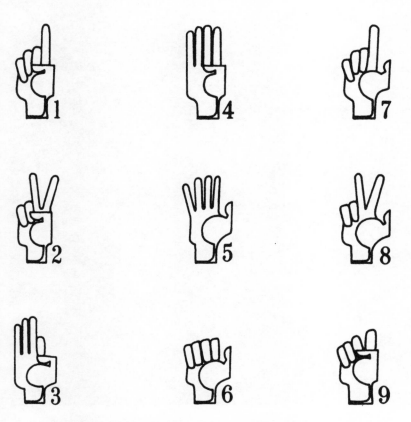

Hand signs used in Japanese simultaneous-bidding auction.

Electronic auctioning of fruits and vegetables in Osaka, Japan. (Photographs, courtesy Toka Osaka Tobu Seika K.K.)

Bidders waiting for auction to open.

Buyer operating keyboard.

Auction room with signboard showing amount bid (upper screen) and number of bidder (lower screen).

Mario Piatelli conducting auction of real property. (Photograph, courtesy Piatelli Co.)

wise, the withholding of goods from markets already well supplied. The rational feeding of markets by producers tends to keep differentials between markets at a minimum, at least in transactions involving the sale of semistandardized goods. It is not surprising, then, that in the auctioning of fish and produce, for example, there is a generalized relationship between markets thousands of miles away from one another. There is, however, no perfect correlation between any two markets, because supplies cannot readily be shifted from an oversupplied market to one of short supply. Thus prices in the two markets tend to pull away from each other. But as there is another factor that can correct for this deficiency (see following subsection), the generalization that such prices tend toward equality is sound.

The student of auctions may wonder whether this principle is applicable to nonstandardized merchandise, such as antiques. In contrast with the commodity auction markets described above, those in which antiques are sold do not usually have the same degree of communication; even more important, the items are not comparable because they are not standardized. Except in the very general sense that antiques of a certain type are fetching better prices in London than in New York, there is apt to be little relationship between antiques sold in one market and those sold in another. The market for a fine Meissen ware figurine in Fresno, California, for example, would bear little relationship to that in New York. Given the differing market conditions, there would be hardly any shifting of demand and supply conditions to equalize the two markets.

Communication among markets.—Goods are not likely to be shipped from one market to another in order to adjust prices. The telephonic and teletype information that is available to buyers in many markets, however, permits them to purchase in an auction where prices are favorable rather than in another where prices are unfavorable, from their standpoint. Intermarket buying is possible in part because the buying representatives of large distributors, assigned to various markets, are in close communication with their head offices. Checks on prevailing prices in different markets, combined with telephonic communication with his buyers, enable a distributor to engage in arbitrage by instructing buyers in certain markets to purchase and those in others to withhold purchases, with a resulting tendency toward price equalization among markets.

The efforts of individuals in their own behalf at most commodity auctions also tend to equalize prices. One type is the buyer who needs goods but is free to purchase his requirements in the market where he finds himself or in another market, depending on the relative price situation. His timing of purchases may also be flexible, so that he can purchase or postpone purchasing, depending on the strength or weakness of the market. By giving or withholding patronage, even the speculator who buys only when he thinks it is favorable to him assists in stabilizing prices and in equalizing prices among markets (see table 6).

Generally speaking, on a basis of the foregoing, the relationship among markets in the same orbit is such that prices will be roughly equal except for transportation costs. This generality, however, does not apply to the sale of nonstandardized items. For one thing, auctions in which such items are sold are not apt to be in operation at the same time, and therefore lack the advantage of communication. For another, the items are seldom identical, and close comparability is not to be expected. Nevertheless, the prices of comparable nonstandardized goods do not get too far out of line for any considerable period of time, because buyers can obtain information about prices fetched at different auctions. By attending those at which prices tend to be soft and acting in accordance with the information derived, they may exert an equalizing influence.

Intermarket communication.—The auction method of selling is usually employed in commodity fields at the primary distribution level. Producers sell to wholesale distributors, who in turn sell to retailers who are one step closer to the ultimate consumer. Bidding by such dealers is influenced by what they expect to get for the goods they want to buy. Information about demand in secondary or tertiary markets, and about the factors that influence it, is therefore essential to intelligent bidding in primary markets, and communication between bidders and agents in consumption markets is crucial.

In the fish industry, as in others, the price the commodity will fetch in the consumer markets largely determines its price in the primary market. Traders in the primary market must consider such questions as "Are the goods moving?" or "How is the weather?"

TABLE 6　　　　207

MODEL: FACTORS INFLUENCING INTERMARKET PRICE RELATIONS

SUPPLY FACTORS	DEMAND FACTORS	MARKET COMMUNICATION
1. Feeding markets by suppliers on a basis of the most profitable alternative opportunities.	1. Instructions to buyer-agents located in various markets who are advised by principals to purchase or not to purchase.	1. Between suppliers and markets.
2. In-transit diversion of shipments.	2. Purchase of requirements by principal buyer who is flexible as to both place and time of acquisition.	2. Among two or more markets: *a.* At the same distribution level. *b.* As between market levels (depending on relative market conditions).
3. Withdrawal of supplies by seller by bidding in the goods.	3. Purchase for own account by speculator who buys only under soft market conditions for sale in other markets at what he hopes will be a higher price (thus engaging in a kind of arbitrage transaction).	
4. Withdrawal of goods by auctioneer for possible sale at a more favorable time.	4. Purchase by auction company which may buy goods for its own account when prices are too low (as in the case of tobacco in the United States).	

The information gained thereby, combined with knowledge of other consumption factors such as the day of the week, which is particularly important in fish markets, guides the dealer-buyer in his bidding at auction.

Sometimes, as in Japan, sales in both the primary and the secondary stages of the fish market are conducted by the auction method. The existence of back-to-back auctions makes for the possibility of a profit squeeze between the price paid by a buyer in the first auction and the price he receives when he consigns it for sale in the secondary market. Traders in the primary market must therefore be particularly careful to keep themselves informed about the characteristics of and the price behavior in the secondary market. Generally speaking, if they are to avoid a squeeze, the market prices should move together. There will, however, tend to be a difference in prices between the two markets approximately equal to the service and transportation costs.

Communication of market intelligence between different market levels is also important in the wool trade. Much of the wool sold at auction in Australia is exported to England, where it is transformed into wool tops and sold to spinners. Obviously, wool traders in Australia would need to keep an eye on cabled market reports of prices of tops in England. Conversely, English buyers and sellers of tops, which are traded on the basis of private treaty, must watch the wire reports, transmitted daily, of wool prices in Australian auctions. In this instance, then, the relationship between prices in the primary market and those in the secondary market works both ways.

Legal Aspects

15 A CLEAR understanding of auctioning is difficult, if not impossible, without consideration of legal issues. The following analysis of the key aspects of the law applicable to auction selling, though not definitive, is sufficient for the purposes of this volume.

Theory of the Auction Transaction

The nature of a contractual arrangement might seem of little significance, except perhaps to a legal philosopher. It behooves buyers and sellers in auction operations, however, to acquaint themselves with the legal aspects of an auction transaction, because the rights and obligations of participants in an auction are indubitably influenced by law.

English-type auction.—In any buyer-seller transaction, there is an offer by one party and an acceptance by the other. The question arises as to which trader makes the offer and which trader accepts it, thus concluding the contractual arrangement. Either of two opposing theories is applicable to auctions of the English type. (1) The putting up of the goods by the auctioneer may be considered a legal offer, while the bid by the would-be buyer may be viewed as an acceptance of the offer, conditional upon the absence of higher bids. (2) Conversely, the bidding on the goods by the would-be buyer may be viewed as an offer, while the knocking down of the lot to the buyer may be considered an acceptance, conditional upon payment for the goods and services.

A difficulty in reconciling these conflicting views is that in certain auction transactions the seller places a reserve price on some or all of the items, while in others the items are sold without reservation. Sometimes the auctioneer gives no overt indication as to whether property is to be sold with or without reserve. If, however, the goods are given a reserve price, the theory that the offer is made by the seller and acceptance by the buyer is hardly applicable. Once a bid is received, a sales contract is in effect, and it would have to be abrogated if the seller decided to withdraw the item at any point below the reserve price.[1] When there is a reserve price, therefore, it seems to me that the buyer makes the offer and the auctioneer accepts, and that there is no contract between seller and buyer before the merchandise is awarded to the high bidder. The weight of judicial opinion supports this view, which is based on the well-established point of law that a bidder may withdraw from the competition at any time before the fall of the hammer.

Does the seller have a right to withdraw the property from sale prior to the fall of the hammer? Again, we must keep in mind that goods may be auctioned either with or without a reserve price. If there is a reserve price, the seller may legally withdraw the goods by direct action of the auctioneer, or indirectly by having a colleague bid on the item or by recognizing a phantom bidder. The problem is more complex when goods are sold without a reserve price. The vendor then is tendering the goods to the highest bidder, rather than receiving an offer from a would-be buyer. In other words, the offer would appear to be made by the vendor and ac-

---

1 For a discussion of auctioning with and without a reserve price, see Nicholas Unkovic, "The Three Types of Auction Sales," *Dickinson Law Review*, XXXIV (June, 1930), esp. 235–243; N. C. Contakos and B. Sandler, "Contracts—Offer and Acceptance—Auctions," *Boston University Law Review*, XII (April, 1932), 240–243; "Sale by Auction with a Reserved Price and Reservation of Right To Bid," *Solicitors' Journal*, LXXXII (July 2, 1938), 539; and D. Napley, "Withdrawal of Property from Auction," *Law Journal*, CII (June 6, 1952), 312–313.

cepted by the buyer, because after the initial bid is made the vendor has a contractual obligation to sell the item at whatever price it will bring. Any withdrawal then would seem to vitiate the agreement, making such a violation actionable. It follows, inferentially, that the seller may withdraw property before bidding starts. Even after a bid is made, he has some recourse to law, if he can show that ruinous prices have been caused by the price-depressing activities of buyers.

In summary, in an auction sale understood to have a reserve price, the theory of buyer-offer and seller-acceptance clearly appears to be superior to that of seller-offer and buyer-acceptance. In a sale without reserve, the theory of seller-offer and buyer-acceptance possesses a clear-cut advantage in explaining the nature of the transaction. Because of this dichotomy, it has been suggested that the statutes relating to auctioning be redrafted so as to recognize the need for different theories. If the suggestion were followed, the relevant statute would read: "At an auction, the auctioneer merely invites offers from successive bidders unless by announcing that the sale is 'without reserve,' or by other means, he indicates that he is making an offer to sell at any price bid by the highest bidder." [2]

Other types of auctions.—In a Dutch auction, the issue is more clear-cut than in an English auction. The auctioneer who calls quotations in descending order, or the clock whose indicator moves downward, is making offers to bidders. The first, or successful, bidder is accepting the offer. This conclusion would appear to hold true even when there is a reserve price.

A different theory is called for in other auction systems. In Japanese simultaneous bidding, offers are made by the bidders, and the auctioneer accepts the best among them. In haphazard bidding schemes, where bids are made blindly, the principle that applies to the Japanese and English systems would appear to hold true. An opportunity is provided by the auctioneer for bidders to make offers, which are then accepted by the auctioneer as the seller's agent. Again, this theory is applicable only to reserve-price situations, as in English-type auctions. Consideration of which theory underlies other auctioning methods goes beyond the scope of this book, but it may be pointed out that no all-purpose theory exists to

2 Quoted in Leonard D. Bodkin, "Auction Sale—without Reserve," *Notre Dame Lawyer*, XXI (June, 1946), 332.

cover all auction systems. Each transaction must be considered individually if one is to determine which of the two theories is more applicable. The need for sound theory becomes even more important when conditions are more complex, as when goods "sold" at auction are destroyed by fire before they are physically delivered or paid for.

Price-Enhancing Tactics of Auctioneers

Because auctions have traditionally been employed to settle estates and to satisfy creditors in bankruptcy proceedings, it has been the expectation of the courts that auctioneers would seek to obtain the highest possible prices, or "top dollar," as they refer to it. They have even been permitted to overstate, with impunity, the worth of the goods that are up for sale in order to increase proceeds. Nevertheless, even sympathy for widows and orphans does not allow the courts to condone fraudulent price-enhancing activities by vendors and their agents. Such activities fall into a number of categories.

Use of confederates.—One device is the employment of a puffer or by-bidder, who makes fictitious bids in order to raise prices.[3] A puffer has been defined as a "person who, without having any intention to purchase, is employed by the seller at an auction to raise the price by fictitious bids, . . . while he himself is secured from risk by a secret understanding with the seller that he shall not be bound by his bids."[4] One who bids at a public sale not because of any desire to purchase but merely to run up the price is not considered a puffer, however, if his bid is recognized as the highest and he can be compelled to accept and pay for the property.

It has been broadly held by judicial pronouncement that puffing is forbidden by law, and that contracts resulting from such tactics are void, or voidable, as contrary to public policy.[5] Decisions

---

3 Peck v. *List,* 48 Am. R. 398, 23 W. Va. 338, 375 (1883).

4 "Auctions and Auctioneers," in *Corpus Juris Secundum* (Brooklyn: American Law Book Co., 1937), VII, 1256. But see *McMillan* v. *Harris,* 110 Ga. 72, 35 S.E. 334 (1900). It might, however, require a Solomon to determine whether a bidder in these circumstances is so obligated, and hence, whether he is a puffer or a legitimate bidder.

5 See the discussion of this point in *Corpus Juris Secundum,* VII, 1256.

handed down in these cases apply to situations in which the price was allegedly enhanced and a sale was actually executed at the inflated price. It appears reasonable to assume that puffing is illegal only in auction sales without a reserve price which are advertised as such, and in auctions with a reserve price in which the bidding is above that price. When bidding is below the reserve price, puffing could not affect the would-be buyer and would therefore be legitimate. Moreover, it is within the right of a vendor to expressly reserve the right to bid in the conditions of sale, although such a provision presumably would be without legal effect if the sale was advertised as one without reserve.

Recognizing phantom bids.—The practice of trotting or running is a price-enhancing technique that precludes the necessity of employing a confederate. If the auctioneer finds himself with only one bidder, he pretends that he has another bid ("one-legged" trotting), or if he has no bids at all he pretends that he has two ("double" or "two-legged" trotting).

Although legal decisions on this subject are rare, one may argue by analogy that if puffing is against public policy, so too is the use of phantom bids. This view is supported by David Napley, who states that "if the auctioneer runs up the price by pretending to receive, from various parts of the auction rooms, biddings which are not in fact made (sometimes called 'taking bids out of the air'), the sale will not be upheld." [6] This opinion, while probably sound, is without much force as a practical matter. The use of phantom bidders is common in auctions, and even if detected is not likely to be challenged by would-be buyers. Moreover, Napley's indictment of the stratagem is too broad. Certainly he goes too far in condemning the practice when he states that the position of a vendor using phantom bids is insupportable even if they are made before a reserve price is reached.[7]

In my view, the legitimacy of phantom bids depends on whether there is a reserve price and on whether that price has been reached. If the sale has been advertised as without reserve, the recognition of phantom bids is unethical, and probably illegal. On

6 David Napley, *Bateman's Law of Auctions* (11th ed.; London: Estates Gazette, 1954), p. 160, citing *Heatley* v. *Newton,* 19 Ch.D. 326, 45 L.T. 455, 51 L.J. Ch. 225 (1881).

7 *Ibid.,* p. 161.

the other hand, if there is a reserve price and it has not been reached, the recognition of fictitious bids is acceptable because it cannot disadvantage the buyer, except perhaps by misrepresenting the degree of interest in the article being auctioned. If the high bid exceeds the reserve price, running by the auctioneer is ethically questionable, and may also be legally actionable. The victim of the allegedly inflated price would have to prove, however, that prices were run up by the use of fictitious bids, a difficult if not impossible task.

Price-Depressing Activities by Buyers

The law, at least in the United States, recognizes that buyer competition is the *sine qua non* of auction selling. According to one judicial pronouncement, a "sale at public auction is based upon the purpose and policy of obtaining the worth of the property by free and fair competition among the bidders." [8] The law looks with disfavor on business tactics such as chilling, stifling, and damping, which are designed to affect buyer competition by discouraging would-be buyers from starting or continuing to bid, with a resulting adverse effect on prices. Tactics that impair competition fall into two categories: those that are individually implemented and those carried out by two or more persons banded together (i.e., collusion). [9]

Individual implementation.—Some price-depressing activities are characterized by an independent effort on the part of an individual. Such effort may take the form of attempts to prevent attendance, to restrict bidding by those in attendance, or to disrupt or disturb a sale that is in progress.

1. Precluding attendance at auctions. One way of impairing prices is to discourage attendance at an auction, thus enabling the would-be buyer to purchase the property with little if any opposition. In a case developing out of such an attempt to chill a deal, an individual purchased a piece of land at a court sale at a price substantially depressed because of the absence of competition. The buyer had allegedly made widespread misrepresentations to other

8 *Nash* v. *Elizabeth City Hospital Co.,* 180 N.C. 59, 104 S.E. 33, 35 (1920).
9 In preparing this section, I have leaned heavily on *Corpus Juris Secundum,* VII, 1255–1256.

potential purchasers that he was going to bid on the land for the decedent's heirs. The court found for the plaintiff in a suit to set aside the sale.[10] In a similar case, the widow of a decedent asked others to absent themselves from a foreclosure sale because the property to be auctioned constituted her sole support. As the only bidder, she was able to buy the land at a very low price, but after the purchase she signed it over to others. In the suit to set aside the sale, the court held that "any act . . . which prevents a fair, free, and open sale, or which diminishes competition, and stifles or chills the sale, is contrary to public policy and renders the sale null and void." [11]

2. Discouraging bidding. In a case falling into this category, a man bought land at a trustee's sale after obtaining, for a consideration, agreements from other interested parties to refrain from bidding. As a result, land worth $10,000 was purchased for $1,800. One of those adversely affected entered a bill to seek recovery of interest lost in the land, on grounds of fraud. In deciding the case, the court found that the action of the defendant constituted chilling of bids at a public sale, and that it operated as a fraud upon the person for whose benefit the sale was conducted. "Prospective bidders at a public sale," said the court, "cannot fraudulently agree together to refrain from bidding one against the other, and to do so renders the sale to any one of the confederates void." [12]

In another case, the goods of a deceased person were being sold at public auction, and the decedent's son was selected by a private party to act as his agent for the purchase of the goods. Sympathetic people who might otherwise have wanted to buy the goods would hardly bid against the son, who would ostensibly be seeking only to buy back family property that was being sold by court order. Because the private party who employed the son used this chilling tactic for his own gain, the court found that it was a clear-cut case of stifling a sale within the meaning of the law.[13]

3. Disrupting a sale. The plaintiff in one case was selling a large cargo of tea. Numerous bidders were in attendance, and bidding

10 Bethel v. *Sharp*, 25 Ill. 173, 76 Am. Dec. 790 (1860).

11 Herndon v. *Gibson*, 20 L.R.A. 545 (1893).

12 Fulgham v. *Burnett*, 151 Miss. 111, 117 So. 514, 516 (1928).

13 Rodgers v. *Rodgers*, 13 Grant's Ch. Rep. (Ont.) 143 (1867). See also *Nash* v. *Elizabeth City Hospital Co.*, 180 N.C. 59, 104 S.E. 33 (1920).

was lively. The sale proceeded quietly until the defendant was refused some merchandise, on which he evidently thought he had been high bidder, on the ground that he had violated one of the conditions of sale. Angered by the decision, he disrupted the proceedings by importuning the assembled crowd to "throw up" their purchases, and then moved to "adjourn." A large number of buyers retired, despite counterefforts on the part of the auctioneer. The decision in this case went to the plaintiff with costs; he had not sought damages because he wanted to prevent future demonstrations rather than cover any immediate monetary loss.[14]

Most of these practices involve some form of fraudulent activity designed to depress prices, such as exploitation of a sympathetic attitude toward members of a decedent's family who are ostensibly attempting to buy property that is being sold to settle an estate. Should a bona fide impecunious widow dissuade potential purchasers from bidding so she could buy the property at a low price, however, no fraud would be perpetrated against those who refrained from bidding, and perhaps the courts would not regard her activities as chilling. But what about possible creditors of the estate whose claims might not be satisfied? Great wisdom would indeed be required to reconcile conflicting points of view in such a case.

Cooperative implementation.—If the worth of an object or a piece of property is to be established by the auction method, would-be buyers must compete freely against one another so that the one with the highest demand price prevails. Yet collusion is just as natural to some buyers as competition. They think in terms, not of intensifying competitive efforts, but of avoiding competition by agreeing not to bid against one another in order to obtain the property at a lower price.

To my knowledge, there is no legislation in the United States specifically outlawing buyer collusion or ring operations. Decisions based on common law, however, have held that fraudulent agreements not to bid are illegal in a public sale.[15] Moreover, antitrust laws which proscribe trade-restraining activities apply to actions of buyers as well as of sellers, and presumably cover collusive behavior. But no one would think of employing the artillery of anti-

---

14 *Furness* v. *Anderson*, 1 Pa. L.J. Reps. 324 (1842).
15 *Corpus Juris Secundum*, VII, 1255, citing *Fulgham* v. *Burnett*, 151 Miss. 111, 117 So. 514 (1928).

trust enforcement to kill the sparrow of ring activities as practiced in specific instances, even in the absence of jurisdictional questions. Continuing ring operations and organized efforts to depress prices would enlarge the target and could possibly justify the use of heavier weapons.

The law, although prohibiting collusion for price-depressing purposes, does not proscribe joint purchases at an auction when the purpose is legitimate, even though the result may be a reduction in prices. Agreements not to bid are voidable or not, depending on whether the intent is to chill the sale. Some combinations are formed simply to share the financial burden and distribute the risk. The courts have even recognized that cooperative bidding at an auction sale may enhance rather than depress prices, because individual members of a syndicate may not have been financially able to bid alone. This view was expressed very clearly in a court case more than a century ago:

> It is true that in every association formed to bid at the sale, and who appoint one of their number to bid in behalf of the company, there is an agreement, express or implied, that no other member will participate in the bidding; and hence, in one sense, it may be said to have the effect to prevent competition. But it by no means necessarily follows that if the association had not been formed and each member left to bid on his own account, that the competition at the sale would be as strong and efficient as it would by reason of the joint bid for the benefit and upon the responsibility of all. The property at stake might be beyond the means of the individual, or might absorb more of them than he would desire to invest in the article, or be of a description that a mere capitalist, without practical men as associates, would not wish to encumber himself with. . . .
>
> These observations are sufficient to show that the doctrine which would prohibit associations of individuals to bid at the legal public sales of property, as preventing competition, . . . is too narrow and limited for the practical business of life. . . . Instead of encouraging competition, it would destroy it. And sales, in many instances, could be effected only after a sacrifice of the value, until reduced within the reach of the means of the individual bidders.[16]

Although collusive buying activities in an auction sale are not, per se, violations of common law, the courts have taken a dim view of buying behavior that is intended to have a damping effect on the market. Nevertheless, they have not been successful in bringing

16 *Kearney* v. *Taylor*, 15 Howard (56 U.S.) 494, 520 (1853).

such activities under control, partly because of their inherent weakness as law-enforcing agencies. Without question, however, the failure to control collusion stems also from the tenuous nature of auction activities, which makes it difficult to marshal evidence.

Although legislation specifically aimed at buyer collusive activities is very rare, agreements among buyers at auctions are condemned in England by the Auction (Bidding Agreements) Act of 1927.[17] This statute proscribes both the giving and the asking of money or other consideration for abstaining from bidding in a sale by auction, "either generally or for any particular lot." Actually it makes undisclosed bidding agreements illegal; bona fide joint bidding is permitted if a copy of the agreement is deposited with the auctioneer.

Apparently little has been accomplished by the enactment of this law. Although ostensibly covering ring activities generally, in actual practice the law fails to provide a remedy in all situations. For one thing, it applies only to chattels. Moreover, it is not applicable to the auctioning of some merchandise, such as fish, because buyer agreements do not provide inducements not to bid, unless an opportunity to buy needed supplies at a reduced price is interpreted as an inducement. Another weakness is that evidence of price-depressing activities which will stand up in court is extremely difficult to obtain. More important, it may not be worth the time and effort required to bring such matters to court, especially if other solutions are available.[18]

Warranties

A warranty has been defined as a "statement . . . made by the seller of goods, . . . having reference to the character, quality, or title of the goods, by which he promises . . . that certain facts are or shall be as he then represents them." [19] It is somewhat like a

17 For a complete discussion of this enactment, see B. S. Yamey, "Bidding Agreements at Auctions," *Butterworth's South African Law Review* (1955), pp. 78–80.

18 One solution, although not applicable to fish auctions, is an agreement by dealers to abstain from collusive activities and to punish members who violate the rule. See also pp. 191–192.

19 Henry Campbell Black, *Black's Law Dictionary* (4th ed.; St. Paul, Minn.: West Publishing Co., 1951), p. 1758.

guarantee in that it insures a buyer against a default in the sales transaction or a defect in the property sold. Warranties in auctions involve important legal considerations which are of interest to both sellers and buyers. Goods sold at auction may be expressly warranted, although they often are not; usually, if not always, a warranty is implied.

Any warranty of goods at auction is assumed to be given by the vendor as owner and is binding on him. An auctioneer has no authority to bind the seller by an express warranty of quality or title unless instructed to do so.[20] As agent of the vendor, however, the auctioneer may involve himself by making an unauthorized representation concerning the quality or the authenticity of the item being sold. The buyer must decide whether or not he can legally rely on representations made by the vendor or his agent, and whether, in the absence of clear-cut statements or of any statements at all, he can seek redress under the law. It is his responsibility to familiarize himself with his rights and obligations in auctions.

Goods sold at auction are either listed in a catalog, which may describe them in detail, or are displayed in advance of the sale. If a catalog is available, as it usually is for sales of art objects, a buyer may reasonably expect to rely on its descriptions. A gross misdescription on which a buyer did in fact rely may be grounds for voidance of a sales contract. Qualifying phrases, such as "more or less," "thereabout," "estimated to contain," or "nearly," lessen the seller's responsibility but do "not protect him against the consequences of intentional misstatements or gross carelessness." [21] Warranty of sales by sample in effect guarantees that the bulk of the commodity will be equal to the sample, and that the sample fairly represents the quality of the commodity.

Goods are specifically warranted in certain fields, as in the sale of stamps. In many instances, however, neither the authenticity nor the quality of the goods is guaranteed. The usual motto in auctions is *caveat emptor:* "Let the buyer beware," or "take care." [22] The

---

20 See *Corpus Juris Secundum*, VII, 1252–1253, 1261, 1268–1269.

21 See *ibid.*, p. 1253, citing *Dennerlein* v. *Dennerlein*, 46 Hun. 561 (1887), appeal dismissed, 111 N.Y. 518, 19 N.E. 85 (1888), and *Foley* v. *M'Keown*, 4 Leigh (31 Va.) 627 (1833).

22 *Black's Law Dictionary* defines *caveat emptor* as follows: "Let the buyer beware (or take care). . . . This maxim summarizes the rule that a

intention to put the risk on the buyer is often expressed in the conditions of sale of particular auctions, but the effect on the buyer of the vendor's disclaimer of liability is difficult to determine in the absence of fraud. It is up to the buyer to inform himself about the condition of and the title to the property. He is aided by his right of inspection, which offers protection under the law to both purchaser and vendor. The vendor, however, cannot completely divorce himself of responsibility even when goods are sold as is, because there is an implied warranty as to the actual existence of the items sold "in form and substance as advertised." [23] A decision in a court case concerning the sale of chattels held that a seller impliedly warrants the title of the goods. [24]

The law and good business practice require reasonable care in the preparation of descriptions of property to be sold at auction. Although many auctions are conducted without the use of a catalog (for example, the sale of fish, tobacco, and livestock), oral representations as to the quality of the goods are often made. A "simple commendation," or even excessive praise, of property is not, however, necessarily an undertaking on the part of the owner that the chattel is what it is represented to be. The law, in other words, recognizes "dealer talk" as simply a form of salesmanship characteristic of the auction. [25] If an auctioneer, who has no authority to bind a seller as to the quality of or the title to goods without specific instructions, [26] makes a misrepresentation on a "material" matter without authorization, and if damage results, he may be liable to prosecution.

Despite the potential gains to be made by purchasing goods at auction, the buyer must realize that he is running a risk regarding

purchaser must examine, judge, and test for himself. . . . the purchaser takes risk of quality and condition unless he protects himself by a warranty or there has been a false representation" (p. 281).

23 *Corpus Juris Secundum*, VII, 1248: ". . . an auctioneer selling goods 'as are' impliedly warrants the existence of the goods in form and substance as advertised."

24 *Gray* v. *Walton*, 52 N.Y. City Super. Ct. 534 (1885).

25 See *Corpus Juris Secundum*, VII, 1269, citing *McGrew* v. *Forsythe*, 31 Iowa 179, 181 (1870).

26 *Ibid.*, p. 1248: "An auctioneer has no authority to bind the seller by a warranty of the quality or the title of the goods sold, unless specially instructed so to do, or unless authorized by statute."

authenticity, quality, and even title. He must beware lest he become emotionally involved and therefore lose his powers of rational thinking. It would be a good policy for the layman to assume that all the goods he is considering purchasing at auction are being sold as is on a *caveat emptor* basis. Instead of relying on representations or supposed representations made by the vendor or the auctioneer, the buyer, especially the uninitiated buyer, should inform himself about product quality, authenticity, and so forth. Hence, sound buying procedure requires careful inspection of the goods before bidding and precise judgment on the worth of the item to the prospective buyer.

Legislative Restrictions

Police power is "the power vested in the legislature by the Constitution to make, ordain, and establish all manner of wholesome and reasonable laws, statutes, and ordinances, either with penalties or without, not repugnant to the Constitution, as they shall judge to be for the good and welfare of the commonwealth, and of the subjects of the same." [27] The state has the right to legislate for the protection of public health, morals, safety, and general welfare, without favoring one group at the expense of another. It is under this power that many business activities are controlled.

In the eyes of the law, conducting auctions is a legitimate business activity, although it may be reasonably regulated by state or municipal authority. The term "regulate" is not synonymous with "prohibit," for it implies continued existence of the operation. Regulation as applied to auction selling may be defined as "authority reasonably to control or restrain by invoking the conditions under which sales of property at auction may be made." [28] Thus, auction selling is not subject to arbitrary interference by legislative means, but neither is the right to sell goods at public auction absolute. It may be thought of as a privilege extended by public authority, a privilege that may be withheld unless there is compliance with reasonable regulations, including licensing require-

27 Quoted from 11 Am. Jur. 972 in James A. Ballentine, *Law Dictionary with Pronunciations* (2d ed.; Rochester, N.Y.: Lawyers Co-operative Publishing Co., 1948).

28 *Gordon* v. *City of Indianapolis,* 204 Ind. 79, 183 N.E. 124, 125 (1932).

ments.[29] It was decided in one case, for example, that a sale on a descending-price basis was an auction within the terms of an ordinance requiring the auctioneer to obtain a license.[30]

The ostensible purpose of regulatory legislation relating to auctioning is to prevent abuse and fraud. Regulations that are reasonable are within the police power of the state, and should be found valid under the power granted municipalities by the state. Most enactments regulating auctions take the form of municipal ordinances. A San Francisco ordinance regulating sales by public outcry [31] (1) prohibits such sales in streets; (2) prohibits such sales in stores without a permit from the chief of police; (3) requires a successful applicant to pay a fee of $150, give a bond for $10,000, and provide a certificate of good character; (4) requires permittee to maintain inventory of stock or itemization of cost-price and make quarterly reports to the chief of police; and (5) requires every employee of an auction firm to secure a permit and file a bond.

Auction sale regulations must have a valid purpose, such as the prevention of fraud, and must be reasonably related to their ostensible purpose. Regulations that have been held valid by the courts include (1) requiring a license and the payment of a reasonable fee to conduct auctions; (2) demanding a bond of auctioneers for performance of contractual obligations; (3) requiring the keeping of a sales book signed by purchasers; (4) limiting the number of sales days for certain types of auctions, such as purported closeouts; and (5) singling out a particular product for special treatment (for example, confining auction sales of jewelry to daylight hours).

Auctions are often viewed with jaundiced eye by the established business community of a municipality. The antipathy of businessmen may be based on the "shady" aspects of some auction operators or on their own dislike of competition from auction houses. Some legislation ostensibly designed to regulate auctions is therefore actually enacted with the intent of prohibiting them, although such laws would be vulnerable to adverse judicial action. Since power to

29 For a fully documented discussion see *Corpus Juris Secundum*, VII, 1241–1244, from which most of the material in this section was drawn.

30 *Village of Deposit* v. *Pitts*, 18 Hun. (N.Y.) 475 (1879).

31 *Hirsch* v. *City and County of San Francisco*, 143 Cal. App. 2d 313, 300 P.2d 177 (1956), lists the provisions of the ordinance.

regulate auctions does not include the right to prohibit them, court decisions have struck down, as unreasonable restrictions on business operations and therefore unconstitutional, enactments (1) requiring that an auction may take place only at a location where the merchant has been in business for at least ninety days preceding the sale; (2) requiring a merchant to have been in business one year before conducting a public auction; (3) prohibiting the auction of certain types of items, such as jewelry; (4) limiting auction sales to six days in any one year; and (5) prohibiting the auctioning of merchandise in a public place that opens immediately into a public way or street.

The reasoning of the courts in handing down decisions on the legality of regulatory enactments is instructive. For example, the regulation limiting the auctioning of jewelry to daylight hours was designed, at least ostensibly, to prevent the sale of cheap jewelry as genuine at a time when artificial lights might facilitate fraud. Despite a diversity of opinion, the weight of authority favors the constitutionality of legislation confining sales of jewelry to daylight hours.[32] Some court decisions have held that illumination developments of recent years have made such a regulation no longer necessary, and that it is an arbitrary restriction on sales activities. On the other hand, as one court has said, "to say that because the candle and the lamp light have been succeeded by electric light, deception and fraud cannot be perpetrated, . . . may not be true in fact. With the improvements in science and manufacture, imitation jewelry and precious stones are much more like the real article than ever before. To detect the imitation is now much more difficult."[33] This court decided that the regulatory enactment was "an attempt to meet present-day conditions and not a mere continuance through ignorance of dead legislation."[34]

In summary, because of the possibility of fraudulent activities on the part of auction houses, regulation by public authorities is a proper legislative function. On the other hand, auctions are perfectly proper marketing mechanisms and should be neither out-

---

32 *Levy* v. *Stone*, 97 Fla. 458, 121 So. 565, 566 (1929), supports this position because of the weight of authority and the superiority of reasoning.

33 *Biddles* v. *Enright*, 239 N.Y. 354, 146 N.E. 625, 628, 39 A.L.R. 766 (1925), affirming 203 N.Y.S. 920, 208 Ap. Div. 790 (1924).

34 *Biddles* v. *Enright*, 146 N.E. 625, 627 (1925).

lawed nor arbitrarily restricted. As in any legislative effort, the regulations applying to auctions must be properly related to a real hazard, and not used to protect one type of marketer against another. Because they are adopted for the purpose of protecting auction patrons from fraudulent activities, customers who believe they have been deceived should complain to the proper authorities. On the other hand, city authorities that have arbitrarily refused licenses to legitimate auction operations should be taken to court for appropriate action.

Other Legal Issues

In addition to the legal issues discussed in this chapter—the theory of auction transactions, price-enhancing and price-depressing activities by sellers and buyers, warranties, and regulatory restrictions—other legal matters are taken up elsewhere in this book. The legal meaning of the term "auctioneer" and the auctioneer's legal rights and obligations are analyzed in chapter 8. Chapter 10 includes a discussion of conditions of sale. There is a supplementary treatment of the law applying to buyer rings in chapter 13. Issues that have legal overtones are entirety bidding (chap. 11) and co-operatively set price floors (chap. 16).

Legal questions may also arise in considering the differences between public and private auctions (chap. 2). For example, should an auction sale be considered "public" or "private" when it is not open to the public but when attendance is by invitation? Or when the auction is patronized only by those engaged in certain types of business? A further question is: What is the effect of the regulatory framework within which a public auction may operate? More specifically, should the circumscriptions that apply to public auctions also apply to private auctions? Should those who operate private auctions be licensed? Are puffing and chilling proscribed in private as well as in public sales? These questions are merely raised here; considerable research would be required to provide firm answers.

An interesting legal question is the relationship of the fall of the hammer to the termination of the transaction. Certainly the hammer is commonly used to terminate the bidding and thus to conclude a sales transaction, yet I have seen an auctioneer in a world-famous auction house reopen the bidding after he had indicated the awarding of the property by the use of the hammer, allegedly because he had failed to detect a would-be buyer in the act of bidding. In view of the traditional use of the gavel in knocking goods down to buyers, however, the law might well support a complaining bidder to whom goods had been awarded by the fall of the hammer only to be sold later to someone whose bid was subsequently recognized.

These treatments of the legal aspects of auctioning are in no sense intended to convey professional legal advice. I want simply to broaden understanding of the auction mechanism, in its legal as well as its marketing aspects. An aggrieved individual in any auction transaction should seek the advice of a competent attorney; my analysis, however, may help to point the way to circumstances that call for legal action.

Reserve Prices and
Price Floors

16 IF GOODS are sold at auction without reservation or with no price floor, the vendor takes whatever price he can get for his goods. But some goods are auctioned with the proviso that they will be sold only if the highest bid equals or exceeds a certain minimum figure.

Individually Set Reserve Prices

In any one auction session the full value of an item may not be reached, either because buyers with the highest demand prices are not in attendance, or because such buyers have selected one of their number to buy the item on a noncompetitive basis. A seller establishes a reserve price in order to avoid "giving an item away" in a temporary soft-market situation. The term "reserve" as applied to auction prices refers to a vendor's right to bid on his own property or, more often, to a price determined by the vendor or his agent, the auctioneer, below which the property is not sold. This reserve price is usually an estimate of the value of an article by an expert who specializes in that type of merchandise.

Nature of the reserve price.—Theoretically a reserve price may be set at any level the seller chooses; thus it may be set and reset by the seller even while a sale is in process. No contract exists between seller and buyer indicating what the reserve price is, or even that there is to be one, although an auctioneer would be chary of representing a principal who could not make up his mind. In the sale of real property, where the upset price may be determined by the amount of encumbrance, even bids exceeding that figure may require the approval of the vendor before the property is awarded to the high bidder.

In setting reserve prices, the goods are appraised before the auction starts and a minimum price is established for each item on which it is deemed advisable. A certain antique ceramic piece may be examined by an expert who, guided by the reputation of the manufacturer or the artist, the condition of the piece, its particular worth, and recent price trends of similar art objects, renders a judgment as to the amount it should bring, or its present market value. The figure he sets is the minimum, or the reserve, price.

The auctioneer may not go below this minimum valuation in selling the item, at least not without further instruction from the vendor. The fact that the item is reserved may or may not be announced, so long as the event has not been publicized as a sale without reserve. Even if the existence of reserve prices is announced, the amount of the reserve on each item may or may not be revealed; usually it is not. In some auctions the large bulk of items may be sold without reserve, with only a few carrying a reserve price. In that event the auctioneer is likely to identify the items placed on reserve.

Placing a reserve price on an item does not guarantee its sale at that price, or at any price. On the contrary, it may make the item more difficult to sell, particularly if the reserve price is not realistic. Reserve prices, although useful at times, should therefore be applied with great care. An astute auctioneer does not accept a commission for the sale of property on which the reserve price is, in his judgment, too high.

The auctioneer does not necessarily start the bidding at or above the reserve price, even though he knows the item is not to be sold for less than that figure. When he asks for an initial bid instead of relying on the crowd to start the bidding, he may begin at a point below the reserve price. By doing so he may bring into competition more individuals than would otherwise join in the bidding; once attracted, they remain for awhile and so serve in the price-enhancing process. Even if they later drop out, they will still have forced others to bid higher than they would otherwise have done in order to acquire the item.

If the bidding for an item is lively, the price may go far above the reserve level. It is the auctioneer's prerogative to decide whether or not to announce that the reserve price has been reached. Some authorities think that such an announcement has a damping effect, as bidders may be reluctant to pay more than the estimated value of a piece of property. But one experienced auction official prefers to inform the assembled buyers that the item is now "in the room" when the reserve price has been reached; he has found that such an announcement often stimulates bidding, especially when it is apparent that genuine bidders have hung back until they were certain there was to be a sale.[1]

Even a wisely set reserve price may not be reached in any one auction session. The auctioneer then either announces withdrawal of the item, stating the reason, or knocks it down to a fictitious bidder. The vendor or his agent may buy in an item at any time before it is knocked down, provided that the "buying" price is below the reserve price. Because of the publicity given the "selling" price, however, the seller derives an advantage from buying in the item at a level as close as possible to the reserve price.

Usefulness of the reserve price.—The setting of a reserve price on goods sold at auction has two purposes: (1) to avoid sacrificing an item when only a few buyers are interested in it; (2) to prevent ring operations from eliminating competition and hence depressing prices.

Through the use of reserve prices, an auction firm either obtains estimated market prices or postpones the sale of the merchandise until the market is more favorable. The reserve price, by preventing a sale under disadvantageous conditions, may also avoid the setting of a false value, which could have long-run effects on the selling price of similar items. It is important, therefore, that the auctioneer, when buying an item for the vendor, run the price up through fictitious bids to a point just below the reserve. In this way the price at which the item is "sold" will approximate its estimated value.

1 Geoffrey G. Rogers, "The Sale of Real Estate by Auction," *Chartered Auctioneer and Estate Agent*, XLIII (Nov., 1963), 526.

The danger that an item subject to a reserve price will not be sold may be averted by noting the name of the highest bona fide bidder at the time the merchandise is withdrawn and later trying to negotiate a sale with him at a satisfactory price. In fact, when an item is being overtly withdrawn it is not unheard of for the highest bidder to request the auctioneer to make his bid known to the owner, so that the latter can weigh the offer when he is considering whether to reauction the item or attempt to find a private buyer.

Of secondary importance is the use of the reserve price in combating the activities of buyer rings. Placing reserve prices on the goods prevents their sale at artificially depressed levels. The device, in brief, is designed to take the profit out of buyer collusion.

A serious weakness of the reserve-price method of auctioning is the cost in terms of customer goodwill. Some auctioneers refuse to sell on a reserve-price basis because they feel that bidders expect an occasional bargain, which a reserve price denies them, and, further, that bidders expect goods to be sold to bona fide buyers rather than being bought in by the house. In certain areas (London, for example) the use of reserves in the sale of antiques is commonplace; in others (such as Beverly Hills) it is unusual. This difference stems mainly from the fact that in Great Britain most of the auction patrons are dealers (who could easily collude), whereas in the United States they are mainly private collectors (who could not so easily collude).[2]

In deciding whether to use reserve prices, a seller must balance the absence of fully competitive conditions against the goodwill of buyers. In some instances the threat of buyer rings practically demands the use of reserves. In others, the danger of rings is negligible because the market is made up largely of collectors rather than dealers, and collectors seem to prefer that goods be sold without reserve.

Selling goods on a reserve basis by auction method is suitable to any auction system, whether English, Dutch, Japanese, or whatever, although in the United States and Britain it is usually thought of as applied to the English auction system. In the Dutch system, if the downward movement of quotations reaches the reserve price before a bid is registered, the goods are withdrawn. Similarly, if none of

2 See "The Ever Young Pursuit of Antiques," *Fortune*, LXI (June, 1960), 162.

the simultaneous bids in the Japanese system equal or exceed the reserve price, the goods are withdrawn.

The setting of a reserve, or upset, price is very common in auctioning antiques, though it may be difficult to determine because the items are unstandardized.[3] In fact, if it is possible to estimate the worth of an item accurately, why employ the auction system at all? The ordinary take-it-or-leave-it sales system would appear to be practicable in such an instance. But because neither a high degree of precision in evaluating unstandardized items nor static conditions prevail in an actual market, the enterprising vendor looks to the auction for maximizing returns.

The decision to have reserve prices is the responsibility of the vendor, but the actual setting of such prices is often delegated to the auction house. Leading auction firms have members who are specialists in certain lines, and they also employ consultants from museums or universities to supplement the evaluation efforts of employees. Because of the several variables—authenticity, quality, physical condition, and market trends—the appraising task is very difficult, and at times mistakes are made. Overvaluation may result in an aborted sale, whereas undervaluation provides opportunities for ring operations.

Cooperatively Set Minimum Prices

In some commodity fields price floors are established for certain varieties of goods put up for auction, below which the commodity is withdrawn from sale. Goods not salable at minimum prices may be destroyed, as are cut flowers in Holland; they may be processed into lower-price products, as fish is transformed into pet food and produce into cattle fodder; or they may be withdrawn for sale in the future, as tobacco is. The key difference between the reserve price and the minimum price is the fact that the former is set by the individual vendor or his agent, whereas the latter is determined by the cooperative efforts of the several vendors in a field.

Basic considerations.—Price floors are set on certain types and grades of commodities for the purpose of withdrawing excess supplies of goods from the market in order to relieve price pressure.

---

3 But see E. B. Butler, "Auction Prices: Estimated and Realised," *Economic Journal*, LXXI (March, 1961), 114–120.

To accomplish this purpose, the amount the market will take at various prices could be estimated, and then it might be possible to control the supply, and in turn the market price. But the objective can be achieved more effectively by using price as a controlling mechanism for determining the "correct" supply for the market.

Because price is used as an indicator for the diverting of supplies in a minimum price system, the key problem is the setting of minimum levels. The principle is to consider price elasticity, or responsiveness of amount taken to price changes, and to avoid setting levels above the point where stimulation of sales by price reductions is possible. At the same time, public authorities must seek to preclude monopolistic gains that might accrue from artificially created supply situations. The impact of lost sales may be borne either by the individuals whose product has been withdrawn or by all producers collectively.

The next important aspect of minimum price auctions is the withdrawing of surplus goods from the market in order to maintain prices at profitable levels. There is little doubt that the withdrawal of supplies, even of a modest amount, will prevent a precipitous fall in prices. The minimum-price method therefore provides a kind of safety valve for relief of the pressure of supply on prices.

A minimum-price schedule is often concerned with two different prices: the minimum price, and the price obtained by selling the surplus goods diverted to secondary uses. The minimum price, however, is not really a price in the sense of a figure at which a sale is consummated, but is simply a price point below which goods are withdrawn from sale. Moreover, there is likely to be a wide gap between the minimum price and the price obtained for the surplus goods. In a simple minimum-price plan, the owners of the goods withdrawn from the market receive payment based on the revenue obtained from the secondary-use processors. The price these processors pay is determined by the cost of comparable supplies available from alternative sources.

Applicability in auction operations.—The use of price floors in commodity auctions is fairly common. In Great Britain, for example, various ports have an unofficial system of minimum prices for certain kinds of fish. Trawler owners throughout the country (in Hull, Grimsby, Fleetwood, Milford Haven, Swansea, Cardiff,

Lowestoft, and Granton) have been utilizing minimum prices for years. The price minimum is set, and the fish that are not sold at or above that figure are withdrawn from the market. This surplus is sold for other uses, such as the manufacture of pet food and fertilizer. Pressure on prices is relieved both by withdrawing excess supplies from the market and eliminating the psychological factor of purchase postponement by buyers waiting for further price declines. In the whitefish trade, each catcher bears the loss occasioned by the failure of his fish to reach the minimum-price level, but he does receive a partial recompense from the sale of goods for secondary use. The system thus gives catchers an incentive to strive for high quality. Integrated companies that process as well as market fish may find it advantageous to buy their own supplies at minimum prices, despite a loss, in order to avoid an even heavier loss resulting from the sale of the fish for nonfood uses.

Some of the soft-price difficulties that develop in a market are caused by individual producers whose product is too poor in quality to be sold at the minimum price, but some come from the fact that the product is in heavy supply. Goods of high quality may thus remain unsold simply because of an excess supply. Because the identity of the producer whose goods are unsold is largely a matter of chance, depending on the order of sale, it would seem logical that individual producers and producers as a whole share the burden of unsold goods. Implementing such a plan may be difficult, but it is not impossible. The main point is to avoid premiums for producing large quantities of low-quality product. Goods of high quality left unsold would be a group responsibility, but unsold goods that are below standard would be the responsibility of individual producers.

Guaranteed Returns

The principle of a guaranteed return, even in its most basic form, goes a step further than the simple minimum-price scheme. In addition to providing price floors, it guarantees producers a certain return on the unsold goods, though at a level lower than the minimum price.

Basic principles.—The guaranteed-return system inevitably brings control of production, and is thus the ultimate in market control. Often such a system is inaugurated because of the prevalence of soft-market conditions in a commodity field. If adopted, the system may aggravate the supply situation, especially when the guaranteed price is an attractive one and no controls are imposed on production.

To offset the danger of overproduction, the minimum price is sometimes put at a level low enough to discourage low-quality production for sale at the guaranteed price. Another approach is to guarantee a fairly high price, but then add production controls. A participant in a guaranteed-price plan must agree to produce only a certain amount of a commodity or to cultivate only so much acreage. He benefits from the plan by receiving substantially more for his goods than he would have received from their sale for secondary use. Moreover, returns from the goods sold at auction prices, plus returns from those that are withdrawn and yield only the guaranteed price, are presumably larger than returns obtained if supply is uncontrolled. Thus the three price quotations inherent in any guaranteed-price system are, proceeding from highest to lowest: (1) the minimum price at which the goods not attaining that level are withdrawn; (2) the guaranteed price that producers receive for goods unsalable at or above the minimum; and (3) the price at which surplus goods are sold for secondary use.

In a guaranteed-return system, some way must be found to make up the difference between the amount guaranteed the producer and the amount received from a secondary-use processor. There are two possibilities: the losses can be absorbed by a government agency, or underwritten through an insurance plan to which producers contribute. Contributions may be made on a basis of the number of units sold through the auction at prices above the minimum level. Supply is controlled by means of this system, and the income of producers is leveled over a period of time by insurance.

The system in practice.—Two examples of the application of the guaranteed-price principle follow.

1. Auctioning is extensively used in the Netherlands in the sale of commodities at the primary distribution level. Notable in the Dutch auctioning scheme is a system of minimum-price levels, accompanied by payment of compensation prices to growers for unsold surpluses. A levy on each unit of goods sold at auction goes

into a fund from which producers are paid for unsold goods. This plan is, in essence, a kind of insurance scheme designed to absorb surpluses.[4]

The levy on sales is calculated at a rate that allows for the accumulation of an amount large enough to compensate producers for unsold surpluses in times of seasonal oversupply or temporary soft-market conditions. Produce that remains unsold at minimum prices at the auction becomes the property of the insuring agency, which holds it for disposal. The compensation price received by the grower of the unsold goods is usually about 80 percent of the minimum price, but for highly speculative crops it may be as low as 50 percent.

The key to the control of short-term supply in the Dutch system is the minimum price below which goods are withdrawn from the market, just as in any price-floor scheme. The level of minimum prices must be low enough to ensure maximum sales—that is, prices must be set at points below which sales can no longer be stimulated—but high enough to ensure continued production of adequate supplies to satisfy present and future demands. To complement the minimum return granted the grower, the Dutch system provides for acreage control to reduce, if not to preclude, the opportunity for unprincipled growers to produce for surplus.

2. The price-support system used in American tobacco markets is also a kind of guaranteed-return plan. Goods are taken off the market when they are unsold in the auction at support prices, and growers who participate in the related acreage-control program are permitted to take out nonrecourse loans on the goods that are withdrawn from the market. Growers are thus guaranteed a specified return for unsold goods, but may redeem them later if prices move to higher levels.

The plan used in tobacco markets differs from other guaranteed-price plans in several ways. In it the support price and the guaranteed price are the same. Moreover, the agency assuming the responsibility of supporting the price through loans is an arm of the United States government, rather than a cooperative insurance organization. The most fundamental difference, however, is that

4 *The Dutch Auction System of Marketing Fruit & Vegetables: A Lesson for English Growers?* (London: Agricultural Co-operative Association, *ca.* 1950), p. 5.

the goods withdrawn from the market are not destroyed or processed for secondary uses, but are stored for later sale. Any loss incurred in the subsequent sale is borne by the lending agency, but any advantage gained by sale in a favorable market belongs to the grower-borrower, assuming he wishes to repay the loan.

The auction prices of tobacco are directly affected by the minimum price-support price system in that a floor is provided below which auction prices cannot go. The indirect effect of such a program on prices is difficult to assess in the absence of cost-price information over a period of time. The tobacco plan is further complicated by the acreage-control program, which is not entirely effective because of the possibility of increasing yields on fixed areas by intensive cultivation. Another complication is that supplies of goods not sold at support prices are stored instead of being disposed of, and thus overhang the market. As the stored supplies increase, they tend to depress auction prices because of their pressure on the current market, which in turn could reduce the proportion of goods selling at or above the minimum price.

The inherent danger in a guaranteed-return system is that it may stimulate production by those producing for the guaranteed-price level. For this reason, production control was added. There is, however, a possibility of jumping control barriers in such a plan. Through selection of high-yield varieties, improvements in cultivation, and use of powerful fertilizers, yields have been greatly increased. For example, tobacco yields have doubled in a quarter of a century or so, but unfortunately the quality of the product has declined. At least momentarily, then, higher yield per acre permits producers "to have their cake and eat it too," although eventually production increases necessitate adjustments in acreage, and producers' gains will decline.

Evaluation of Price-Floor Schemes

Sales by auction method in its pure form permit goods to be sold quickly at whatever price the market will bring, without the seller having to protect himself by means of a stop-loss mechanism. There are, however, certain reasons for the seller's adoption of protective devices, such as price floors.

An auction that depends on price floors is a far cry from the pure auction where property is sold at the highest price it will fetch. Some of the price-floor plans are designed to restrict in part the operation of the law of supply and demand. One limitation of certain types of restricted-sales plans is that the vendor who must liquidate his goods promptly may be handicapped.

The reserve device, under which goods must reach the upset price or be withdrawn from sale, although useful for certain purposes, is not without pitfalls. The upset price acts as a protection to the seller in that he may avoid the soft-price trap in a particular auction session. One potential danger, however, is that the sale is merely postponed until a presumably more favorable time which may never eventuate. In the meanwhile, sales fees must be paid, although possibly on a reduced rate for an aborted sale. If an auction becomes so protective, moreover, as to eliminate all possibility of bargains, buyers are not attracted and the auction may be limited in performing its function as a marketing mechanism. For this reason, the withdrawal of merchandise that fails to meet a reserve price may be effected by means of a simulated purchase by a member of the auction firm's staff.

There may be considerable justification for price schemes based on cooperation among producers to withdraw their goods permanently from the market when they do not yield a minimum price, provided consumers are not deprived of needed supplies that they would purchase at lower prices and that the minimum price is not so high as to encourage production that would aggravate soft-price conditions. One argument for a minimum-price system is that supply and demand conditions may force prices down to low levels in one market session, only to push them to high levels in another, and producers cannot operate efficiently without the use of a price-leveling mechanism. In other words, the system is justifiable not so much because it saves individual producers from bankruptcy as because it protects the structure that provides goods needed by consumers.

The minimum-price level should not be so high as to exclude purchases by impecunious consumers or attract low-quality supplies for disposal at the minimum prices. The fact that the production phase of the industry is so organized that a levy is exacted from producers for use when the market is soft should have no effect on the soundness of the scheme.

The most important aspect of minimum-price systems in auctions is the effect they have on prices. Price floors are most effective when the commodities sold are in short supply in relation to the demand, and command prices well above the minima, but then the device is not needed. A direct effect can be expected if supplies are heavy, because no sales will be made at prices lower than the minima. A more subtle effect may result from the withdrawing of supplies of goods unsold at minimum prices, because prices are buoyed up by the prospect of withdrawal. Since buyers know that prices cannot go below the floor and that, if prices do reach the floor, some of the supplies are going to be lost, they may be tempted to make bids at levels above the minima, although some buyers may choose to wait and take the chance of being able to buy at the minimum price.

In individually set reserve-price systems, where there is no obligation to supply the consumer, the would-be purchaser who fails to get a particular vendor's goods as a result of their withdrawal from the market cannot be said to have been seriously affected. When minimum prices are cooperatively set, there is always a danger that the minimum level will be placed higher than market conditions warrant, to the disadvantage of consumers. Sellers clearly control the price to some degree, and any such plan runs counter to public interest unless it simply prevents prices from sinking to levels at which production becomes uneconomical, with a resulting loss of needed supplies. The same dangers prevail with respect to a guaranteed-return system. In such schemes, therefore, public authorities should participate in setting the minima.

Special Problems

17 SEVERAL IMPORTANT miscellaneous problems connected with auctioning remain to be briefly considered. No attempt at exhaustive analysis is made here. The purpose of the following discussion is simply to present the problems in proper perspective.

Price Behavior within an Auction Session

Because auction prices are made by the competitive strivings of varying numbers of rival buyers with differing intensities of desire for constantly shifting quantities of goods, they differ in accordance with the makeup of the buying group in relation to the available supply of goods. Market conditions surrounding the sale of goods at auction are usually very dynamic, with a resulting instability in the factors that determine prices at any moment of time. The characteristic of the auction mechanism is its ability to translate these dynamic conditions into prices that properly reflect existing market conditions.

Substantial differences in prices may occur from one market to another, and even from one session to another in the same market. The most interesting aspect of price behavior, however, is the trend of prices within a given auction session. In view of the nature of the auction operation and the dynamics of supply, demand, and competition as related to auctioning, one can readily understand that prices of commodities that are basically similar or even identical do change during an auction session. In a sale of large numbers of similar items, for example, prices tend to decline; buyers with the most urgent need for a particular item would be expected to fill their requirements early in the session. As part of the demand for the item would then be dissipated, the upward pressure on prices is reduced. This analysis of intrasession price behavior is obviously incomplete, because the trend may be partly offset by the buying activities of speculators who are able to shift buying emphasis from one market to another as favorable purchasing opportunities change.

A sophisticated buyer, cognizant of the behavior pattern described above, may gain an advantage by postponing purchases until later in the auction period. A bargain hunter would be particularly likely to succeed in this maneuver if supply was heavier than usual and a substantial number of competitors did not pursue the same tactics. In any event, intrasession declines in price tend to be relatively modest, because speculator and intermarket buying and the activities of individuals who postpone purchasing in the early part of the session and thus reduce the price variations serve as correctives.

The downward pattern in auction-price behavior is by no means inevitable. Even when urgent requirements are satisfied in the early part of an auction, there are still buyers left with unsatisfied needs. The available supply will also have declined because early buyers have taken part of it. If buyers who postpone their purchases discover that supply is inadequate when they decide to satisfy their requirements, there will tend to be an upward pressure on prices. Furthermore, if demand increases because new orders are communicated from the outside to the broker-buyers, as may well happen, prices tend to move upward toward the end of the auction session. The upward tendency, however, is limited by two facts: (1) as the price increases buyers will shift to more favorable markets; and (2) dealers buying for resale in consumer markets and fearing a squeeze may resist the higher prices. A dealer-buyer is not in business simply to exchange dollars, and he will withdraw from the market if he does not feel the goods can be resold at a profit.

This discussion of price behavior within an auction session refers to units or lots of a commodity which are similar or identical. The concept of price-behavior patterns within a single session has little meaning in an antique auction, where no two items are exactly alike. For example, lot number 1 may be a Chippendale commode, and lot number 10, a pair of Ming vases. The market for one type of item may be firm, while the market for another may be quite soft, depending on the special interests of would-be buyers. And one particular item may fetch one price if sold early in the session and quite a different price if put up later; this kind of price fluctuation is quite likely to occur in country auctions, where buyers are not well informed about the goods in which they are trading.

The actual behavior of prices during an auction session is a challenging question, but so far little has been done except to hypothesize about probable price patterns. Data obviously are needed to confirm or vitiate the hypothetical conclusions presented above, and to throw light on causal factors. There are few if any data at present for prices in relationship to a precise time of each sales transaction, but the increasing use of electronic equipment suggests that they will soon be available. In addition to adequate data, however, more precise information is required as to the quality of each offering, for price differences may depend, not on changing prices, but on varying quality of goods.

Auctions Back to Back

The term "back-to-back auctions" refers to the sale of goods in one market and their resale at a subsequent auction. Nevertheless, a particular item may be sold at auction numerous times over a period of years without falling into the back-to-back category. To be classified as a back-to-back auction, the resale should follow the first auction transaction within a relatively brief period of time.

Back-to-back auction transactions ordinarily refer to those occurring in the normal flow of commerce through marketing channels. Goods are manufactured, processed, or harvested by a producer, sold in a primary market, and subsequently resold at various levels as they move toward consumption markets. It is in the purchase and sales transactions taking place at successive stages in the marketing process that the concept of back-to-back auctions becomes meaningful.

As commodities move from producer to consumer, they are sold

by certain functionaries and bought by others who may in turn resell to still others. The vendor normally expects to make a profit on
the purchase-sale transaction. A merchant-middleman, who acquires title to the goods he handles, may purchase his requirements
at auction in a primary market and resell in a consumption market.
Typically he would expect to sell in the distant market on a firm-
price basis or on a negotiated-price basis, either of which would
give him a degree of control over the transaction. In some instances,
however, buyers purchase goods at auction at the primary level and
sell in distant markets through consignees, who may utilize the
auction in finding buyers for the goods. Goods usually become
more costly as they move from primary markets toward consumption markets because of the value added by distribution. Functionaries at each market level normally buy at one price and sell at a
higher price, even though market conditions remain the same; that
is, they operate on a margin between the cost of the goods to them
and the selling price to subsequent buyers. It is out of this differential that their expenses and profits must come.

More often than not the sale of goods in primary markets is by
auction, whereas other methods are frequently employed at postprimary levels. On rare occasions, goods purchased at auction are
sold at auction at the jobber level in consumption markets. In such
back-to-back auctions the shipper may be squeezed, especially if he
is a distributor who has paid a firm price for the goods rather than
a producer; many of the producer's costs are indirect and need
not be counted in an individual short-term transaction. The reason
for this potential squeeze is that, while prices in primary markets
and consumption markets tend to move together, conditions may
change in the interim between the two transactions. The functionary who has purchased property at a firm price always faces this
risk, regardless of the method employed in the second sale. But he
is particularly vulnerable if the second sale is made by auction
method—especially if there is no reserve price—because he has less
control over the choice of buyers and the precise timing of the sales
transaction.

The danger of a squeeze between the purchase price in one auction and the sales price in a back-to-back auction is probably not so
serious as it appears to be at first glance. In the first place, the purchase and sales transactions may be executed so rapidly as to make
unlikely any change in conditions. Second, the entrepreneur who

operates on this basis works, at least theoretically, on a margin between his buying and selling prices, which the economic system provides him in exchange for the services performed. Thus, even if prices in the two markets do not move precisely together, the trader usually has a cushion against out-of-pocket losses.

It is also possible for market prices to move apart rather than together, so that the owner of the goods may gain in his trading operations. For example, if consumer market prices go up and primary market prices remain the same, the one who purchases in the latter market and sells in the former stands to gain rather than to lose. While gains are obviously much more welcome than losses, the trader ordinarily does not strive to make speculative gains; he desires only to earn the normal trading margin to cover his expenses and perhaps ensure a profit.

The relative rarity of back-to-back auctioning in its technical sense may be due to reasons other than the risk of buying in one market and selling in another. It may simply result from the fact that auctioning is confined largely to sales at the primary level, and commonly is not used at subsequent levels. If we assume an absence of auctioning at postprimary distribution levels, it follows that back-to-back auctions cannot exist.

Fewness of Bidders in Auction Buying

Regardless of how many individuals attend an auction, the number interested in any one item is usually limited. That is, only a few buyers exhibit demand in relation to each transaction.

A condition in which buyers are few is known to economists as an oligopsony. But fewness of buyers in the sense used here is not oligopsonistic, if they are unknown to one another and lack sufficient time to become acquainted and to evaluate one another's potential moves. In many such instances, moreover, the supply of goods is limited; in fact, an item that is up for sale may be the only one of its kind. If demand is active, therefore, two or more buyers may be expected to compete vigorously to acquire property sold at auction.[1]

[1] For a discussion of the complexities arising from fewness of bidders in an actual market situation see Duncan Ridler, "Imperfect Competition and the Cobweb Theorem: A Vegetable Case," *Journal of Agricultural Economics,* XVII, no. 2 (1966), esp. 189–192.

In some auctions, however, not only is the total number of buyers small, but the same buyers are present at each market session. In the primary cigarette tobacco market, for example, the same nine buying companies are represented at each session; each representative knows not only that his actions affect the actions of others, but that he can get more tobacco tomorrow or the next day if he does not fill his quota today. Buyers under these circumstances are likely to exercise restraint, and an unusually large number of tie bids may well follow, as buyers soon get to know one another's price limits and tend to honor them. If the auctioneer breaks the ties by unofficially allocating the lots on some equitable basis to the various buyers (as he may well do), the effect of this "cooperative" effort is to depress prices.

One type of auction in which the same small number of buyers participate each market day is the sale of halibut in Seattle. As this commodity is in high demand, dealers are eager to acquire supplies from the fishermen. There are, however, only half a dozen or so separate halibut buyers at the primary sales level, and so, in economic terms, an oligopsony prevails. Theoretically, a certain amount of restraint in bidding would be expected, because of the interrelating impacts of competitive bidding, but nevertheless bidding for the halibut is very lively.

There are several reasons for this active competition. First, on each market day one or more dealers may urgently need fish to fill specific orders in consumption markets in various parts of the country. Second, halibut dealers are strongly competitive in their distribution activities, and even when they do not need fish they may bid actively to force up competitors' costs. Third, even in this oligopsonistic situation, buyers must think about the continuity of supplies, which may be broken if they practice too much restraint. Finally, a compelling reason is that the Antitrust Division of the Department of Justice would pounce on this operation if it suspected price-depressing activities.[2]

Tuna auctions in San Diego bear a resemblance to halibut auc-

2 In certain instances the Department of Justice has done just that. See, for example, *United States* v. *New England Fish Exchange*, 258 Fed. 732 (1919), modification of decree denied, 292 Fed. 511 (1923); *United States* v. *San Pedro Fish Exchange*, consent decree, *CCH Trade Regulation Reports, Supp. 1941–43*, ¶52669 (1941); *United States* v. *Seattle Fish Exchange, Inc.*, consent decree, *CCH Trade Regulation Reports, Supp. 1941–43*, ¶52887 (1942).

tions in Seattle. Only three or four tuna canners attend each auction sale to buy supplies, thus creating an oligopsonistic situation. They are well known to one another, and have become familiar with one another's business affairs and methods of operating. Furthermore, alternative sources of supply exist in the form of imported fish. As expected, these tuna buyers exhibit considerable restraint in their bidding against one another for immediate supplies of fish. They have no need to go all out in their bidding, nor are they apt to bid goods in at ruinous prices simply to make sure of maintaining a longer-run supply of tuna. On the other end of the transaction, sellers often reject bids they consider too low, simply holding the refrigerated cargo over until the next session. It is significant that in tuna auctions, as in halibut auctions, packers are aware of the watchful concern of the government over price-depressing activities.

Despite its limitations, the auction is generally preferred by fishermen—that is, the sellers of the catch—to the erstwhile private-treaty method of selling. They can be sure that in auction operations the packers will take any supply of tuna at some price. Whether the packers themselves prefer the auction is, however, an open question. At least they tolerate it, even though they buy some of their tuna from affiliated fishermen who sell to them direct at prices established by the auction.

Use of Auction Prices in Nonauction Sales

If substantial quantities of a certain type of goods are sold at auction, it is almost a truism that private-treaty systems automatically become practicable in that field. Auctioning establishes reference prices that serve as a basis for individual negotiation and thus, ironically, precludes the need for auctioning in individual circumstances. The use of auction prices for reference purposes is theoretically sound, assuming that the auction transactions are fully representative of the market. If increasingly smaller quantities of goods are sold at auction, however, the auction price becomes less reliable in reflecting total demand and supply conditions.

As noted elsewhere, the sales volume in fruit auctions in terminal markets of the United States has been decreasing. When the decline first started some years ago, private-treaty traders were able to rely heavily on auction prices for reference purposes in individually negotiated transactions. But as more and more of the fruit bypassed the auctions, less and less confidence could be placed in auction prices as a basis for individual negotiation.

Halibut prices set by the Seattle auction are used as reference prices in other North Pacific ports, particularly Alaskan ports. Differentials between the Seattle auction price and halibut prices in the other markets are based on differences in transportation costs. These differentials vary from time to time, depending on 'the amount of fish needed by processing or shipping companies in a particular port, and on negotiations between sellers and buyers. Again there is the potential danger that more and more of the total supply will short-circuit the auction while reliance is still being placed on auction-made prices for reference purposes.

Another pertinent example is the Hull-Grimsby primary fish market in northern England, which supplies fresh fish to London consumer markets. Some years ago it was found that many buyers needed fish at the beginning of an auction session in order to meet early morning transportation schedules, or to ensure efficient operation of the work force. The resulting heavy competition for fish in the first few minutes of the sale tended to force prices up; after the early peak activity there was an abnormal reduction in demand. To remedy the difficulty, a scheme of early withdrawal was devised several years ago. It permitted buyers to acquire needed supplies before the auction session opened, and to pay for them at prices established later in the session. In actual practice, the prices paid for the fish that are withdrawn are the average of the prices of identical varieties, and presumably similar qualities, landed from the same ship and sold during the subsequent auction session. Top rows of fish must, however, be retained for sale at auction to determine "a fair and reasonable price for that particular variety and quality of fish." [3]

It might seem that the withdrawal of supplies, automatically resulting in a reduction in demand for similar quantities later, would have no effect on the market. But this is not necessarily true, be-

3 R. A. Taylor, *A Report on the Economics of White Fish Distribution in Great Britain* (Hull: Hull University, Department of Economics and Commerce, 1958), p. 111.

cause changes that are qualitative in nature may develop. For example, those who withdrew supplies before the auction session may have had a more intensive demand for goods than those who did not. Moreover, the supplies withdrawn may be of higher quality than the average of all supplies remaining to be sold at auction. These factors could affect market conditions, and the price paid for the fish that were withdrawn could differ from the price that would have prevailed had the goods not been withdrawn. To pursue the question further, if *all* buyers withdrew their supplies early, leaving nothing to sell, there would be no basis for the price of the goods withdrawn. This is not likely to happen, but it does suggest that so large a proportion of the goods could be withdrawn as to make market conditions anything but representative of those that would have obtained had there been no withdrawals. In actual fact, the Hull-Grimsby market places a limit on the percentage of the total supply which may be withdrawn—usually 40 percent of any variety —and on the maximum amount that may be withdrawn from any one vessel.

Auction prices of antiques are also used for reference purposes in private-treaty sales. An associate of mine recently overheard several individuals, undoubtedly dealers, request price information at Parke-Bernet about the preceding day's auction sales, presumably for use in negotiations with clients on related items. Staff members often make available marked catalogs for the purpose of providing such information. One of the world's greatest rare coin auction operations publishes a "priced catalog" after each auction, giving the prices at which the items were sold.

It is not absolutely necessary from the standpoint of effective price making to auction the whole supply of a commodity. To save time and energy, only a part of it need be auctioned, and the balance can be priced on a reference basis. This solution is not always feasible, but will certainly be useful in some circumstances.

Buying Goods Sight Unseen

In some auctions, goods are bought sight unseen. For example, in certain markets fish are purchased by the boatload without prior inspection. Estimates are given, however, concerning the type and size of the fish that are being sold, and inspection is made after the sale when the goods are weighed and classified under the buyer's eye.

One of the most puzzling types of auctions is the sale of sealed packages of goods without disclosure of the contents. These sales are held when the owners of stored goods fail to claim them or to pay storage costs. Usually the buyer bases his bid on the size, shape, and type of container, although sometimes he knows the broad classification of the goods from a label on the outside of the package. But he is really bidding blind; he is gambling that in exchange for a small expenditure he may acquire something of great value. It is a commentary on human nature that bidding on sealed packages is often very lively.

In a sale I witnessed the auctioneer sold several mystery packages for $7 or $8 each; then during a lull he told the audience about a buyer who had found a set of United States coins in mint condition worth $2,500 in such a package. The story, it seemed to me, had a stimulating effect on the bidding. The same auctioneer, in displaying a chest of drawers, would open one of the drawers and exclaim over the contents in a half-serious tone of voice. This tactic aroused the curiosity and increased the activity of the audience.

In some auctions mystery packages are prepared by the auction company. In one instance the auctioneer, after classifying the goods (used machinery) into lots, placed the miscellaneous items—small tools, for example—in boxes, nailing the top shut and putting them up for sale sight unseen. In this kind of transaction the vendor must be truthful in his statements about the contents of the boxes, or he and the auctioneer may face charges of fraud.

One of the most valuable acquisitions I know of at an auction of mystery packages was a trunkful of old comic books bought by two collectors of rare books. The trunk contained early editions, in "mint" condition, of Batman, Flash Gordon, Captain Marvel, and so forth. In this instance, however, the purchasers had information about the existence of the treasure, but they did have to rely on detective work to locate it. They found the storage company, discovered that it was preparing to sell unclaimed items at auction, and decided to buy every trunk put up for sale until they got the right one. After purchasing two duds, the collectors hit the jackpot. By paying $4.16, they obtained a collection of comic books worth approximately $10,000.[4]

Other episodes illustrate the psychological fascination of risking a small investment in the hope of realizing a big gain. For example, one bidder at an auction I attended thought he could not lose much by going as high as $10, or even higher; he had once paid $20 for a box of fine records worth $200. Another said that she would go as high as $15, or would bid as much as she had with her. Such auctions were her hobby; in fact, she took employment just so that she would be able to bid at them. She seemed philosophical about the fact that sometimes one wins and sometimes one loses.

The uncertainty that plays so important a part in mystery auctions may give rise to legal questions. Some years ago a box of old clothing which sold for $9.50 was later found to contain two rings, one a cameo of little value, the other a diamond worth $2,500. In a suit by the vendor to recover the rings, the decision turned on the question as to whether title to the rings had passed to the buyer of the clothing. The key issue, according to the court, was the intention of the parties; because the vendor did not intend to sell rings, or the buyer to purchase them, it was decided that they had not been sold along with the clothing.[5]

Another court case developed from the auctioning of goods salvaged from a shipwreck. The high bidder bought a package ostensibly containing newspapers (cataloged and designated as such), but the contents turned out to be calico. When the seller refused to deliver the goods, the buyer sued for nondelivery. The court found for the buyer on the ground that there was no "mutual mistake," which would have vitiated the sale, but that the parties had contracted to sell and buy a "chance" and therefore accepted the risk of false description of the contents.[6] Unlike the decision cited above, this case seems to be relevant to mystery auctions. Buyers and sellers fully understand that the transaction is a gamble, and no vendor is likely to seek recovery of a valuable item on the ground that he did not intend to sell it. If he does, he is certain to fail. Indeed, a suit

4 Dave Felton, "Batman Escapes from Old Trunk To Fly Again," *Los Angeles Times*, Feb. 8, 1966, Pt. II, pp. 1, 3.

5 *American National Bank of Nashville* v. *West*, 212 S.W.2d 683, 685 (Tenn. Ct. App. 1948), cert. denied by Supreme Ct., July 17, 1948.

6 *Crespin* v. *Puncheon*, 7 V.L.R. 203, 208–209 (Australia, 1881).

for recovery might well ruin further sales of this type, because the essence of the mystery sale is the chance that something of great value may be in a sealed package.

Producer-Distributor Integration

Integration of production and distribution for the purpose of enhancing efficiency is a common phenomenon today. Such integration may take place internally, as when one type of business operation extends its activities into another phase or stage of the business. It may, on the other hand, come about externally, as when a firm at one level of business operations acquires a firm engaged in operations at another level. This type of combination is technically known as forward integration if it moves from production to distribution, and as backward integration if it moves from distribution toward production.

If a firm is so integrated that it produces goods as well as distributes them, one operating division may have to acquire supplies from another. If, further, the firm utilizes auctioning as a sales mechanism, it may be both buyer and seller of the same commodity. For example, one of the processing and distribution facilities of Britain's Ross Group, a large integrated food concern, may bid in the fish caught by the firm's fishing fleet.

It may be argued that such purchases are unnecessary and indeed unfair because the firm is really selling to itself and thus has unlimited buying power. It would therefore make no difference how much the buying department bid for the fish, because no transfer of funds is involved. The transaction consists merely of bookkeeping entries between commonly owned departments of the enterprise. Possibly on the basis of such reasoning, companies owning vessels are not permitted to bid in certain primary fish markets in the United States.[7] This concept that a bidder may bid as high as necessary with impunity if he is buying from a different department of the same company, although intriguing, is hardly valid. It may have an element of truth if one assumes that all of the product

---

7 In the Boston market a government decree "forbade the dealers to bid, directly or indirectly, on fish caught by their own vessels" (Donald J. White, *The New England Fishing Industry* [Cambridge, Mass.: Harvard University Press, 1954], p. 23).

is of the same quality, that various operations of the company have no separate identity, and that only single transactions are being considered. Only if these conditions prevailed could the concern use its buying power with impunity.

These conditions, however, are very unrealistic. In the first place, the segments of an integrated company are in large part separate entities. A buyer of fish for an integrated company would not want to purchase at inflated prices because of possible harm to his operating results. By the same token, the seller would be reluctant to accept a disadvantageous price, even though the buyer represented a part of the same company. Running a business on anything but a competitive basis may well be disastrous to company morale and efficiency. Just as important is the fact that the commodity sold in any primary market may vary widely in species, size, and quality, and the processing department is not apt to need precisely what the producing segment has available. Therefore a firm must often sell the product it owns and buy the one required to meet its special needs. In so doing it helps to create goodwill, for it patronizes other integrated organizations that in turn purchase goods from it.

Whether the auction system is the most efficient selling method for an industry that is vertically integrated is quite a different issue. It might seem at first glance that giant firms that both catch and use fish could find a better way of exchanging goods than auctioning. But just because a system appears to be anachronistic is no proof that a superior system is available. In considering alternative sales methods, one should remember that there are different points of view represented among the traders in any auction situation, and that fishermen—the unaffiliated catchers, at least—are apt to strongly favor the auction system because it is based on overt competition among buyers and because they feel they understand it.

Withholding of Supply Information

The buyer at an auction, at least the professional buyer, expects to obtain all the information possible about the demand for, and the supply of, the type of item he wants to purchase. He needs price data from other sales to indicate the strength of the demand, and data about the supply—that is, the quantity available for sale. Lacking such information, he may pay too high a price for the goods he buys and thus suffer a loss when he resells. It is possible that if the supply is plentiful, for example, a buyer can save money by purchasing later in the auction session at a much lower price. To get supply information, he should look around the market, where a large part of the day's supply may be on display, and also investigate other areas.

The withholding of supply information may affect market prices to some extent. Sometimes, accordingly, auctioneers or vendors purposely withhold such information from buyers, or at least attempt to do so. They may, for example, not allow buyers to preview the goods to be sold. In this event buyers must employ whatever intelligence facilities they possess in an attempt to gain the information needed. I have seen the principle of withholding supply information applied in various markets of the world. In the Manila primary fish market, for example, the goods are lightered from the fishing boats to the market in the early morning darkness by means of amphibious boats, so that buyers do not know the total supply available for sale. Additional supplies are fed into the market as required from the boats at anchor offshore. Such information is also withheld from buyers in the fish markets of Tel Aviv and Haifa, as well as those of Hong Kong.

Whether this strategy would be practical in other types of auctions is not known. It may be possible to feed an excess supply of an item (for example, several hundred bedroom chairs from a defunct hotel) into different auction sessions so as to avoid a glut. Another solution is to encourage the attendance of dealers whose demand for goods is derived, and who can buy up large supplies for resale over a period of time. The withholding of supply is, of course, a different strategy from the mere withholding of information, although the former may be used to supplement the latter.

The question of precisely how the withholding of supply information affects prices is more easily asked than answered. It would appear a priori that such a policy would enhance prices early in the auction session and soften them subsequently. The buyers who need supplies, knowing nothing about quantities available, would have to bid early in the auction session for fear of not being able to satisfy their requirements later. Conversely, buyers whose needs were less intensive could postpone their purchasing, and would eventually discover that supplies were in excess of normal demand. Indeed, in some instances the bottom might drop out of the market at the end of the session because all buyers had satisfied their requirements and there were still some goods unsold. At such times, incidentally, the efforts of speculators may assist in stabilizing the market.

Several aspects of this analysis, however, require further thought. First, the withholding of supply information may work when supplies are not too heavy, but then the price-enhancing device is not really needed. Indeed, if there is a shortage of goods, the firm may disseminate rather than withhold supply information so as to increase prices. Second, it may be possible to withhold supplies from one auction session for sale at another session, thus avoiding a drop in price at the time when buyers become aware of the actual state of the supply. But this strategy is very dangerous, because supplies later on may be even heavier than at present, and the problem will not only have been postponed but possibly intensified.

Finally, the withholding of supply information has a different impact on different buyers. Astute and enterprising buyers undoubtedly engage in intelligence activities to uncover the facts when supply information is lacking. If successful, they have an advantage over others not so informed, and can acquire goods at the most favorable time and thus at the lowest prices. This kind of speculative effort, however, is not for the amateur, who not only lacks information about demand and supply, but would not know how to use it if he did have it.

Price Ceilings

If inflationary forces are strong, direct price controls are sometimes deemed necessary, and may be complemented by the rationing of supplies. When prices are fixed at a point above which traders may not legally buy and sell, inflationary pressure usually pushes them up to the ceiling, where they stay, at least officially.

The setting of price ceilings—as in wartime, for example—renders auctioning impracticable in any meaningful sense, unless ceilings are set so high as to be ineffectual.[8] The key factor in auc-

8 See "Leaf at Auction," *Business Week*, Dec. 23, 1944, pp. 46, 49; "Kettle of Fish: . . . Strikes, Black Market, OPA Troubles, and Allocation Threat," *Business Week*, April 29, 1944, pp. 53–54.

tioning is the bidding up of an item by would-be buyers with the highest bidder taking the goods; if this is not possible, then there is no auction. It does not follow that, when ceiling prices are in effect, goods cannot be sold by firms normally operating on an auction basis, but simply that under such circumstances the auction principle is vitiated. Under shortage conditions, any buyer would take the total supply available at the ceiling price; the goods cannot be awarded to the highest bidder because there can be no highest bidder.

Under a system of price controls, commodities that were formerly auctioned can no longer be sold by that method, but they must still be distributed. Normally the allocation process is automatically taken care of by the price system in a free market; that is, those desiring the goods most intensively and possessing the necessary buying power simply offer more for them than others do. There is enough for all who are willing and able to pay the price. As soon as price ceilings go into effect, automatic allocation goes by the board, and a different method of allocation of needed supplies is required. Incomes are up and supplies are short, most buyers desire to share in the limited supply, and there is simply not enough to go around. If buyers were to bid on the available supplies with a ceiling in effect, they would all bid at the same price.

There are different methods of artificial allocation, and the choice of which one is to be used depends on whether the goods are to go to only one buyer or are to be divided among several buyers. In the latter instance, past experience may serve as a guide. In the English fishery trade, for example, supplies were allocated during World War II on the basis of purchases made in the last prewar year. Percentage figures derived from past records were applied to the total amount currently available. If, as is possible, more was available at the ceiling price than the market could absorb, the English plan provided for shifting from one market to another. The weakness of this allocation scheme was that it froze the existing distribution structure and excluded new entrants.

Auctions were held in the United States and elsewhere during the war, and were reported to be quite profitable, even in legitimate operations. The explanation is that goods were in such short supply that all goods were in great demand, and on some items no price ceilings were in effect. The demand for used electrical refrigerators, which were under a ceiling, was so heavy that auctioneers had to devise an equitable way of allocating them to buyers. Starting at the ceiling price, some auctioneers simply gave each interested individual a playing card and awarded the goods to the person holding the card of the highest denomination. One auctioneer reports that merchandise sold by him at the ceiling price was often immediately resold by the buyer at a substantial profit in a private-treaty transaction.[9] The latter sale was obviously a black-market transaction.

In some parts of the world, price ceilings are in effect on certain food items even when no war is in progress. Although most fish in Lisbon, for example, are sold without a ceiling, one very popular species is still under price controls. I was visiting the Lisbon market a few years ago when a supply of this kind of fish was put up for sale under the Dutch auction system starting at the ceiling price, with a resulting sea of hands from fishmongers (all women). The problem in such a situation is to allocate supplies in some manner, whether equitable or arbitrary. The questions are: who is to receive shares of the goods, and how much is each to receive?

The problem, which apparently still exists in Lisbon, cannot be satisfactorily solved until the ceilings are removed. An unofficial solution sometimes develops in the form of black-market operations. The use of auctioning in a black market is hardly practicable, because it is less secretive than private-treaty arrangements. Moreover, vendors under abnormal shortage conditions can very likely obtain maximum returns without resorting to direct competitive bidding, and therefore tend not to utilize the auction.

Fraudulent Use of the Auction Device

In some cities—London and New York, for example—there are operations that have the appearance of auction sales but really are not auctions at all. These mock auctions are usually found where foot traffic is heavy, because they are designed to bilk the public and require a constant and fresh supply of customers. They are characterized by (1) the outward appearance of a legitimate auction sale; (2) the use of well-known brands of goods as bait to induce passersby to enter the premises; (3) the sale of surprise packages, as "evidence of good faith," which are to be delivered later in the proceed-

9 George H. Bean, *Yankee Auctioneer* (Boston: Little, Brown, 1948), p. 153.

ings and therefore serve to detain the suckers—"jamming," as it is known in the trade; (4) the "selling" of high-quality merchandise to stooges, ostensibly at substantial discounts, in order to set up the suckers for the "kill"; and (5) the "auctioning" of "flash" goods to suckers after skillfully replacing legitimate goods with junk merchandise.[10]

Although it does not seem possible that such tactics could succeed with otherwise intelligent people, they are surprisingly effective in the hands of skilled operators. Much sleight of hand is practiced by the "slicker" who conducts such sales. He may, for example, suggest the purchase of a surprise package as evidence of good faith at a point in the proceedings when it appears that the buyer is in a position to gain from such an investment. A touch of larceny in the hearts of victims who think they are going to get something for nothing is an essential ingredient of a mock auction. On the contrary, such operations are costly to those who patronize them, most of whom can ill afford foolish expenditures. Another unfortunate result of this unscrupulous practice is that legitimate auctions, which are usually operated on an open and honest basis, suffer from the bad name given them by fraudulent activities.

Contrast, for the moment, a genuine auction with a mock auction. First, in a real auction people are invited to attend; they are not tricked into attending. Second, while goods are often offered on a *caveat emptor* basis, the would-be buyers are permitted, and often encouraged, to examine the merchandise before bidding. Third, there is no switching of merchandise in a genuine auction, no using of quality goods to attract buyers who are then sold junk. In short, real auctions are not designed to victimize buyers, but to sell goods openly at prices competitively made by rival buyers.

Much time and thought have been devoted to planning legislation to bring mock auctions under control.[11] One of the difficulties is that those who conduct fly-by-night sales are clever enough to avoid entanglements, once they know what the law specifically prohibits. They are constantly on the lookout for police officers, and lie

10 A description of a mock auction in London is given in Appendix C. See Carlton Brown, "Auction Sale This Day," *New Yorker*, Aug. 7, 1937, pp. 19–23, for a detailed description of a mock auction in New York City.

11 *Parliamentary Debates, House of Lords*, "Mock Auction Bill," Official Report, CCXIV (March 12, 1959), 1122–1152.

low when any visit the premises. Operators of mock auctions even use a cryptic phrase to warn that a detective is in the house—"Bring out item number seven!"

Neither the United States nor Great Britain has effective legislation against mock auctions. Although they are declared illegal by the Uniform Commercial Code, which is in effect in many jurisdictions of the United States, the language of the statute is weak: "Every person who obtains any money or property from another, or obtains the signature of another to any written instrument, the false making of which would be forgery, by means of any false or fraudulent sale of property or pretended property, by auction, or by any of the practices known as mock auctions, is punishable by imprisonment . . . or by fine." [12] Mock auctions do not come within the scope of Britain's Auctions (Bidding Agreements) Act of 1927, which was designed for the entirely different purpose of controlling collusive activities among buyers.[13] A mock auction may be thought of as a conspiracy among vendors. Although in both the United States and Great Britain statutes that proscribe deceitful practices in any form may be invoked against the operators of mock auctions, convictions on a basis of fraudulent behavior are almost impossible to obtain. The complainant would have to prove intent to cheat or deceive on the part of the accused, a very difficult task indeed.

12 *California Penal Code,* sec. 535 ("Mock auctions").

13 David Napley, *Bateman's Law of Auctions* (11th ed.; London: Estates Gazette, 1954), pp. 171–172.

Conclusions

18 AT ONE time the auction method was applied chiefly to sales by court order for liquidation of estates or settlement of bankruptcy cases. Although such sales exist today, at most auctions goods, and even real property, are freely offered by their owners, who believe the auction superior to other sales methods.

On the basis of this study of auctions we are able to conclude that there is much more than meets the unpracticed eye in this ancient marketing mechanism. Various aspects of the auctioning process have been analyzed in order to give the reader a glance at what is beneath the surface. From the buyer's point of view, the auction is a game in which would-be purchasers compete against one another to acquire goods and to force one another to pay more for them, or, alternatively, act collectively to outwit the seller and obtain the property at a price below its worth. Like most games, auctioning is interesting not only to participants but to spectators as well. In fact, as in sporting events, some spectators or participants place wagers on the outcome.[1]

Many questions about auctioneering are still unresolved. For example, although we have substantial

1 See "Art Auctions: Latest Inflation Hedge," *Business Week*, March 3, 1951, p. 23.

knowledge about the different auction systems and how they work, we know much less about their application to differing sales tasks. We are not well informed about their comparative efficiency or about their specific effects on prices.

Auctioning is employed in various parts of the distribution system throughout the world. Like any other distributive mechanism, it is particularly useful in the performance of certain tasks; indispensable in some marketing situations, it is practically useless in others. In the sale of fresh fish, it is almost universally found at the primary distribution level, but seldom at the retail consumer level. This pattern suggests that auctioning is more a special-purpose selling device than one possessing general applicability.

To determine the relative marketing efficiency of auctioning as compared with other sales methods, one must first choose the criteria to be used. First is the need to get the job done effectively and promptly. At times the key task is to determine what price accurately reflects the market conditions prevailing at the moment, and for this task auctioning is well qualified, even in a dynamic market situation. Through this mechanism prices can be determined on a tailor-made basis to fit the particular market situation. Sometimes auctioning is the only feasible way to approach the problem.

The second criterion is the cost of getting the job done in terms of manpower requirements. Whereas pricing can be accomplished by one person in a fixed-price situation, or by two individuals in a private-treaty arrangement, in an effective auction system many buyers have to devote much valuable time to the bidding process, through which they indirectly make prices. In certain circumstances, however, the benefits of the system outbalance the higher cost.

One of the most important conclusions, then, is that the auction method is absolutely essential to the solution of certain marketing problems. This remarkably effective price-making mechanism is particularly useful in fields so diverse as fresh fish and antiques, where prices are not stable but may have to be reestablished at each sales session and for each transaction. If prices are set by other methods in such sales operations, it is only because they are established, in part at least, by the auction mechanism.

One of the fields in which the auction is essential is the first sale of fresh fish. Here, the supply of goods in proper quality and adequate quantity, and the demand for goods, based on consumption habits and even on the effect of weather conditions, govern the prices that clear the market each day. Although auctioning is less important in the sale of antiques, where prices are not so mercurial, it is still extremely useful as a direct-selling mechanism, and indirectly as a device for providing authentic market prices which serve as a basis for prices in individually negotiated sales.

That variations do exist in antique items there can be no question. For example, a silver George II snuffer tray that sold at Christie's for $1,134 in 1959 fetched $7,280 in the spring of 1966 at another auction conducted by the same firm. A Breughel print for which its American owner paid $518 in the early 1950's brought $18,200 at a Craddock & Barnard auction fourteen years later.[2] On the other hand, some items have declined in value. A Landseer painting that sold for $85,000 late in the nineteenth century would, the experts say, bring only a fraction of that figure today. Paintings by Sir Winston Churchill have recently leveled off in value, and promise to have only historical value in the future. In general, however, the prices of paintings, especially of masterworks, will increase. As more and more of the authentic masters find their way into art museums, the supply available to collectors is shrinking, even while a higher degree of interest in fine arts is pushing up demand. Whether values go up or down, however, some form of price-making mechanism is required for the sale of items of variable value, a mechanism that will accurately reflect current market conditions and thus find a price to fit the conditions.[3]

Once it has been decided that the auction method of selling is particularly suited to the performance of a certain marketing task, there still remains the problem of what particular auction system to employ. Again, in a comparative evaluation, as in the comparison of auctioning with other sales systems, criteria must be established. These include (1) the relative price levels that can be attained by use of the various systems; (2) the selling speed potentially achievable by each; and (3) the confidence buyers have in each system.

2 Ray Vicker, "How To Sell A Seurat: London Art Houses Thrive as Prices Soar," *Wall Street Journal,* June 24, 1966, p. 22.

3 For excellent examples of prices recently established for art items through the auction process see "A Catalogue of Costly Beauty," *Fortune,* LXXIV (Sept., 1966), 139–146.

The first of these criteria for measuring the comparative efficiency of different auctioning systems is not so much the highest price bid as the most nearly correct price. This factor is particularly significant in primary markets, where those acquiring the product for sale in distant consumption markets face the risk of loss if the price they pay does not properly reflect demand and supply. The second criterion, speed of selling, has to do with the time required to conduct a sale. Although better prices might be obtained for a lot of goods if more time were allowed for each transaction, buyers and sellers are busy people whose many business responsibilities limit the amount of time they can devote to trading. Speedy auctions may save both time and money. The third and perhaps the most important criterion in the choice of a particular auction method is the confidence buyers and sellers have in its effectiveness to perform a particular sales task.

There are three possible approaches to the problem of comparing auction systems as to their relative efficiency in specific marketing operations: (1) making a theoretical comparison; (2) comparing different systems empirically; and (3) applying controlled experimentation.

Theoretical analysis.—A theorist who applies the three efficiency criteria—price level, speed of sales, and acceptability by buyers—to a particular auction method arrives at a judgment simply through the process of logical thinking. It is possible, for example, to compare the English and Dutch systems conceptually on the basis of the attainable selling price. From the seller's point of view, the Dutch method possesses a short-run theoretical advantage in that each potential buyer tends to bid his highest demand price, whereas a bidder in the English system need advance a rival's offer by only one increment. Theoretically, the Dutch system thus brings higher prices than the English system. If speed of selling is a criterion, it is easier, on a conceptual basis, to separate fast-selling schemes from slow-selling ones than it is to select the fastest-selling plan from a number that are potentially speedy (English, Dutch, and Japanese).

Theoretical analysis does have limitations, however. Practically nothing can be said by the theorist about the attitude of buyers toward a particular auction method. Attitudes, which are determined by environmental conditioning, cannot be pondered in the abstract. The principal weakness of this approach, however, is that it deals mainly in tendencies, and the analyst is not always able to perceive subtle factors that might in practice offset such tendencies. Concepts relating to comparative efficiency of auction systems therefore remain hypothetical, unless they can be tested for soundness. One way of checking conceptual conclusions is to seek confirmation from empirical data derived from the marketplace.

Empirical comparison of markets.—This approach is often attractive to the layman because he is apt to perceive the problem as a simple one of comparing results in two markets that employ different systems. Actually, however, it is difficult to make a meaningful comparison if the marketplaces have been selected merely because they use different auction systems. Conditions vary tremendously from market to market, and any difference found is likely to be compounded by other variables.

To illustrate the untenability of such an empirical comparison, consider the Hull and Grimsby markets in northern England. The Dutch auction system is used in Hull, and the English auction system is used in Grimsby, just across the Humber River. Although these auctions may take place at identical hours, sell essentially the same types of goods, cater to the same type of buyers, and so forth, the uncontrolled variables—varieties of fish in different proportions, size and quality of product, and even the precise time the lots are sold within the auction session—tend strongly to vitiate any conclusions concerning the superiority of one over the other. As a further complication, prices in Hull and Grimsby must remain fairly close together, regardless of the auction system employed, because the two ports serve closely related consumer markets. Therefore the discovery of identical or almost identical results between the two markets would not necessarily mean that the systems per se produced the same results.

Controlled experimentation.—Since we cannot find auctions that are identical in every respect but the system utilized, we cannot assess differences in effectiveness by selling merchandise by one auction system and then reselling it by another; furthermore, it would be difficult to test the effectiveness of individual auctioneers by having one sell a lot of goods and then have another resell them. It is possible, however, that the difficulties of using raw empirical data for comparing different auction methods could be overcome by applying modern controlled experimentation techniques. Although it is theoretically feasible to select test and control mechanisms from numerous markets on a random sample basis, and thus largely eliminate the otherwise uncontrollable control groups, such a course is not practicable as applied to a comparative study of auction systems, because there is a paucity of comparable mechanisms.

Thoughtful colleagues have suggested that light might be thrown on the question of comparative efficiency of auction systems by the application of laboratory experimentation. All recognized variables except the one that is being measured could be kept constant, and others could be properly distributed by random selection techniques. Laboratory experimentation, moreover, might enable us to discover inherent differences in two or more methods qua method. The scientific approach might also be used to evaluate the effectiveness of auctioneers through comparison of the price levels attained at simulated auction sessions handled by different individuals. While it would not be practicable to run a control without an auctioneer, a completely inexperienced one might be used in the English system as a basis for comparing the effectiveness of two or more skilled ones.

One cannot expect giant forward steps to be made from the application of laboratory experimentation to the problem of auction efficiency; one can only hope that dark corners will be illuminated. For example, it might be possible to test the hypothesis that the English system develops more competitive spirit than the Dutch system and thus results in higher prices. On the other hand, it might be possible to test the hypothesis that the Dutch system produces higher prices because the high bidder, lacking the guidance afforded by the English system, tends to bid his maximum demand price in order to acquire the item. Another area of investigation is that variations in results under different systems may depend on the intensity of buyer desire.

The foregoing suggests that not only the auction method, but also each type of auction, is to some extent a special-purpose device. The specific task to be performed must be considered in evaluating a particular auction system. Some types of auctions may be very useful for certain tasks but not for others. For example, the hand-shake auction could not be used to sell tobacco, or the Dutch clock to sell real estate. It does not follow that only one auction method properly fits each sales task, although it is true that a certain task may call for a type of auction with specific characteristics, such as speed, which are unimportant in other situations. It is most important, finally, that the buying group making up the market have full confidence in the auction system utilized.

What kind of future can be envisioned for auctioning in the rapidly changing age in which we live? The trend clearly indicates a growth potential. Some fields, such as antiques, in which auctioning is prevalent are experiencing great expansion because consumer purchasing power is stronger and interest in fine paintings, antique furniture, art objects, and so forth is growing. Although of the estimated $3 billion a year spent for art objects throughout the world less than $500 million flows through auction houses, the amount spent in auctions of antiques has quadrupled in the past ten years.[4] In the field of real estate the usefulness of auctioning is just being discovered. The auction method of sale is especially applicable to some kinds of property. I have a friend in the real estate business who believes auctioning is just as effective as, and often superior to, other sales methods in the solution of almost any real estate sales problem. Auctioning also shows an upward trend in the sale of used cars at the wholesale level, for which it is almost perfectly suited. Expansion in this field is inevitable because of the constantly rising demand for automobiles.

Another aspect of the increasing applicability of auctions is the opportunity for their use in emerging countries. The continuing need of producers for protection from capitalist-distributors seems typical of underdeveloped countries. It is almost a truism that economic freedom follows in the wake of political freedom. With the tremendous upswing in emerging countries in these dynamic times, the unshackling of producers is bound to follow; it will probably come, in part at least, through the medium of the auction. Properly operated, the auction ensures the producer-vendor a fair market price, thus enabling him to remain free of the toils of the capitalist-buyer, his erstwhile creditor.

We should not, however, overlook the possibility of a downward trend in the application of auctioning to certain types of sales operations. In some fields the auction system may have outlived its use-

4 Vicker, *loc. cit.*

fulness. The sale of fish is a good example. The integrated business organizations that operate in the Hull-Grimsby market in England have become important in both selling and buying at auction. Some critics point out that when one segment of an integrated firm buys merchandise from another segment, the transaction is without substance. The harshest critics argue that an integrated firm, in the purchase of its own product, can outbid a nonintegrated firm with impunity because the transfer of title, regardless of the price, is merely a bookkeeping transaction. As noted earlier, this argument is faulty in certain respects.

Other elements, however, compound the problem and thus militate against auction selling of fish. One important factor is that the end product of fisheries is being sold less and less in its fresh state and more and more in processed form. The trend toward frozen fresh fish fillets is a good example. The end products, in contrast with the fresh product, tend to have fairly stable retail prices. When prices are steady, daily price making is no longer necessary; prices can be negotiated for a period of six months or even a year, possibly with an escalation provision. If and when this condition becomes prevalent, the auction will no longer be absolutely essential, and may give way to private-treaty arrangements.

This reasoning process, however sound, neglects the important factor of quantity. Only when the product is in short supply, as in wartime, would a buyer agree to take all the seller had to offer at a fixed price. Either an individually negotiated term contract would have to specify quantity, or the buyer would control the fisherman's activities, reserving the right to tell him when to fish and when not to fish. The auction system is thus superior to individual negotiations in one important respect, and this is not even to mention the fisherman's preference in a particular method of sale.

In auctions, the market price is automatically adjusted to existing supply and demand. Even in the southern California tuna industry, whose end product is a canned grocery item with substantial price stability, the auction system is almost universally preferred to a system of negotiated prices. Under the former, fishermen are free to catch all they can instead of having to adjust the amount they catch to the needs of the buyers.

Although in some fields auctions are more effective than other sales methods, they still are not so efficient as they might be. In the tobacco industry, for example, auction selling is very rapid and, in performing a given task, very efficient. But sales efficiency might be substantially enhanced by combining lots of identically graded tobacco for sales purposes. Unfortunately, however, each farmer prefers to have his tobacco sold separately, and it is most important to tobacco companies (which buy the tobacco) and to warehousemen (who handle it) that the farmers be contented. This observation brings us back to the acceptability factor: an auction system may be the most efficient mechanism in existence, but it will be useless if it is not favored by those who market their goods through it.

In the study of auctions and auctioneering, many problems remain unresolved. I hope, however, that the analysis in this volume has pointed up areas that require more intensive investigation, and that scholars in economics and marketing will be stimulated to continue the work. This study is the beginning, not the end, of the task of seeking an understanding of a fascinating marketing mechanism, the auction game. The promise of further effort would be ample compensation for the years of arduous work which the project entailed.

Appendixes

Appendices

Appendix A

TYPICAL CONDITIONS OF SALE FOR AUCTIONS,
DRAWN FROM DOCUMENTARY SOURCES

BOOKS IN EIGHTEENTH-CENTURY ENGLAND

I. That he who Bids most is the Buyer, but if any Dispute arises, the Book or Books to be put to Sale again.

II. That no Person advances less than Sixpence each bidding, and after the Book arises to One Pound, no less than One Shilling.

III. The Books are in most elegant Condition, and supposed to be Perfect, but if any appear otherwise before taken away, the Buyer is at his Choice to take or leave them.

IV. That each Person give in his Name, and pay Five Shillings in the Pound (if demanded) for what he Buys, and that no Book be deliver'd in Time of Sale.

V. The Books must be taken away at the Buyer's Expence, and the Money paid at the Place of Sale, within Three Days after each Sale is ended.

Any Gentleman who cannot attend the Sale, may have their Commissions receiv'd and faithfully executed . . . [by the auctioneer].

ANTIQUES IN LONDON

1. The highest Bidder to be the Buyer; and if any dispute arises between two or more Bidders, the Lot so in dispute shall be immediately put up again and re-sold.

2. The Auctioneer has the right to advance the bidding at his absolute discretion. No person to advance less than 1s.; above Five Pounds, 5s.; and so on in proportion.

3. In the case of Lots upon which there is a reserve, the Auctioneer shall have the right to bid on behalf of the Seller.

4. The Purchasers to give in their Names and Places of Abode and to pay down 5s. in the Pound, or more, in part payment, or the whole of the Purchase-Money, *if required;* in default of which, the Lot or Lots so purchased to be immediately put up again and re-sold.

5 (*a*). Each Lot is sold by the Seller thereof with all faults and defects therein and with all errors of description and is to be taken and paid for whether genuine and authentic or not and no compensation shall be paid for the same.

(*b*). CHRISTIE, MANSON & WOODS LTD., act as agents only and are not responsible for the correct description, genuineness, authenticity of or any fault or defect in any Lot and make no warranty whatsoever.

6 (*a*). The Lots are to be taken away at the Buyer's expense and paid for within THREE DAYS from the sale.

(*b*). Upon the failure of a Buyer to take away and pay for any Lot in accordance with this condition, the money deposited in part payment shall be forfeited and at the entire option and discretion of CHRISTIE, MANSON & WOODS LTD. and without prejudice to any other rights or remedies (i) any such Lot may be re-sold by public or private Sale, and the deficiency (if any) attending such re-sale shall be made good by the said defaulting Buyer or (ii) any such Lot may be handed by CHRISTIE, MANSON & WOODS LTD. to HUDSONS LTD., Wilton Road, Victoria Station, S.W.1, by whom such Lot will be held in store at the expense of the Buyer and will be released by the said HUDSONS LTD. upon payment of the accrued cost of removal, storage and insurance.

7. To prevent inaccuracy in delivery, and inconvenience in the settlement of the Purchases, no Lot can on any account be removed during the time of Sale; and, unless that is waived, the remainder of the Purchase Money must absolutely be paid on delivery.

ANTIQUES IN NEW YORK

The property listed in this catalogue will be offered and sold by Parke-Bernet Galleries, Inc. ("Galleries") as agent for the "Consignor" on the following terms and conditions:

1. All property is sold "as is" and neither the Galleries nor its Consignor makes any warranties or representations of any kind or nature with respect to the property, and in no event shall they be responsible for the correctness of description, genuineness, authorship, attribution, provenience or condition of the property and no statement in the catalogue or made at the sale or elsewhere shall be deemed such a warranty or representation or an assumption of liability. With respect only to Impressionist, Post-Impressionist and modern paintings, drawings and sculptures, if, within twenty-one days after sale of any property the Galleries, in its best judgment or that of such experts as it may consult, determines that there is valid doubt as to authenticity or attribution, and if the property is returned to the Galleries within that time, the Galleries as agent

of the Consignor may rescind that sale of the property and refund the purchase price.

2. The Galleries reserves the right to withdraw any property at any time before actual sale.

3. Unless otherwise announced by the auctioneer at the time of sale, all bids are to be for a single article even though more than one article is included under a numbered item in the catalogue. If, however, all of the articles under a numbered item are either specifically designated by the auctioneer at the time of the sale or designated in the printed catalogue as a "Lot," then bids are to be for the lot irrespective of the number of items.

4. The Galleries reserves the right to reject a bid from any bidder. The highest bidder acknowledged by the auctioneer shall be the purchaser. In the event of any dispute between bidders, the auctioneer shall have absolute discretion either to determine the successful bidder (in which event his determination shall be final) or to re-offer and resell the article in dispute. If any dispute arises after the sale, the Galleries' sale record shall be conclusive as to who was the purchaser, the amount of the highest bid, and in all other respects.

5. If the auctioneer, in his sole and final discretion, decides that any original bid is not commensurate with the value of the article offered, he may reject the same and withdraw the article from sale. Or, if the auctioneer, having acknowledged an original bid, decides that any advance thereafter is not of sufficient amount, he may reject the advance.

6. Title will pass to the highest bidder on the fall of the auctioneer's hammer, the risk and responsibility for the property thereafter to be the purchaser's. The name and address of the purchaser of each article or lot shall be given to the Galleries immediately on the conclusion of the sale thereof and payment of the whole purchase price, or such part thereof as the Galleries may require, shall be made immediately by the purchaser and the property removed from the Galleries' premises at the purchaser's risk and expense. If the foregoing Conditions or any other applicable conditions herein are not complied with, in addition to other remedies available to the Galleries and the Consignor by law, including without limitation the right to hold the purchaser liable for the bid price, the Galleries, at its option, may either (*a*) cancel the sale, retaining as liquidated damages all payments made by the purchaser or (*b*) resell the same without notice to the purchaser and for the account and risk of the purchaser, either publicly or privately, and in such event the purchaser shall be liable for the payment of any deficiency plus all cost, including warehousing, the expenses of both sales and the Galleries' commission at its regular rates. All property not removed by the purchaser within three days from the date of sale may be sent by the Galleries to a warehouse for the account, risk and expense of the purchaser.

7. Unless the sale is advertised and announced as an unrestricted sale, or as a sale without reserve, the Consignor has reserved the right to bid personally or by agent; and if the Consignor or his agent is the highest bidder, less than full commissions may, under certain defined circumstances, be payable.

8. Unless exempt by law from the payment thereof, the purchaser will be required to pay the combined New York State and New York City sales tax, namely, 5 per cent if within New York City; 2 per cent outside New York City.

9. The Galleries, without charge for its services, at its discretion and without responsibility for errors, may undertake to make bids on behalf of responsible persons approved by it, including the Consignor, subject to the Conditions of Sale and to such other terms and conditions as it may prescribe.

ANTIQUES IN LOS ANGELES

1. The property in this sale will be sold subject to the following terms and conditions:

2. The word "Gallery," wherever used, means the firm of Marvin H. Newman Auctioneers.

3. The Gallery has exercised reasonable care to describe correctly the property to be sold but we do not warrant the correctness of description, signature, marks, insignia, genuineness, authenticity or condition of said property. All items sold without recourse.

4. A substantial deposit shall be made by the purchaser to apply on all purchases, but in no event shall there be less deposit than 25% of the purchase price of all items at any time.

5. The highest bidder is to be the Buyer. If any dispute arises at the time of sale between two or more bidders, the lot so in dispute shall be put up again and resold. If there be no advance, then the article shall go to the person from whom the auctioneer recognized the last bid. The auctioneer may decline any bid made by any persons who, in his judgment are not responsible, reliable bidders.

6. Unless otherwise announced by the auctioneer at the time of sale, all bids are to be for a single article though more than one article is included under a numbered item.

7. The buyer may come to the platform and examine any article before making his bid.

8. Articles purchased and not removed within 24 hours following the sale may be turned over by the Gallery to a carrier to be delivered to a storehouse for the account and risk of the purchaser and at his cost. If the purchase price has not been paid in full, the Gallery may at its option and in addition to all other remedies provided by law either cancel the sale, and any partial payment already made shall thereupon be forfeited as liquidated damages, or it may resell the same without notice to the buyer and for his account and risk, charging its established commission, and hold him responsible for any deficiency.

9. The lots to be taken away at the buyer's expense and risk upon the conclusion of the sale, and the remainder of the purchase money to be absolutely paid on or before delivery; in default of which the undersigned will not hold themselves responsible if the lots be lost, damaged or destroyed, but they will be left at the sole risk of the purchaser. Goods will be delivered on presentation of a receipted bill presented by anyone.

10. Except as herein otherwise provided, title will pass to the highest bidder upon the fall of the auctioneer's hammer, and thereafter the property is at the purchaser's sole risk and responsibility.

11. Purchasers buying merchandise with the intention of accepting delivery of such merchandise at some point outside of this state, must make arrangements for shipment prior to bidding, otherwise California Sales Tax will be added to the bill.

12. Any bid which is not commensurate with the value of the article offered, or which would be a gross injustice to the owner or Gallery, or is merely a nominal or fractional advance over the previous bid, may be rejected by the auctioneer if in his judgment such bid would be likely to affect the sale injuriously.

13. If an article purchased cannot be delivered in as good condition as the same was at the time of sale, or should any article purchased be stolen or misdelivered, or lost, the undersigned is not to be held liable in any greater amount than the price bid by the purchaser.

14. The Gallery, subject to these Conditions of Sale and to such terms and conditions as it may prescribe, but without charge for its services, will undertake to make bids for responsible parties approved by it when covered by a 25% deposit.

15. The buyer will be required to pay all taxes prescribed by law, in addition to the purchase price, unless the buyer is exempt from the payments thereof.

16. The Galleries will facilitate the employment of carriers and packers by purchasers but will not be responsible for the acts of such carriers or packers in any respect whatsoever. Packing done by the Gallery is at the sole risk of the buyer.

17. These Conditions of Sale cannot be altered except in writing by the Gallery or by public announcement by the auctioneer at the time of sale.

18. The Conditions of Sale shall be known as a contract between buyer and seller and be a part thereof.

19. In the event suit is instituted by The Gallery against the Buyer to enforce any of its rights arising out of any transaction in the course of the sale, the Buyer agrees to pay in addition to all other sums which may be due The Gallery, reasonable attorney's fees and costs.

ANTIQUES ON PACIFIC COAST

1. Terms cash (or check), payable before leaving the premises. You must pay each day you buy. Merchandise may be removed during or following the sale or at such time as specified by the auctioneer.

2. Reasonable care has been exercised to catalogue and describe correctly the items to be sold but we do not warrant the correctness of description, genuineness, authenticity, or condition of the items and bidders are held to have satisfied themselves as to this before bidding. In case typographical or other errors are discovered, the auctioneer will announce them and memoranda will be kept of such corrections, which will take precedence over the printed matter in the catalogue. The auctioneer acts as selling agent only, but will use every effort to protect the interest of both the buyer and the seller.

3. The highest bidder to be the purchaser but in event of any dispute between bidders, the auctioneer may in his discretion determine who is the successful bidder or the auctioneer may re-offer and re-sell the article in dispute to the highest bidder thereafter and his decision shall be final and binding on all parties.

4. No article shall be moved or packed until a receipted bill has been presented to one of the auctioneer's assistants and the items thereon checked over to avoid mistakes.

5. Regards article sold but not paid for by the customer or articles resold at the request of the buyer (at the end of the sale). Any loss attending such resale shall be made good by the defaulter at the sale.

6. The auctioneer reserves the right to refuse a bid if in his opinion such a bid may render sale injurious. For the convenience of absent buyers, bids will be accepted in advance of sale. Leave your bid with the party giving out catalogues. Please leave check for the amount of the bids with your name and address. The difference between the sale price and the bid, or the whole check if the bid fails, will be returned at once.

7. The auctioneer will facilitate the employment of shippers and packers for purchases, but will not be responsible for the acts of shippers or packers in any respect whatsoever.

8. In addition to the purchase price the buyer will be required to pay government excise tax (clocks and silver) unless the buyer is exempt from the payment thereof.

9. All articles sold "as is" whether specified or not & all measurements are approximate.

FISH IN SEATTLE

1. SELLERS. The exchange shall be open without discrimination to all persons desiring to sell catches of fish.

2. BUYERS. The exchange shall be open without discrimination to all buyers who (*a*) have their own places of business on the Seattle waterfront, (*b*) have safe dock locations and moorage facilities sufficient to safeguard vessels from damage at all times when catches are being discharged, (*c*) have handling facilities capable of discharging fish with reasonable speed and safety, and (*d*) are financially able to pay for purchases at all times and to post performance bond if requested to do so by exchange.

3. TIME OF LISTING. The exchange shall be open for business Monday through Friday of each week, holidays excepted. Trips shall be listed for sale on the exchange not later than 8:30 A.M. each day except Friday. On Friday, two sales will be held. Trips shall be listed not later than 8:30 A.M. for the first sale and not later than 2:00 P.M. for the second sale.

4. HAILINGS. Hailings are to be listed on the exchange by the master of the vessel or by someone authorized by him to do so. A leeway of twenty per cent on all size-grades of fish is to be allowed. This twenty per cent is to be applied on either over or under hailing but not both on the same kind of fish. On all fish weighing out over or under this leeway, the buyer may make a deduction of twenty per cent in price to offset the shortage or overage. Penalties shall apply only where buyer is injured by mis-hailing.

5. DELIVERY. All fish sold on the exchange, except trips sold at the second sale on Friday, shall be delivered at the buyer's dock in Seattle by 1:00 P.M. on the date of sale and shall be discharged by the buyer on the date of sale; provided, that in the event the buyer buys two fares of fish, he may defer the discharge of one fare until the following morning. Any master who does not wish to wait until the next day to discharge can avoid doing so by notifying the exchange manager of such desire before the day's bidding begins. In the event the trip is not delivered to buyer by 1:00 P.M., the buyer shall have the option of refusing the catch. All trips sold on the second sale on Friday shall be discharged on Saturday. Any trip not delivered to buyer's dock by 1:00 P.M. Saturday may be refused by buyer.

6. GRADING.

(*a*) There shall be three size classifications of halibut, with separate bids permitted on each, as follows:

(1) SMALL. This shall consist of all halibut measuring at least 26 inches or more in length from the tip of the lower jaw to the middle of the tail up to but not including 11½ pounds in weight, dressed with heads on, or all fish weighing from 5 to 10 pounds, dressed heads off.

(2) MEDIUMS. This shall consist of all halibut weighing 11½ to 68

pounds, dressed with heads on, or 10 to 60 pounds, dressed heads off.

(3) LARGE. This shall consist of all halibut weighing 68 pounds and over, dressed heads on, or fish weighing 60 pounds and over, dressed heads off.

(*b*) There shall be two additional grade classifications, as follows:

(1) SECOND QUALITY MEDIUMS. . . . This classification shall be purchased at 4¢ per pound less than first quality mediums.

(2) SECOND QUALITY LARGE. . . . Second quality large shall be purchased at 4¢ per pound less than first quality large.

(*c*) There shall be only one classification of small halibut. Small halibut with surface blemishes measuring one-half inch or less across shall be taken as first quality. All small halibut not taken as first quality shall be considered as unmarketable and shall not be purchased.

(*d*) SABLEFISH. There shall be only one grade of sablefish, provided, however, that if the opening bid so designates, all sablefish weighing less than five pounds shall be paid for at one-half the price bid. The fish paid for at half the bid price shall not include any sablefish five pounds or over regardless of condition.

(*e*) MIXED COD. Mixed cod shall be sold in one grade only. Separate bids for each kind of cod are permissible.

(*f*) HEADS. Fish shall be weighed out either heads on or heads off at option of seller. If fish are weighed heads on, a deduction of twelve per cent shall be allowed for heads and two per cent for ice and slime only shall be allowed. In the event buyer wishes to use heads, he shall pay one cent per pound for them.

(*g*) WEIGHING. All fish of doubtful weight shall be weighed by buyer. Whenever possible, buyer shall locate a scale next to the grading table with its platform level with the grading table for use in weighing doubtful fish at the breaking point between medium and large. . . .

(*h*) CULLS. All fish not accepted by the buyer shall remain the property of the seller.

(*i*) DISPUTES. In case of a dispute as to grading of fish between buyer and seller, the fish shall remain the property of the seller.

7. EXCHANGE CHARGE. All dealers who have been accepted as bidders on the exchange shall pay $10.00 per month to the exchange. . . . For this charge, the exchange prior to each sale will supply the dealer with names and catches of all vessels listing fish for sale. A minimum [auction] charge shall be $2.00. One-half of the charge or $1.00 per $1,000.00 may be deducted by buyer from the seller while the remaining half shall be absorbed by buyer. . . .

8. BIDDING. No bid of less than $10.00 will be accepted. Buyers shall bid on exchange in person or through authorized representatives; provided, however, this requirement may be waived at option of exchange manager whenever circumstances warrant.

9. AMENDMENTS. Additional rules and amendments may be made at any time without notice by the exchange management.

FISH IN HONG KONG

. . . .

6. (1) All commercial firms or individuals, holding a licence for sale by retail of marine fish granted by the Chairman, Urban Council or the District Commissioner, New Territories, intending to bid at the market, shall first register their names as bidders at the office of the market or with the marketing inspectorate.

(2) A bidder registered in accordance with paragraph 6 (1) above may add to his name the name or names of not more than two persons employed and nominated by him for the purpose of bidding at auction sales in his absence.

7. Each commercial firm or individual registered under para. 6 shall be issued with a chop and a badge. The cost of the chop and the badge shall be paid by the bidder. The use of the chop and the badge shall be the responsibility of the commercial firm or individual in whose name the chop and the badge were issued. The chop and the badge shall be surrendered when a commercial firm or individual has notified the manager or a marketing inspector of their/his intention of withdrawing as a bidder. The cancellation of a chop and badge may be carried out at any time and without stating any reason therefor.

8. Each bidder buying on credit shall provide adequate guarantors of reputable standing subject to the approval and satisfaction of the Director or a marketing inspector.

9. (1) A bidder may deposit a sum of money with the market against which he may purchase marine fish. In no case may the bidder be permitted to purchase marine fish in excess of the amount he has on deposit.

(2) Any bidder purchasing marine fish on credit shall pay the full price of the fish sold to him, as stated on the market bill, by noon on the day following that on which the fish was purchased or within 24 hours of the presentation of such bill, whichever is the later.

10. Each commercial firm or individual who intends to register as a bidder under para. 6 shall be required to provide his business and private address, personal photographs and any other relevant information required.

11. Commercial firms or individuals not registered at the market under para. 6 shall not be permitted to bid at auction sales.

12. The manager may, in certain circumstances, appoint a member of the staff of the market to bid as agent for a principal whose identity may or may not be disclosed, as the manager shall deem fit, provided that:

(a) the principal is not a registered bidder;

(b) before the auction commences, due notification shall be given to the auctioneer and to the other bidders that a member of the staff of the market will bid in the auction as agent;

(*c*) the principal can show cause why he should not register himself as a bidder to the satisfaction of the manager.

13. All sales of fish shall be by public auction, except that fish may be sold after auction hours by negotiation subject to the approval of the manager and with the consent of the seller who should state the minimum price acceptable to him. Such sales will be conducted on a cash basis.

14. When marine fish is sold by auction, each lot is prima facie deemed to be the subject of a separate contract of sale. The sale is complete when the hammer falls or as is otherwise customary and, after that time, no bid may be retracted.

15. A bid shall be signified in any manner customary in public auction sale, e.g. a nod of the head, the raising of a hand, a verbal remark or statement which can be taken as an assent by the auctioneer that the maker of such remark or statement wishes to record a higher offer for the marine fish being sold than any offer previously made.

16. A bid is not binding until accepted by the completion of sale. Any withdrawal of a bid must be clearly indicated to the auctioneer and to the other parties bidding before the completion of sale is signified by the auctioneer.

17. The acceptance of a bid implies a binding contract on the bidder to pay the full price on the declared weight shown on the auction voucher without condition. The bidder shall not be entitled to revoke his bid in any circumstances after it has been accepted.

18. The seller or his agent may place a reserve price on the marine fish and if, in the bidding, this price is not reached the auctioneer shall declare that the marine fish is not sold for the reason that the reserve price has not been reached. The auctioneer shall not sell any marine fish on which a reserve price has been placed and which, on the bidding, has not been reached without the express permission of the owner of the marine fish or his representative. The auctioneer may, however, at his discretion, re-open the bidding at some later time for marine fish not sold because the reserve price on it was not reached in the bidding, with a view to reaching the reserve price.

19. The seller need not notify the bidder that he has placed a reserve price upon his marine fish but he shall, before the auction commences, inform the auctioneer of the reserve price. In the event of his not doing so, he shall not be entitled after the marine fish has been knocked down to declare that he will not sell.

20. Any marine fish not sold as a result of the seller exercising his right under para. 18 remains the sole responsibility of the seller. If storage space for fresh marine fish is available in the market, marine fish not sold may, at the discretion of the market manager, be handed over to the market authorities and be kept on the market floor until the following day. A storage charge of two dollars per picul or part thereof may be charged for this service and the market accepts no responsibility for the marine fish so handed over. In the

case of salt/dried marine fish not sold, it may be left in the market until the following day if the owner desires, and a charge of fifty cents per picul or part thereof may be charged on all salt/dried marine fish so deposited. Any marine fish so stored will be at the owner's risk. Any marine fish handed over to the market authorities for cold storage will be charged in accordance with cold storage charges.

. . . .

25. The commission deducted from the selling price of all marine fish sold at the market shall be variable but shall not exceed 10%.

26. The Director shall determine from time to time, as necessary, the percentage commission to be deducted in respect of marine fish sold at the market.

27. The amount of commission to be so deducted shall be calculated to the nearest cent. 0.5 of a cent being reckoned as the next cent above.

28. The amount of commission so computed shall be deducted from the selling price of the marine fish before the seller is paid.

. . . .

30. Each seller whose marine fish is sold shall be paid the selling price less commission as soon as possible after the sale of the marine fish unless he should wish to direct otherwise.

31. The market will not recognise any error in under-payment once the seller has left the presence of the paying-out officer.

32. Payment will only be made to the seller on production of the authorized collecting note duly signed and initialled.

. . . .

FURS IN LENINGRAD

1. The show bundles of the goods intended for sale at the Auction may be inspected in the House of Fur Auctions of V/O "Sojuzpushnina" every day from 9 A.M. until 1 P.M. and from 2 until 5 P.M. from the 14th to the 23d of July inclusive, and also during the Auction sales at the same hours.

2. Goods will be sold by public auction. The auction sales will last about 10 days.

Unless otherwise stipulated, each bid is understood to refer to one piece.

The highest bidder is considered the Purchaser of the lot. If several bidders offer the same price, the first bidder shall be deemed the Purchaser.

The settlement of all disputes shall be left to the decision of the Management of the Auction sales, which also reserves the right to offer any lot for sale a second time.

Any claims in connection with each lot sold at the Auction must be brought to the notice of the Management before the beginning of the sale of the next lot. After the sale of the next lot has started the Purchaser will not be entitled to withdraw his bid for the previous lot and the Management will not recognize any claim in connection with this lot.

3. The Auction Management is authorized to withdraw any lot before it has been sold without explanation of the reasons.

4. Purchasers of goods at the Auction are required to pay the full value or at least 30% on account of the value of the purchased goods to the State Bank of the USSR in Moscow for V/O "Sojuzpushnina." Such payment is to be effected by cable transfer to the account of the State Bank of the USSR with one of the Bank's correspondents stated below.

The balance is to be paid out of an irrevocable confirmed Letter of Credit to be opened by the Purchaser by cable with the State Bank of the USSR in favor of V/O "Sojuzpushnina" payable on presentation of the shipping documents to the State Bank of the USSR, Moscow, or its branches in the USSR.

All charges in connection with the cable transfers of the advance payments and the establishment of Letters of Credit as well as Banking commission charges are borne by the Purchaser.

The Letters of Credit are to be opened through one of the . . . correspondents of the State Bank of the USSR abroad. . . .

When effecting payment and opening Letters of Credit the Purchasers are to state in their instructions to the appropriate corresponding bank that the amount in question is intended in payment of goods purchased at the Leningrad Auction Sales.

5. Payment will be deemed to have been effected on the date V/O "Sojuzpushnina" has received confirmation from the State Bank of the USSR in Moscow that V/O "Sojuzpushnina's" account has been credited with the corresponding amount.

6. Should payments not be effected before August 23d, 1958 V/O "Sojuzpushnina" is entitled to consider the contract violated, to dispose of the goods at its discretion and to reimburse any losses incurred from the advance payments received from the Purchaser.

7. Goods will be dispatched to their destination only after V/O "Sojuzpushnina" has received full payment or an advice to the effect that the Purchaser has opened a Letter of Credit for the full value of the goods, or after the Purchaser has effected the advance payment and has opened a Letter of Credit for the remaining amount as per § 4.

If the advance payment is not effected by the Purchaser in accordance with § 4, V/O "Sojuzpushnina" is entitled to consider the contract violated and to dispose of the goods at its discretion and to claim for losses incurred. The Purchaser is not entitled to any surplus obtained.

8. The Purchaser must give V/O "Sojuzpushnina" his shipping instructions in writing immediately after the sale.

The goods will be packed in accordance with V/O "Sojuzpushnina" standard.

9. V/O "Sojuzpushnina" bears the entire risk for the goods from the moment of the sale up to the time of their dispatch from V/O "Sojuzpushnina's" warehouse.

Freight and insurance in transit to be borne by Purchasers. Custom house expenses in the USSR to be borne by V/O "Sojuzpushnina."

10. V/O "Sojuzpushnina" carries out Purchasers' instructions to ship the goods by sea to any European port, or by air to Helsinki, Stockholm and London or by railway to Helsinki and to insure the goods in transit against marine and war risks and pilferage.

11. In case of a total or partial loss of the goods all insurance claims to be referred by Purchasers to the Insurance Company direct.

12. All claims and disputes are to be settled by the Foreign Trade Arbitration Commission at the USSR Chamber of Commerce in Moscow.

STAMPS IN LONDON

Every lot offered at this auction is offered subject to the Philatelic Auctioneers' Standard Terms and Conditions of Sale which are as follows:

1. The highest bidder for each lot shall be the purchaser thereof. If any dispute arises as to the highest bidder the Auctioneer shall determine the dispute and may put up again and re-sell the lot in respect of which the dispute arises.

2. (*a*) The bidding and advances shall be regulated by and at the discretion of the Auctioneer, and he shall have the right to refuse a bid.

(*b*) The purchaser of each lot shall at the sale if required (i) give his or her name and address to the Auctioneer, and/or (ii) pay into the hands of the Auctioneer at his discretion either the whole or part of the purchase money. If any purchaser fails to comply with the foregoing conditions the Auctioneer may put up again and re-sell any lot in respect of which such failure is made; if upon such re-sale a lower price is obtained for such lot than was obtained on the first sale the difference in price shall be made good by (and a debt due from) the purchaser in default upon the first sale.

(*c*) Where an agent purchases on behalf of an undisclosed client such agent shall be personally liable for payment of the purchase price to the Auctioneer and for safe delivery of the lot to the said client.

3. (*a*) The Auctioneer reserves the right to bid on behalf of Clients and Vendors, but shall not be liable for errors or omissions in executing instructions to bid.

(*b*) The Auctioneer reserves the right before or during a sale to group together lots belonging to the same Vendor, or to split up and/or to withdraw any lot or lots.

4. Each lot shall be at the purchaser's risk from the fall of the hammer and must be paid for in full before delivery and must be taken away at his or her

expense by a purchaser in the United Kingdom within seven days of the date of sale and by a purchaser overseas within a reasonable time. If any purchaser fails to pay in full for any lot within the said time such lot may at the Auctioneer's discretion, be put up for Auction again or sold privately; if upon such re-sale a lower price is obtained for such lot than was obtained on the first sale the difference in price and the expense of such re-sale shall be made good by (and a debt due from) the purchaser in default upon the first sale.

5. The Auctioneer shall not be liable for any default of the Purchaser or Vendor.

6. (*a*) Unless otherwise indicated each lot is sold as genuine and properly described.

(*b*) If after the sale the purchaser of a lot shall prove it to be not genuine or wrongly described the purchaser shall be at liberty to reject the lot provided he or she— (i) being within the United Kingdom within seven days or being overseas within a reasonable time of the date of the sale give notice in writing to the Auctioneer of intention to question as the case may be the genuineness or description of the lot, AND (ii) within thirty days of the date of the sale (or, in exceptional cases, such longer time as may in the Auctioneer's discretion be allowed for expertising) returns such lot to the Auctioneer. NOTE: The onus of proving a lot to be not genuine or wrongly described lies with the purchaser. Proof of the inability of an Expert Committee to express a definite opinion will not discharge such onus.

(*c*) No lot may be rejected if subsequent to the sale it has been immersed in water or treated by any other process unless the Auctioneer's permission to subject the lot to such immersion or treatment has first been obtained.

(*d*) Lots stated to contain collections and/or undescribed stamps must be taken with all faults and errors as to numbers (if any), and by reason of the foregoing a purchaser of any such lot shall have no right to reject the same.

TEA IN LONDON

1. The highest bidder shall be the buyer, but the Seller shall have the right to withdraw any lot before or during the Sale. Any alteration of quantity owing to short landed, missing or damaged packages, when possible to be announced in the Sale. Any dispute that may arise shall be settled by the Auctioneer whose decision shall be final. Samples will be "on show" at the Warehouse not later than 10 A.M. on the Wednesday preceding the auction. Any teas not on show to be withdrawn. Buyers shall be deemed to have bought on the basis of the "show package."

2. Buying Brokers or Agents purchasing at this Sale must declare in writing their Principals (to be approved by the Selling Broker) within 24 hours after the purchase, or be held personally responsible as Principals. Any Buy-

ing Broker or Agent who purchases for any person under age shall be held personally responsible as Principal.

3. Buyers shall pay to the Selling Brokers a deposit as is stated in the Catalogue at the time of sale if demanded by the Auctioneer or on the Monday following the day of sale provided that weight notes have been delivered to the Buyer by 5 P.M. on the previous Thursday. The remainder of the purchase money shall be paid on or before ——— (the Prompt Day) * on delivery of the Warrants. The delivery of the Warrants (or other documents of title to the tea) by the Selling Broker to the Buyer on payment of the purchase money shall be deemed to be delivery of the tea to the Buyer. Interest at the rate of £5 per cent. per annum shall be allowed on amounts paid by way of deposit and on the remainder of the purchase money from the day of payment to the Prompt Day. The tea shall be paid for by Buyers at the Customs or Warehouse landed weight with Customs or Warehouse tare. Draft as usual. Rent to commence from Prompt Day. The landed weight shall include the odd ounces which the packages may weigh in excess of the inscribed weight. The only tea which may be taken from the packages (without payment) before delivering them to the Buyers shall be that drawn for Merchants' samples and for necessary inspecting purposes.

4. These teas have been weighed, inspected, bulked in the country of production or, if necessary, in the United Kingdom and tared, and will be reweighed, papered and leaded down by the evening of the day after the day of Sale. All packages will be nailed down within six days of the day of Sale. All packages will be put in merchantable condition. Delivery will be given on the day after the day of Sale, and up to the delivery of the Weight Notes, on notice being given (in writing) to the Selling Broker the day before delivery is required. The Buyer to have the option of refusing any packages as to which the above conditions have not been complied with. Three Clear Working Days are to be allowed for delivery of Weight Notes. The Buyer to have the option of refusing to accept any lot or lots for which Weight Notes have not been delivered by the evening of the third day, by giving a written notice to that effect to the Selling Broker on the following morning, if, on application, he cannot then obtain them. Missing packages, if equal to bulk, and not more than 5 per cent., are exempted from this Condition, and are to be taken by the Buyer at the original price and prompt if tendered within fourteen working days from the day of Sale.

5. No claim for difference in the bulk from the show package will be entertained unless notified in writing to the Selling Broker within Five Working Days from the Day of Sale. No allowance will be made on account of any damage, rubbish, false package, or unequal goodness, found, or alleged to be found, after the tea has been taken from the Warehouse.

6. All tea sold at this Sale, shall be at the risk of the Sellers to the extent only of the sale price until the Prompt Day, unless previously paid for. In the

* I.e., 90 days after the day of the sale.

event of the whole or any portion of the tea being destroyed or damaged by or as a result of fire prior to the delivery of the Warrants to the Buyer, the Contract for the whole or such portion shall be cancelled and the Deposit paid in respect of it shall be returned.

7. Lot Money * to the Selling Broker as usual.

8. If any Buyer shall fail to comply with the above Conditions, the Sellers shall be at liberty to resell the teas either by public or private sale, the deficiency, if any, with Interest of Money, from the Prompt Day, Warehouse Rent, and all other charges and damages of every kind, to be chargeable to such Defaulter, and be recoverable against him at Law.

9. Any dispute that may arise concerning any parcel sold in this Catalogue to be referred to two Arbitrators (who must be Members of either of the Indian Tea Association (London), the Ceylon Association in London, the South Indian Association in London, the Pakistan Tea Association (London), London Committee, Nyasaland Tea Association Ltd., the Indonesia Association (Inc.), the Tea Buyers' Association, the Tea Buying Brokers' Association of London, or of the Tea Brokers' Association of London), one to be chosen by each disputant, and such Arbitrators are to appoint an Umpire, if necessary. The Arbitration fee shall be Two Guineas to each Arbitrator, and Two Guineas to the Umpire, if required to act, including attendance at the Warehouse if necessary. The incidence of Arbitration Fees shall be in the discretion of the Arbitrators or of the Umpire making the award.

WOOL IN FREMANTLE, WESTERN AUSTRALIA

1. The highest bidder for each lot shall be the buyer, the Selling Broker reserving to themselves or their agents the right to bid once for each lot, and if any dispute shall arise between the bidders for any lot, it shall be decided by the Auctioneer, unless one of the claimants advance, in which case the lot shall be put up again, the bidding to be then confined to disputing parties, and no buyer shall retract his bidding. No bid shall be less than ¼d. per lb. . . . The Auctioneer reserves the right to refuse any bid without giving any reason for so doing.

2. The Buyer shall, if required by the Selling Broker at any time during or after the sale, pay to the Selling Broker a deposit of £25 per cent upon the Selling Broker's estimated value of the lot purchased, and shall sign these Conditions of Sale. . . .

3. The Buyer shall pay to the Selling Broker a delivery charge of 13/- per full-weight bale and 6/3 per light-weight bale on all bales of wool realising 3¾d. per lb. or over; on all wool realising under 3¾d. per lb. 5/9 per bale; on fadges or butts, 4/- each; on bags or sacks of wool, ¼ each; and the Selling Broker shall deliver to any destination ordered by the Buyer within the

*I.e., 4d. for each six chests, payable by the buyer to the selling broker.

Fremantle City limits as prescribed by the Master Carriers' Association of Fremantle free of charge. Provided that where a Buyer and Selling Broker have made arrangements for the local delivery of wool outside of ordinary working hours, the Buyer shall pay to the Selling Broker all additional costs incurred by the Selling Broker by reason of delivery outside of ordinary working hours. Where wool is ordered to be delivered to destinations outside Fremantle City limits, the additional cost shall be on Buyer's account.

Buyers have the right to take delivery at store door and in consideration of so doing shall be allowed current rates of cartage for destinations within Fremantle City limits.

4. The wool shall be paid for in cash before delivery, but not later than the Fourteenth day after sale, or any agreed extension thereof. When payment is made within Fourteen days after sale (or any agreed extension of prompt), rebate interest of 5¼ % per annum shall be allowed to the buyer for the unexpired period. No deduction of interest shall be allowed for more than 14 days within the prompt period.

The Selling Broker shall, immediately after prompt or any agreed extension of prompt, account to the Vendor for the proceeds of wool sold, and thereupon remit to the Vendor the net amount due to the Vendor on the general balance of account between the Vendor and the Selling Broker.

5. The Buyer shall pay interest on all amounts not paid on the due dates at [specified] rates. . . .

6. During six days from the time of sale every reasonable facility will be given by the selling broker for the examination of any portion of the bulk not previously on view, after which no allowance will be made for faults, errors of description, difference of weights, or other claim of any nature whatever, except as provided for in the Wool Selling Rules, Regulations and Conditions of Sale. Should it appear to the buyer that any bale or bales materially differ from those exhibited, any dispute or claim made by the buyer in respect of such difference shall (if not forthwith arranged) be referred to the decision of two indifferent persons, one to be chosen by Selling Brokers the other by the buyer—who shall, if they disagree, nominate an umpire, and the award of such arbitrators or umpire shall be conclusive on the parties, provided the same be made in writing within the said six days. . . .

7. If any wool be not removed by the buyer from the warehouse of the Selling Broker within 28 days from the date of sale, it shall be subject to a charge for storage . . . except in such cases where delivery orders have been lodged with the Selling Broker within twenty-one days and the vessel concerned is ready to receive such wool from the Selling Broker within twenty-eight days from date of sale then no extra storage shall be charged. But in no case shall removal of the wool by the Buyer be delayed beyond a period of twenty-eight days from date of sale without the consent of the Selling Brokers. In the event of an extension of the prompt, the free storage period shall be extended by the same number of days.

8. The Selling Broker shall insure and keep insured the wool against loss or damage by fire from the fall of the hammer until the wool is paid for in full in an amount equal to its invoice value. . . . Subject as aforesaid the Seller and the Purchaser shall be responsible for the insurance of their own respective interests.

9. If, owing to strike, the Buyer has no opportunity of shipping his wool (the onus of proof of which shall be on the buyer), the obligation of the Buyer under Clause 4 to take the goods within fourteen days (or any agreed extension thereof) shall be suspended for such periods as may be reasonably necessary to give the Buyer opportunity to ship and receive Bills of Lading. The obligation of the Buyer to pay for the goods in cash before removal shall remain unaffected. No charge shall be made to the Buyer for interest, storage or insurance in respect of the period of such suspension and neither the Selling Broker nor the vendor shall be entitled to receive payment until the expiry of the period for payment by the Buyer including any extension thereof or period of suspension. . . .

If any question shall arise as to whether there is a strike within the meaning of this condition or as to the buyer's inability to ship his wool as the result thereof, or as to what period of suspension may be reasonably necessary owing thereto, such question or questions shall be referred to the Joint Committee, whose decision shall be final and binding on all parties.

If the Committee are unable to agree the matter shall be referred to an independent arbitrator to be mutually agreed on by the Committee. The decision of the arbitrator shall be final and binding on all parties. . . .

10. If the weighing and/or delivery of the goods sold, or any portion of them, shall be hindered or prevented by reason of any general or partial strike, lock-out or combination of workmen, the period or periods within which such weighing and/or delivery shall be effected shall be extended for so long as shall—under the circumstances of the case—be reasonable.

11. That in default of compliance with the Conditions of Sale the Wool shall be resold by Public Auction or Private Contract, with or without notice, at the risk of the former purchaser, who will be held responsible for all loss and expense arising out of such re-sale.

12. The Auctioneer will accept the bids of any buyer only on the express condition that such buyer is not acting on behalf of a principal resident in any country which is at war with Great Britain. The Selling Brokers reserve to themselves the right of cancelling any purchase made in violation of this condition.

13. Unless otherwise stated in Catalogue tare allowance will be 11 lbs. per bale, 2 lbs. per bag and actual tare on fadges.

14. The Joint Committee referred to in these conditions shall consist of two persons appointed by the Western Australian Wool & Produce Brokers' Association and two persons appointed by the Western Australian Wool Buyers' Association.

AGRICULTURAL COMMODITIES IN THE NETHERLANDS

. . . .

Article 3
Through the Board the [cooperative] association acts as seller for the members and for other suppliers (non-members). The Board is represented by the auction-master with and respecting the sales.

Article 4
The Board determines time and place of the auctions after having consulted with the committee of buyers. . . .

Article 5
Those breaking through any article of these rules or participants misbehaving or hindering in any other way a good course of things will be ejected from the buildings and the grounds of the auction association by the Board or by the auction-master.

Article 6
Auctioning takes place on a descending scale and in the way announced beforehand by the auctioneer.

The first and second word (time of asking) is with the auctioneer. A sale is effected as soon as the seat number of the buyer is recorded in lights on the dial of the auction clock.

The auctioneer is qualified to announce previous to each and every auction sale how much of the goods put up for sale should at the least or may at the most be bought.

Article 7
The auction-master is entitled to declare a sale null and void in case and as soon as this should be necessary in consequence of engine-trouble (breakdown of the clock), misunderstanding and such-like.

. . . .

Article 10
The auction-master is qualified to prevent horticultural products that are apparently unfit to be eaten (and products that do not come up to the minimum requirements of quality) from being put up for sale. The auction-master is entitled to have these inferior goods removed from the auction.

Article 11
By merely sending in (delivering) their products to the auction suppliers will be considered having instructed the association to sell on a descending scale the goods in question. Recalling this instruction and taking back the products sent in (delivered) may not take place unless with permission of the auctioneer.

. . . .

Article 13

The produce delivered to the auction will be inspected before the sale. The inspection is done by the auction's inspector appointed by the Board. He checks quality and grading and writes down his finding on the auction/delivery-note. In case the suppliers can not agree with the decision of the inspector, they have the right of appeal to the auction-master who will decide on legal and fair grounds in the last resort.

. . . .

Article 19

. . . auction sales are ready-money transactions, so that payment of the amounts due must be made immediately after the invoice or auction-note has gone to the buyer. These payments are to be made in the pay-office of the cashier of the auction who has power to discharge for the amounts received on behalf of the association.

If and so far as the Board consents to paying otherwise than cash, payment is to be made not later than on Saturday of the week following that in which the purchases are made or so much sooner as the Board will determine. . . .

. . . .

Article 21

The auction-master determines the order of succession in which the arrivals will be auctioned.

Buyers are not allowed to needless touching the products supplied to the auction or to utter their opinion about the products, neither in approving nor in disapproving sense.

. . . .

Article 23

The products are auctioned by number or weight. The auction-master may consent to another way of sale only in exceptional cases.

Article 24

When the auctioning takes place "by word of mouth" (e.g. in case there is no Dutch Clock or in the event of the auction clock getting out of order), the auctioneer decides whom of the two or more buyers calling "mine" at the same time will be considered as the actual buyer.

Article 25

A buyer may not make more than two mistakes during one auction sale, and only in case these errors are caused by any disturbance, in the discretion of the auctioneer.

The lot with which the mistake has been made, may not be bought again by the same buyer.

The auctioneer, too, may make mistakes and then the parcel put up for sale is not awarded and will at once be auctioned again; a second error with the same lot is not allowed to the auctioneer. A mistake will not be rectified, if another parcel has already been auctioned after the lot in question.

In exceptional cases, however, the auctioneer may consent to retrieving an error in contravention of above rules.

.   .   .   .

Article 27

Auctions . . . [where the goods are offered for sale by the auctioneer's staff] are auctions for which the products are taken up from the suppliers by the personnel of the auctions, which places, checks and provides the goods with lot numbers.

After being sold the products are handed over to the buyers by the personnel of the auction on behalf of the association (or by the agents of the sections). Buyers are then owners of the goods.

.   .   .   .

Article 32

The auction-master and the supplier have the right to "hold off" and withdraw from the sale a parcel offered (by using the press-button in question); in that case the parcel is registered as being held off. For parcels withdrawn from the sale no selling commission is charged.

A parcel which was held off, may be auctioned again, but generally only after all other parcels have been sold. If the parcel is held off once again by the supplier, he will have to pay selling commission of the "holding off" price.

A parcel is not considered as being held off, but as being not auctioned in case it is not awarded (granted) in consequence of governmental measures.

Article 33

Before the products are delivered, the buyer may be requested to pay first the amount due. This request may be made without reasons given. If a buyer does not comply with (accede to) such a request, the purchase is considered to be refused (declined) and the products are considered not allotted (granted). Products that are not assigned (awarded) in pursuance of the regulation in the previous paragraph, are auctioned once more as soon as possible for account of the buyer mentioned in the same paragraph.

Article 34

If for any product a maximum price is fixed by the government and this maximum price is outbid, the parcel will be divided and distributed according to the governmental instructions given.

.   .   .   .

Article 37

The products bought are immediately for account and risk of the buyer. When the buyer does not take delivery of the products bought on the day of acquisition, the auction may charge the buyer for all the expenses attached to the keeping etc.

If the products bought are not taken up within ——— hours, the Association is qualified to proceed to reselling for account of the buyer. . . .

Article 38
Every buyer is supposed to have seen the goods he bought. However, the buyer may appeal to the auction's inspector within ——— hours after the end of the auctioning (but never after the parcel has left the auction-ground) in case he should be of opinion that grade, weight, number or quality of the products do not correspond with what has been offered with the sale.

⋅ ⋅ ⋅ ⋅ ⋅ ⋅ ⋅ ⋅ ⋅ ⋅ ⋅ ⋅

Article 43
The auction guarantees to the suppliers the proceeds of the products sold by the auction in behalf of the growers, however, with the exception of the proceeds of so-called "administrative" products auctioned. A certain percentage of the proceeds of the products is charged (as a selling commission representing the cost of the service) to all the members/growers of the auction association. This percentage will be deducted from the total amount to be received by the growers and this percentage will be equal for all the members/growers. This selling commission is fixed by the general meeting of the association.

A certain selling commission is also charged to the suppliers non-members. This commission may not be less than the auction commission fixed by the association for the suppliers members.

⋅ ⋅ ⋅ ⋅ ⋅ ⋅ ⋅ ⋅ ⋅ ⋅ ⋅ ⋅

Article 45
No products are delivered to the auction and sold on other conditions than on those described in these rules, so that each and every supplier and buyer at the auction is considered to be acquainted with these terms and is presumed to have accepted them.

The auction-master is qualified to proclaim complementary regulations before the beginning of the sales by auction. As far as these supplementary prescriptions are also material to the buyers, the committee from among the buyers . . . should be consulted beforehand.

Appendix B

REPRESENTATIVE ADVERTISEMENTS OF AUCTION SALES

Lynn Walters Antique Auction
TREASURES FROM OVER THE SEA
IMPORTANT AUCTION
OVER 450 ITEMS — RARE
CHOICE PIECES DIRECT
FROM FRANCE & ENGLAND

CHOICE BRITISH FURNITURE: Choice inlaid Victorian mahogany settee; Oak roll top desk; Bureau bookcase; Superior Sheraton bow front display cabinet; Mahogany credenzas; Oak buffet; Sideboards; Burr walnut pedestal cabinet; Jacobean sideboard; Overmantel; Elegant fitted burr walnut wardrobe; Commodes; Games & sewing table; Large dining table fitted leaf; Draw leaf dining tables; Occasional tables; Tile top table; Occasional & dining chairs & sets of chairs; Sheraton inlaid chair; Windsor bedroom & arm chairs; Pine spindle back farm chair; Rush seat ladder back chairs; Rush seat stools; Gout stool; Oak stool; Mahogany music stools; Music cabinet; Oak reversible table; tea trolley; Oak Hall stand; Postal box; Brass bed with rails; Blackwood stand; Horse martingales; Violin & case; Fender; Barometers; Mahogany cake stand; Antique wolf rug; Patch work quilt; Large white embroidered banquet table cloth; Microscope; Printing press; Scales & weights; Mahogany box; Bellows; Lacquer box; Coal cabinet; Photo album; Books; Bible; Book rest; Table mirror on stand; Ebony elephants; Carvers in case; Riding crop; Hunting knife; Swords; African hand carved spears; etc.

•••

* XXXXXXXXXXXXXXXXXX

* X   PUBLIC EXHIBITION   X

* X   SUNDAY APRIL 24   X

* X   10 AM & DURING SALE   X

* XXXXXXXXXXXXXXXXXX

* SALE & VIEW AT CARPENTERS UNION HALL

* 7500 VAN NUYS BLVD.

* VAN NUYS, CALIFORNIA

* SALE: SUN. APRIL 24, 1966

* SELLING 12:30 SHARP TILL ALL IS SOLD

* ALMA'S LUNCH AT HALL

•••

COLLECTION CLOCKS: German grandfather clocks; Assorted French, English & European wall clocks; French cartels; Wooden mantel clocks; Chiming 3pc clock sets; English 400 day mantel clock under glass dome; Superior 3pc French clock sets; Superior & elaborate large French brass 3pc mantel clock set etc.

FINE FRENCH, ENGLISH AND GERMAN PORCELAINS: Coalport; Royal Dux; Dresden; Wedgwood; Mason Ironstone; Bisque; Delft; Silver-lustre; Spode; Celadon; etc. in Superior pair Dresden capped vases; Superior Wedgwood biscuit barrel; Superior pair English Rockingham vases; Superior coalport china vase; Superior pair Royal Dux figures; Superior china 28pc tea service; Figure groups; Dogs; Comports; Wall plates & plaques; Jardinieres; Tureens; 3 tier flower holder; Vases & sets of vases; Mortar; Creamers & sugar bowls; Cake comports; Ginger jars; Ashets; Cheese dishes; Beer stein; Plate stands; Biscuit barrels; Spice jars; Milk pitchers; Jugs; Cups & saucers; Toby jug; Powder bowl; Tea pots; Shoes; Mugs; Butter dishes; Toilet sets; Slop Bucket; etc.

SUPERIOR ENGLISH BRONZE OF DAVID & THE LION

FINE SILVERPLATE: Cake baskets; Coffee pots; Tea pot; Cream jug; Ladle; Tray; Pickle fork; Cocktail shakers; Vase; Fish knives & forks; Servers; Carving set; etc.

FINE OIL PAINTINGS BY WORLD KNOWN ARTISTS: Oil painting; Oil paintings on silk signed N. EDWARDS; Water colors; Tapestry; Prints; Engravings; French Frame; Silhouette; etc.

Lynn Walters, Auctioneer------------Clackamas, Ore.

CUSTOMERS PLEASE NOTE: Every effort is made to have this flyer accurate, but it is dependent on boat arrivals, customs, clearance etc. Subject to change without notice. Thank you, LYNN WALTERS.

No Limit   No Reserve

PUBLIC AUCTION

Discontinuing Sawmill Business to Concentrate on Veneer Work
Tues. SEPT. 21 — 10:00 a.m.
Freres Lumber Co. & Mt. Jefferson Lumber Co.
Lyons, Oregon
$1.3 Million Facility

[Partial map of Oregon showing location of Lyons]

TERMS OF SALE

25% deposit on award of bid; balance within 4 days. Cash, certified checks, personal or company checks or irrevocable purchase orders are acceptable for deposit only and full payment must be made before removal of purchase. Everything will be sold "as is, where is." ALL SALES FINAL. Cost and responsibility of removal of purchases remain with the purchaser, although every effort will be made to facilitate removal. While quantities and descriptions are believed to be correct, there are no guarantees. The auctioneers or advertising counsel will not be held responsible for advertising inaccuracies or discrepancies. Copies of our regular terms & conditions will be posted on the premises. We hope you enjoy our methods and make many advantageous purchases.

/s/
_____
Milton J. Wershow

PUBLIC AUCTION

HOUSES

STATE OF CALIFORNIA

TO SELL

Flats, Apts. & Comm'l Bldgs.
to be removed from State Highway Right of Way

AT SITES LISTED

Wed., July 6, 1966		9:30 A.M.
Long Beach, San Pedro	Min. Bid.	Deposit
6745 Johnson Ave.	$100	Amt. of bid *
4-br. HWfl. Stucco Hse.		
6725 Lime Ave.	$100	Amt. of bid *
2-br HWfl. Stucco Hse.		
6750 N. Lime Ave.	$100	Amt. of bid *
2-br. HWfl. Stucco Hse.		
200 E. Coolidge St.	$100	Amt. of bid *
2-br. HWfl. Stucco Hse.		
124 W. 65th St.	$100	Amt. of bid *
2-br. HWfl. Stucco Hse.		
674 Upland Ave.	$100	Amt. of bid *
2-br. HWfl. Stucco Hse.		

Thurs., July 7, 1966		10:00 A.M.
Duarte		
2300 E. Huntington Dr.	$500	$500

DRIVE-IN DAIRY BLDG. & EQUIPMENT:
43' umbrella canopy, refrigerators,
freezer & cooler bldg., misc. fixtures.

Fri., July 8, 1966		9:00 A.M.
Castaic		
31655 N. Castaic Rd.	$300	$300
2 steel fr. corru. metal Industrial Bldgs.		

Glendale, Los Angeles		10:00 A.M.
511 N. Verdugo Rd.	$300	$300
3-br., 1¾ ba. HWfl. Stucco Hse.		
5155 Delaware Ave.	$ 50	Amt. of bid *
garage		

* $300 is maximum deposit required.
Deposits must be made in cash, cashier's check,
money order or certified check.
For further information call MA. 0-3600.
Sales conducted by State Personnel.

PUBLIC AUCTION
LAND

STATE DIVISION OF HIGHWAYS TO SELL ON
WEDNESDAY, JULY 13, 1966 AND FRIDAY, JULY 15TH
ALL SALES AT THE SITE AT TIME INDICATED
DEPOSIT MUST BE MADE IN CASH OR CASHIER'S CHECK
WEDNESDAY, JULY 13TH, 1966

2,417 AC.   9:30 A.M.   ZONE R-4
Yockey Street and Cannery, City of Garden Grove, County of Orange.
Minimum Bid $51,300.00. Deposit $5,100.00.

31,735 SQ. FT.   10:00 A.M.   ZONE A-1
End of Palm Street, north side of Garden Grove Freeway, City of
Garden Grove. Minimum Bid $12,750.00; Deposit $2,000.00

38,187 SQ. FT.   10:30 A.M.   ZONE C-2
South of La Veta Avenue at Flower Street, City and County of Orange.
Minimum Bid $32,000.00; Deposit $3,700.00.

9,178 SQ. FT.   11:00 A.M.   ZONE R-1
945 Sherwood Lane, City of Santa Ana, County of Orange. Minimum
Bid $14,900.00; Deposit $2,200.00. Improved with: 7-Room Stucco Residence; 2-Car Attached Garage.

6,162 AC.   1:15 P.M.   ZONE C-2
Adjacent to Garden Grove Freeway, northerly of Garden Grove Boule-
vard. City & County of Orange. Minimum Bid $127,500.00; Deposit
$8,100.00.

12,002 SQ. FT.   2:00 P.M.   ZONE R-1
Northwesterly of the intersection of Pearce & Blackbird Streets, City of
Garden Grove, County of Orange. Minimum Bid $5,000.00; Deposit
$1,200.00

FRIDAY, JULY 15TH, 1966

7,097 SQ. FT.   9:30 A.M.   ZONE R-1
Southwesterly of Davenrich Street and Cedardale Street, City of Santa
Fe Springs. Minimum Bid $4,000.00; Deposit $1,025.00.

5,046 SQ. FT.   9:40 A.M.   ZONE R-1
Southwesterly intersection of Davenrich Street and Cedardale. Minimum
Bid 3,000.00; Deposit $875.00.

5,839 SQ. FT.   10:00 A.M.   ZONE R-1
Southwesterly Intersection of Cedardale Drive, formerly Syringa Street.
Minimum Bid $3,500.00; Deposit $950.00.

12,396 SQ. FT.   10:15 A.M.   ZONE R-1
10529 Longworth Street, City of Santa Fe Springs. Minimum Bid

$15,500.00; Deposit $2,250.00. Improved with: 1-Story Single Family Residence & 2-Car Garage.

5,709 SQ. FT.   10:30 A.M.   ZONE R-1

10837 Benfield Street, City of Downey. Minimum Bid $9,500.00; Deposit $1,650.00. Improved with: 1-Story Stucco Residence.

For Further Information Call MA 0-3600
Sales Conducted by State Personnel

PRIVATE AUCTION
by INVITATION ONLY

Would You like to invest $1,000,000 PREPAID INTEREST AND close escrow prior to Dec. 31st?

Would you like annual income in excess of $500,000?

Would you like to own two of Southern California's most prestigious properties? (Santa Monica) $10,000,000.00

If so, please write to us on your company letterhead stationery telling us of your requirements. We will mail selected invitations to qualified investors only, to attend an exclusive private auction to be conducted at The Westwood Room of The Century Plaza Hotel on Tuesday, November 22nd, commencing at 11 A.M. Upon this occasion, bids will be entertained for the sale of two of the most prestigious properties in the most prestigious location of the Santa Monica Bay area of Southern California overlooking the Pacific Ocean. Brokers will be protected who register their clients in advance. Any investor looking for substantial income, a tax shelter of great proportions and a large depreciation factor should not hesitate to investigate an opportunity of this magnitude.

PRINCE AUCTIONEERS, INC.
8630 Wilshire Blvd., Beverly Hills
(213) OL. 7-7777 · OL. 5-4444
Real Estate Auctioneers

MYSTERY
AUCTION
(Who knows, you may get
a Rembrandt for 25¢)
Saturday, Oct. 29, 1966
9:30 a.m. to 5:00 p.m.

3016 Wilshire Blvd.
Santa Monica

We'll be auctioning off a batch of mystery boxes. Who knows what they contain? They've never been opened.

We're also auctioning off some things you can see, like appliances, televisions, living room and dining room furniture, rugs, etc.

BEKINS
Moving & Storage
Ken Hauter
Auctioneer

Appendix C

DESCRIPTION OF A MOCK AUCTION FROM
A PARLIAMENTARY DEBATE

"I [Lord Denham] could describe the course of a mock auction sale in one sentence by using the jargon of the mock auctioneer: 'The pitch-getter gets the pitch, and then hands over to the top man, who first nails the mugs, then runs out the Hinton lots and finally gazoomphs the sarkers.' Perhaps I had better construe. The 'pitch' is the audience to whom the goods are sold, and the only job of the 'pitch-getter' is to collect an audience inside the shop where the sale is to take place. When he has done that he hands over to the 'top man' or auctioneer, who then 'nails the mugs'—that is, sorts out the 'mugs' from the rest of the audience, and ensures (by a method which I shall explain later) that they stay in the shop until the sale is over. Then he 'runs out,' pretends to sell, the 'Hinton lots,' those lots which are never in fact sold, and finally 'gazoomphs,' or cheats, the 'sarkers,' those of the 'mugs' who have enough money on them to be worth his while. This description may not make the matter very much clearer to your Lordships, but it should certainly show you the amount of good faith there is in this type of sale." *

1. A "pitch-getter" stands behind a table at the entrance to a shop on which there is a sign "Clearance Sale." On the table before him are fine-quality articles—cigarette lighters, alarum [sic] clocks, and so on—which the pitch-getter informs the gathered group are to be sold at "giveaway" prices inside. "This fine cigarette lighter will be sold for as little as one shilling" is a typical statement.

2. Then, having attracted the "mugs," he moves the table inside through the entryway, taking the "mugs," or most of them, with him.

3. The "top man" (i.e., the auctioneer) now goes to work on the "mugs." The first thing he must do is to isolate the gullible. With that objective in

* *Parliamentary Debates, House of Lords*, "Mock Auctions Bill," Official Report, CCXIV (March 12, 1959), 1122. The rest of this summary is condensed from Lord Denham's description of the steps in mock auctions (*ibid.*, pp. 1122–1128).

mind, he offers a sealed package at auction which is quickly bid up to 10s., say, by the shills; having established this "value," he then offers the others present the same proposition at the same price, explaining to them that only those who have shown confidence in the operation by purchasing one of the sealed packages will be permitted to participate in the balance of the sale. Although the money is collected, the sealed packages are not given to the buyers, but instead each gets a token that entitles him to one of the sealed packages later. Thus the "sarkers" ("mugs" with money or the "live" ones) are nailed down.

4. Having isolated the sarkers and nailed them down, the top man then "auctions off" some genuine articles that (a) mugs bid on but never seem to be able to buy (only the stooges get them), and on which (b) the "buyer" is always given a substantial rebate (e.g., 19s. back on the purchase of a 20s. lighter). At this point free merchandise may ostentatiously be given away to the suckers to cover up the "knocking down" of the good merchandise to the housemen.

5. The final step is to "shear the sheep," as it were. The auctioneer says, "We are coming to the last lot," and indicates that he has several items in this lot but that only one is to be sold (for advertising purposes), and the highest bidder will take it. (Actually, these items are such things as a cheap wrist watch, inexpensive table lamp, etc., all having been made especially for this purpose and none of which the "mugs" have seen before.) Lively bidding ensues, partly because the impression has been created that a portion of the money will be returned, and the item is bid up to perhaps £5. The auctioneer gives a choice of items to the winner.

At this point the auctioneer stops the proceedings, after a stooge has whispered in his ear, to announce that he has heard that some of those present suspect the sale is rigged and believe the opportunity to buy is being given only to house people. He then asks the sarker who has just been awarded the merchandise whether he has ever seen any of the people in the store before. When the sarker answers "No," the auctioneer says that the only way to disprove the untrue statement is to allow others who have bought sealed packages the same purchasing opportunity. The auctioneer's assistants "try" to stop him from doing so, saying that he is too "generous," but the auctioneer is adamant. So he and his assistants collect £5 from each of the sarkers, and the auctioneer says: "All right, you have trusted me and now I am going to reward you. I am going to give you something in addition to what you have purchased," and holds up a fountain pen and pencil in an attractive cardboard box.

The "mug" is handed a carrier bag in which the main item that he has chosen (e.g., cutlery) and his pen and pencil set are placed; then the auctioneer opens one of the sealed packages and pulls out a bottle of scent, which also goes into the bag. Each sarker is then given a bag containing his purchases, and the sale is over. When he arrives home, the sarker finds that he has purchased, for £5 10s., merchandise worth possibly 5 to 20s.

Bibliography

BOOKS

"Auctions and Auctioneers," in *Corpus Juris Secundum*. Vol. VII. Pp. 1239–1273. Brooklyn: American Law Book Co., 1937.

Bailey, Emma. *Sold to the Lady in the Green Hat*. New York: Dodd, Mead, 1962. 213 pp.

Ballentine, James A. *Law Dictionary with Pronunciations*. 2d ed. Rochester, N.Y.: Lawyers Co-operative Publishing Co., 1948.

Bancroft, Frederic. *Slave Trading in the Old South*. New York: Frederick Ungar Publishing Co., 1959. 415 pp.

Bean, George H. *Yankee Auctioneer*. Boston: Little, Brown, 1948. 247 pp.

Behrman, S. N. *Duveen*. New York: Random House, 1951, 302 pp.

Berenson, Bernard. *Sketch for a Self-Portrait*. New York: Pantheon, 1949. 185 pp.

Black, Henry Campbell. *Black's Law Dictionary*. 4th ed. St. Paul, Minn.: West Publishing Co., 1951.

Brough, James. *Auction!* Indianapolis and New York: Bobbs-Merrill, 1963. 224 pp.

Carter, John. "The Auction Room," in Milton Grundy, *Money at Work*. London: Sweet & Maxwell, 1960. Pp. 147–170.

Cassady, Ralph, Jr. "The Marketing of Fishery Products in the U.S.A.," in Ralph Turvey and Jack Wiseman, eds., *The Economics of Fisheries*. Rome: Food and Agriculture Organization of the United Nations, 1957. Pp. 180–205.

Diary and Correspondence of Samuel Pepys, Esq., F.R.S. With a Life and Notes by Richard Lord Braybrooke. Deciphered, with Additional Notes, by Rev. Mynors Bright, M.A. Vol. II. New York: Dodd, Mead, 1887. 355 pp.

Durant, Will. *Caesar and Christ*. The Story of Civilization: Part III. New York: Simon and Schuster, 1944. 751 pp.

Duveen, James Henry. *Art Treasures and Intrigue*. Garden City, N.Y.: Doubleday, Doran, 1935. 324 pp.

———. *Secrets of an Art Dealer*. New York: E. P. Dutton, 1938. 288 pp.

Frank, Tenney, ed. "Rome and Italy of the Empire." Vol. V of *An Economic Survey of Ancient Rome*. Baltimore: Johns Hopkins Press, 1940. 445 pp.

Getty, J. Paul, and Ethel Le Vane. *Collector's Choice*. London: W. H. Allen, 1955. 360 pp.

Hahn, Harry. *The Rape of La Belle*. Kansas City, Mo.: Frank Glenn Publishing Co., 1946. 274 pp.

Herodotus. *The Histories of Herodotus*. Trans. Henry Cary. New York: D. Appleton and Company, 1899. 568 pp.

Hollander, H. Louis. "Public Auction of Stocks and Bonds," in *1958 Appraisal and Valuation Manual* (Washington: American Society of Appraisers, 1958), pp. 129–138.

Lightner, O. C. *Buying at Auction*. Chicago: Hobbies Publishing Co., 1942. 146 pp.

Mankowitz, Wolf. *Make Me an Offer*. London: Andre Deutsch, 1952. 108 pp.

Mead, Walter J. *Competition and Oligopsony in the Douglas Fir Lumber Industry*. Berkeley and Los Angeles: University of California Press, 1966. 276 pp.

Mercer, George, ed. *The Auctioneers' Manual*. 11th ed. London: Estates Gazette, 1961. 323 pp.

Napley, David. *Bateman's Law of Auctions*. 11th ed. London: Estates Gazette, 1954. 593 pp.

Oxenfeldt, Alfred R. *Pricing for Marketing Executives*. San Francisco: Wadsworth Publishing Co., 1961. 88 pp.

Partridge, Bellamy. *Going, Going, Gone!* New York: Dutton, 1958. 253 pp.

Reitlinger, Gerald. *The Economics of Taste*. London: Barrie and Rockliff, 1961. 518 pp.

Sotheby and Co. *The Ivory Hammer: The Year at Sotheby's*. New York, Chicago, and San Francisco: Holt, Rinehart and Winston, 1963. 254 pp.

Van Waay, S. J. Mak. *Schets Van Het Veilingwezen in Nederland*. Tweede Druk. ("Survey of Auction Operations in the Netherlands." Second Printing.) Amsterdam: Uitgave Kampert en Helm, 1942. 95 pp.

White, Donald J. *The New England Fishing Industry*. Cambridge, Mass.: Harvard University Press, 1954. 205 pp.

Wraight, Robert. *The Art Game*. New York: Simon and Schuster, 1965, 1966. 224 pp.

PAMPHLETS AND ARTICLES

Agricola. "Sales by the Clock: The Clock Auction System," *Estates Gazette*, March 31, 1962, p. 909.

"Alleged Auction Ring Frauds," *Waste Trade World and Iron & Steel Scrap Review*, Sept. 16, 1950, p. 8.

Allsop, Kenneth. "Sotheby's Strives for a New Record," *New York Times Magazine*, Dec. 9, 1962, pp. 42, 52, 57–58.

"Antique Shops Make New By-Laws," *Times* (London), Dec. 18, 1964, p. 5.

"Art Auctions: Latest Inflation Hedge," *Business Week*, March 3, 1951, pp. 22–23.

Ash, Peter. "The First Auctioneer: Origin of Sales by Auction of Real Property," *Estates Gazette* (Centenary Supplement), May 3, 1958, pp. 33, 35, 37.

———. "Revocation of an Auctioneer's Authority," *Estates Gazette*, Oct. 8, 1955, pp. 426–427.

"Auctioneer," *The Auctioneer*, V (Sept., 1954), 2–6.

"Auctions by Wire: Nine Large U.S. Cities and Florida Citrus Market Are Linked by Selevision," *Business Week*, Jan. 13, 1945, p. 85.

"Auctions Present Christmas Lures," *New York Times*, Dec. 6, 1964, p. 74.

The Auction System of Horticultural Marketing in the Netherlands. 2d ed. The Hague: Central Bureau of Horticultural Auctions in the Netherlands, 1959. 61 pp.

"Auction via Early Bird: Satellite Takes Bids in Transatlantic Art Sale," *Los Angeles Times*, May 25, 1965, Pt. I, p. 2.

Battista, Rocco J. "More about the Auction: The Auctioneer's Place in Retail Selling," *Journal of Retailing*, XXVI (Winter, 1950), 162–168.

Beckwith, Ethel. "Friends Shocked at Auctioneers Fraud Indictment," *Sunday Herald* (Bridgeport, Conn.), Sept. 19, 1965, p. N 27.

Bird, Kermit, and Arthur Wallace. *Oklahoma Livestock Auctions: Developments and Changes*. Oklahoma State University Agriculture Experiment Station with cooperation of Economic Research Service, USDA. Processed Series P-393. Oct., 1961. 32 pp.

Bodkin, Leonard D. "Auction Sale—without Reserve," *Notre Dame Lawyer*, XXI (June, 1946), 327–332.

Bookbinder, Bernie. "Going to an Auction?" *The Auctioneer*, XIV (Oct., 1963), 17.

"Breaking the Ring," *The Economist*, Sept. 15, 1956, p. 869.

"Britain: Trouble in Never-Never Land," *Time*, July 24, 1964, p. 82.

Broaddus, Mrs. H. Montague. "How To Behave at an Auction," *American Home*, XVIII (Nov., 1937), 38, 110–111.

Brooks, John. "Annals of Finance: One Dollar for the Lot," *New Yorker*, April 27, 1957, pp. 110–128, 131–132.

Brown, Carlton. "Auction Sale This Day," *New Yorker*, Aug. 7, 1937, pp. 19–23.

———. "Auction Sale This Day," *Reader's Digest*, XXXI (Oct., 1937), 33–36. (Condensation of *New Yorker* article, Aug. 7, 1937.)

Butler, E. B. "Auction Prices: Estimated and Realised," *Economic Journal,* LXXI (March, 1961), 114–120.

Canaday, John. "Inside an Art Auction," *New York Times* (Western ed.), May 3, 1963, Sec. L, p. 7.

Cassady, Ralph, Jr. "Market Measurement in a Free Society," *California Management Review,* II (Winter, 1960), 57–66.

"A Catalogue of Costly Beauty," *Fortune,* LXXIV (Sept., 1966), 139–146.

"Cattle Auction Barn Profits by Keeping Customers Cool—and Warm," *Air Conditioning, Heating & Refrigeration News,* Sept. 11, 1961, p. 12.

Chappell, Russell. "The Auctioneer's Big Bid," *Newsweek,* Feb. 3, 1958, pp. 78–80.

Cherington, Paul T. "Auctions," *Encyclopaedia of the Social Sciences,* II (1930), 309–310.

Clark, Carl M., and Wilmer Browning. *Organization of the Looseleaf Tobacco Auction Market.* Kentucky Agricultural Experiment Station, University of Kentucky. Bulletin 599. June, 1953. 94 pp.

"Confessions of a Wheeler-Dealer in Antiques," *True,* XLVII (Aug., 1966), 60–61, 82–84.

Contakos, N. C., and B. Sandler. "Contracts—Offer and Acceptance—Auctions," *Boston University Law Review,* XII (April, 1932), 240–243.

Converse, P. D. "Tobacco Auctions Evaluated," *Journal of Business of the University of Chicago,* XVI (July, 1943), 147–159.

"The Curious Case of the Chippendale Commode," *Sunday Times* (London), Nov. 8, 1964, pp. 8–9.

"A Curious Survival," *The Conveyancer,* XVII (Dec., 1931), 76.

"A Curious Survival: Sale by Candle," *The Conveyancer,* XVII (May, 1932), 138.

"A Curious Survival: Sale by Sand Glass," *The Conveyancer,* XVII (May, 1932), 139.

Cusack, Frank. "Push-Button Auctioneering," *Ford News* (April, 1957), pp. 39–43.

DeKrey, W. Warren, and Maurice D. Olson. *Livestock Auctions in North Dakota.* North Dakota Agricultural Experiment Station, Department of Agricultural Economics. Bulletin no. 422. June, 1959. 56 pp.

Dengler, H. W. "Holly Auction," *American Forests,* LXVIII (Dec., 1962), 4–6.

Dougherty, Richard. "Madison Ave. Firm To Sell Antique Cars," *Los Angeles Times,* Sept. 11, 1966, Sec. B, p. 3.

"Dutch Auction," *World Book Encyclopedia,* IV (1961), 316.

The Dutch Auction System of Marketing Fruit & Vegetables: A Lesson for

English Growers? London: Agricultural Co-operative Association, *ca.* 1950. 15 pp.

" 'Dutch Clock' Makes Grade in Open Tobacco Auctions," *Financial Post,* Nov. 8, 1958, p. 10.

Dyer, Walter A. "Antique Stuffing," *Ladies' Home Journal,* XLV (May, 1928), 16, 17, 42.

Edmonds, J. K. "$2 Million in Big Equipment Moved Out in Five Auctions," *Financial Post,* Oct. 26, 1961, p. 32.

" £8,500 Paid for a Watch," *The Times* (London), July 9, 1963, p. 12.

Elz, D. K., and G. E. Brandow. *Marketing and Pricing Pennsylvania Tobacco.* Pennsylvania State University, College of Agriculture, Agricultural Experiment Station. Bulletin 713. Sept., 1964. 32 pp.

"The Ever Young Pursuit of Antiques," *Fortune,* LXI (June, 1960), 160-167, 214, 219-221, 224.

Felton, Dave. "Batman Escapes from Old Trunk To Fly Again," *Los Angeles Times,* Feb. 8, 1966, Pt. II, pp. 1, 3.

Ford, E. C. "First, Probably Only Slave Auction in Kansas," *Negro History Bulletin,* XVIII (March, 1955), 143-144.

"$40,000 Bid for Old Auto," *Christian Science Monitor,* Aug. 13, 1966, p. 3.

Frederick, John H. "Auction," *World Book Encyclopedia,* I (1961), 735.

"Furriers Flock to London Mecca," *Business Week,* March 8, 1958, pp. 88-90.

Gall, Peter. "Eager House Hunters Snap Up New Homes at 'Distress' Sales," *Wall Street Journal,* May 10, 1965, pp. 1, 14.

George, Edward F. "Auctioneer's Refusal To Accept Highest Bid," *Law Quarterly Review,* LXV (July, 1949), 310-311.

Granger, E. M., Jr. "The Auction Business . . . As I Have Lived It," *Hoard's Dairyman,* Dec. 10, 1957, p. 1188.

Gruen, F. H. "Goulburn, Forward Prices and Pies," *Review of Marketing and Agricultural Economics,* XXVIII (June, 1960), 85-96.

Hamilton, Doris H. "Autographs: Bidding at Auction," *Hobbies,* LX (April, 1955), 108-109.

"Happy Bibliophile: Cuban Collector Buys Manuscript of Lincoln's Gettysburg Address," *Life,* May 16, 1949, pp. 145-148.

Hirshberg, Richard L. "Auction," *Encyclopedia Americana,* II (1963), 534.

Hoffman, Marilyn, "Meet Manhattan," *Christian Science Monitor,* July 16, 1963, p. 6.

Holtzman, Jerome. "What Price Rembrandt?" *United Mainliner* (Feb., 1965). Unpaged.

Hook, Ralph C., Jr. "The Role of Auctions in Merchandising," *Implement & Tractor,* Oct. 23, 1954, pp. 26-28.

"How To Go to an Auction," *House & Garden*, CIX (May, 1956), 118–119, 208–209.

Hyam, Leslie A. "Manners and Morals of the Auction Room," *Atlantic Monthly* (March, 1962), pp. 117–118.

"Idol's Costly Eye," *Life*, Jan. 18, 1963, pp. 45–46.

International Art Market, III (Aug., 1963), 121–144.

Ivamy, E. R. H. "Conditions of Sale at Auctions and Their Exclusion," *The Solicitor*, XVIII (Sept., 1951), 199–202, 207.

Keilholz, F. J. "Why You Can't Understand Auctioneers," *Saturday Evening Post*, March 18, 1950, p. 17.

Kendall, Elaine. "Everything is Going—Going—Gone," *New York Times Magazine*, March 18, 1962, pp. 67, 69.

"Kettle of Fish: . . . Strikes, Black Market, OPA Troubles, and Allocation Threat," *Business Week*, April 29, 1944, pp. 53–54.

Knox, Sanka. "Art Gallery Ends 2d Best Season," *New York Times*, June 30, 1963, sec. 1, p. 56.

———. " 'Idol's Eye' Gem Sold for $375,000," *New York Times* (Western ed.), Nov. 15, 1962, Sec. L, p. 9.

Koch, Charles R. "Hogs on the Wire," *Farm Quarterly*, XVI (Winter, 1961–62), 70, 71, 84, 86, 88.

Krohn, Klaus-Hinrich, and Arnold Alewell. *Sea-Fish Marketing in the Federal Republic of Germany*. Rome: Food and Agriculture Organization of the United Nations, 1957. 143 pp.

Kular, Robert H. "Sales by 'Wire'—Teletype Hog Buying by Dutch Auction—Ontario Packers List Pluses, Drawbacks," *National Provisioner*, July 21, 1962, pp. 19, 22, 23, 43.

"L.A. Man Buys Rembrandt at Cost of $2,234,400," *Los Angeles Herald-Examiner*, March 19, 1965, Sec. A, pp. 1, 5.

Lake, Carlton. "For Sale at Auction," *New Yorker*, Nov. 5, 1955, pp. 139–141, 143–144, 146, 148–154, 157–161.

Lang, Daniel. "A Reporter at Large: Pelikaanstraat Midtown," *New Yorker*, July 10, 1943, pp. 42, 44, 46–53.

Law, Alfred. "Bulls Make Money: Big Angus Auction Opens amid Pomp," *Wall Street Journal*, Oct. 13, 1966, pp. 1, 19.

"Leaf at Auction," *Business Week*, Dec. 23, 1944, pp. 46, 49.

Leap, Norris. "This Auctioneer Helps Doctor Ailing Business," *Los Angeles Times*, Nov. 12, 1961, Sec. E, pp. 1, 3.

Leffingwell, B. H. "New York City Doll-Toy Auction," *Hobbies*, LXIV (April, 1959), 38, 40, 57.

Lemert, Bula. "School for Auctioneers: How To Sell Out—for the Right Price," *Coronet* (Aug., 1966), pp. 130–135.

McLean, Louis. "Auction Anecdotes," *Oklahoma Bar Association Journal*, XXVI (April 30, 1955), 683–686.

McPherson, W. K. "How Well Do Auctions Discover the Price of Cattle?" *Journal of Farm Economics*, XXXVIII (Feb., 1956), 30–43.

Malphrus, Lewis D. *Livestock Auction Operations in South Carolina*. South Carolina Agricultural Experiment Station, Clemson Agricultural College. Bulletin 467. Dec., 1958. 31 pp.

"The Market: Doubleheader," *Time*, April 23, 1965, p. 66.

"Master Auctioneer," *Time*, April 20, 1962, p. 76.

Matthew, Mary. "Angelenos To Buy Art via TV," *Los Angeles Times*, April 15, 1960, Pt. II, pp. 1, 4.

May, Roger B. "Going, Going, Gone! More Americans Sell Real Estate at Auction," *Wall Street Journal*, Sept. 7, 1965, pp. 1, 15.

Meissner, Frank. "Synchronized Fruit Auctions in Denmark," *Foreign Agriculture*, XVIII (April, 1954), 70–71.

Metz, Leonard. "Realtors Frown on 'Distressed' Sales," *Daily Sun* (San Bernardino), May 15, 1965, Sec. B, p. 3.

Metzdorf, Robert F. "Sacribovicide," *Antiquarian Bookman*, XXXIII (June 15, 1964), 2551–2555.

"Million in Mink Sold at Auction," *New York Times* (Western ed.), May 25, 1963, Sec. L, p. 9.

Moore, Marge. "White Mountain Apache Cattle Auction," *Arizona Highways* (Oct., 1957), pp. 2–4.

Napley, D. "Withdrawal of Property from Auction," *Law Journal*, CII (June 6, 1952), 312–313.

Neal, Charles, Jr. "Auction Bidders Go for Broke," *Los Angeles Times*, April 19, 1963, Pt. IV, p. 9.

"New Jersey's Fifty-Million-Dollar Vegetable Garden," *Federal Reserve Bank of Philadelphia Business Review* (Sept., 1962), pp. 16–23.

New York Stock Exchange. *The Modern Auction Market: A Guide to Its Use for Institutional Investors*. New York: New York Stock Exchange, March, 1965. 18 pp.

Norton-Taylor, Duncan. "The World's Fastest Art Market," *Fortune*, LXXIV (Sept., 1966), 134–138, 170, 175, 176.

"Now Closed-Circuit TV Makes a Direct Pitch to Customers," *Business Week*, Oct. 17, 1959, pp. 54–55, 57.

Pauley, Gay. "At Pelt Auction: Minks 'Going—Going—Gone!' " *Los Angeles Times*, Feb. 23, 1962. Pt. IV, p. 2.

Penny, Newton M., and Paul S. Akins. *A Comparative Study of Marketing Tobacco through Auction Warehouses.* Georgia Agricultural Experiment Stations, University of Georgia College of Agriculture. Bulletin n.s. 86. Dec., 1961. 69 pp.

"Peter Wilson, Sotheby's Sublime Auctioneer," *Vogue* (June, 1962), pp. 118–119, 120, 164, 166, 167.

Pollack, Eleanor. "We Visit a Country Auction," *McCall's* LXXXII (July, 1955), 8, 11, 12.

"Prosperity Index: Plant Auctions," *Business Week,* Oct. 15, 1949, p. 31.

"Real Estate Auction Ban Gets Second Look," *Los Angeles Times,* Oct. 16, 1966, Sec. K, Westside ed., pp. 2, 6.

"Record for Art World: Sale of Paintings at Auction in London Brings $2,922,052," *Los Angeles Times,* June 12, 1963, Pt. I, p. 2.

"Record for Auction: Rembrandt Painting Sold for $2.3 Million," *Los Angeles Times,* Nov. 16, 1961, Pt. I, p. 1.

Riddell, G. E. "Farmers in Low Countries Sell by the Clock," *News for Farmer Cooperatives* (Sept., 1950).

Ridler, Duncan. "Imperfect Competition and the Cobweb Theorem: A Vegetable Case," *Journal of Agricultural Economics,* XVII, no. 2 (1966), 181–195.

"The Ring and the Book," *The Economist,* Aug. 11, 1956, pp. 467–468.

Rogers, Geoffrey G. "The Sale of Real Estate by Auction," *Chartered Auctioneer and Estate Agent,* XLIII (Nov., 1963), 517–527.

"Sale by Auction with a Reserved Price and Reservation of Right To Bid," *Solicitors' Journal,* LXXXII (July 2, 1938), 539.

"Sale by Sand Glass," *The Conveyancer,* XVIII (Aug., 1932), 20.

"Sale of Shotguns by Auction," *Chartered Auctioneer and Estate Agent,* XXXIX (Feb., 1959), 92–93.

"Sales by Auction," *Commercial Law Reporter* (South Africa) (Feb., 1956), pp. 44–51.

Sederberg, Arelo. "All the World Goes under Auctioneer's Gavel," *Los Angeles Times,* April 25, 1965, Sec. H, pp. 1, 2.

Seidenbaum, Art. "L.A.'s Lowly Art Auction Image Going, Going, Gone," *Los Angeles Times Calendar,* Nov. 8, 1964, p. 11.

Sherman, Gene. "L.A. Art Patron Buys $2 Million Rembrandt," *Los Angeles Times,* March 20, 1965, Pt. I, pp. 1, 10.

"Silent Auction Scheduled by League Aides," *Los Angeles Times,* March 24, 1964, Pt. IV, p. 2.

Slaughter, L. W. "Antiques at Auction," *Hobbies,* LXIII (Feb., 1959), 42–43, 45; LXIV (March, 1959), 46–47; LXIV (April, 1959), 44–45.

Smith, Col. C. B. "Dairy Cattle Selling," *The Auctioneer*, V (Sept., 1954), 20-21.

Smith, John N., and Harold D. Smith. *Pen-Lot Versus Single-Head Selling of Calves at Maryland Auction Markets*. University of Maryland, Agricultural Experiment Station, 1960. Misc. Publication no. 391. 18 pp.

Smith, Red. "Trot Auction Not Always Final," *Philadelphia Inquirer*, Oct. 25, 1961, p. 45.

Smith, Vernon L. "Experimental Auction Markets and the Walrasian Hypothesis," *Journal of Political Economy*, LXXIII (Aug., 1965), 387-393.

"Son of Rembrandt," *Time*, March 26, 1965, p. 70.

Sosnick, Stephen H. "Bidding Strategy at Ordinary Auctions," *Journal of Farm Economics*, XLV (Feb., 1963), 163-182.

Speight, W. L. "Sales by Auction in the Old Days," *Commercial Law Reporter* (South Africa) (Feb., 1954), pp. 38-40.

Stewart-Gordon, James. "Auctions," *Christian Science Monitor*, July 25, 1962, p. 9.

Stout, Thomas T. *Livestock Auctions in Indiana*. Purdue University, Agricultural Experiment Station. Research Bulletin no. 713. March, 1961. 16 pp.

Sutton, Denys. "The King of Epithets: A Study of James Christie," *Apollo*, LXXXIV (Nov., 1966), 364-375.

Taylor, Frederic. "Auto Auctions," *Wall Street Journal*, Aug. 7, 1963, pp. 1, 11.

"Telephone Egg Auction," *Poultry Processing and Marketing*, LXVIII (Feb., 1962), 104.

Terrel, Elwin. "Auctioneers—Are They Necessary?" *Hoard's Dairyman*, Jan. 25, 1957, pp. 86-87.

Thomas, J. A. C. "The Auction Sale in Roman Law," *Juridical Review*, Pt. I (April, 1957), pp. 42-66.

"Treasury Auctions Off $250 Million in Bonds," *Los Angeles Times*, Jan. 9, 1963, Pt. III, p. 8.

"Tuna Marketing by Auction Tried Again in California," *Pacific Fisherman* (Nov., 1963), p. 9.

"TV Doubles as Art Auction Block," *Business Week*, May 7, 1960, pp. 30, 32.

Unkovic, Nicholas. "The Three Types of Auction Sales," *Dickinson Law Review*, XXXIV (June, 1930), 233-243.

"Used Farm Equipment" (editorial), *Implement & Tractor*, Oct. 23, 1954, pp. 24-25.

Uzanne, Octave. "The Hotel Drouot and Auction Rooms in Paris before and after the French Revolution," *The Connoisseur*, III (Aug., 1902), 235-242.

Vicker, Ray. "How To Sell a Seurat: London Art Houses Thrive as Prices Soar," *Wall Street Journal*, June 24, 1966, p. 22.

Watt, James Muir, and John Widmer Cowee. "Auctions and Auctioneers," *Encyclopaedia Britannica*, II (1964), 742–743.

Westerfield, Ray Bert. "Early History of American Auctions: A Chapter in Commercial History," *Transactions of the Connecticut Academy of Arts and Sciences*, XXIII (May, 1920), 159–210.

"What To Know If You Buy at Auctions," *Good Housekeeping*, CLVI (Jan., 1963), 122.

"World's First Auction Sale of Buttons," *Hobbies*, XLV (Sept., 1940), 30–31.

Yamey, B. S. "Bidding Agreements at Auctions," *Butterworth's South African Law Review* (1955), pp. 73–80.

Yang, Lien-sheng. "Buddhist Monasteries and Four Money-Raising Institutions in Chinese History," *Harvard Journal of Asiatic Studies*, XIII (June, 1950), 174–191.

GOVERNMENT PUBLICATIONS

Australia, Commonwealth of. *Report of the Wool Marketing Committee of Enquiry*. Feb., 1962. Canberra: A. J. Arthur, Commonwealth Government Printer, 1962. 186 pp.

———. Bureau of Census and Statistics. *Wool Production and Utilization*. Statistical Bulletin no. 9. 1960–61. Canberra: 1961. 13 pp.

Australian Wool Board Report and Recommendations on Wool Marketing. Australian Wool Industry Conference, Canberra, July 1964. North Clayton, Vic.: Specialty Press, n.d.

California Penal Code, sec. 535 ("Mock Auction").

California Penal Code, sec. 2328 ("Sale by Auction").

Cook, R. Cecil. *Report by the Honourable Mr. Justice Cook under Section 8 of the Monopolies Act, 1923, Concerning the Trade in Wool*. Parliament of New South Wales, 2d sess., 1959, before the Industrial Commission of New South Wales, no. 305 of 1958. Sydney, N.S.W.: Victor C. N. Blight, Government Printer, 1959. 73 pp.

———. *Further Report by the Honourable Mr. Justice Cook under Section 8 of the Monopolies Act, 1923, Concerning the Trade in Wool*. Parliament of New South Wales, 2d sess., 1959, before the Industrial Commission of New South Wales, no. 305 of 1958. Sydney: Victor C. N. Blight, Government Printer, 1959. 15 pp.

Great Britain. Ministry of Agriculture, Fisheries and Food. *Report of the Committee of Inquiry into the Fishing Industry*. Cmnd. 1266. London: H.M.S.O., 1961. 175 pp.

Jaleel, S. A. *Fish Market and Terminal Karachi.* Karachi, Pakistan: Food and Agriculture Council of Pakistan, Ministry of Agriculture and Works, Feb., 1964. 51 pp.

McMillan, R. B. *Marketing of the Australian Wool Clip.* Department of Industry. Canberra, 1964. 6 pp. Mimeographed.

Parliamentary Debates. House of Commons. "Antique Dealers (Rings)." Official Report, DCCIV (Dec. 23, 1964), 1242–1259.

————. *House of Lords.* "Mock Auctions Bill." Official Report, CCXIV (March 12, 1959), 1122–1152.

Szczepanik, Edward. "A Survey of Fish Marketing in the Indo-Pacific Region." Sec. II of *Report on the First FAO-ETAP International Fish Marketing Training Centre, Hong Kong 11th July–31st August 1954.* Rome: Food and Agriculture Organization of the United Nations, 1955. Pp. 21–111.

U.S. Congress. House. *Report of Special Study of Securities Markets of the Securities and Exchange Commission.* 88th Cong., 1st sess., H. Doc. 95, pt. 2. Washington, 1963. Pp. 40–47.

U.S. Department of Agriculture. *The Changing Role of the Fruit Auctions,* by Alden C. Manchester. Agricultural Marketing Service, Marketing Research Division. Marketing Research Report no. 331. June, 1959. Washington, 1959. 16 pp.

————. *Livestock Auction Markets in the Appalachian Area: Methods and Facilities,* by Clayton F. Brasington, Jr. Agricultural Marketing Service, Marketing Research Division, in cooperation with Agricultural Experiment Stations of Virginia and West Virginia. Marketing Research Report no. 309. March, 1959. Washington, 1959. 75 pp.

————. *Livestock Auction Markets in the Southeast: Methods and Facilities,* by George E. Turner and Clayton F. Brasington. Agricultural Marketing Service, Marketing Research Division, in cooperation with Agricultural Experiment Stations of Florida, Georgia, Louisiana, and Mississippi. Marketing Research Report no. 141. Nov., 1956. Washington, 1956. 99 pp.

————. *Livestock Auction Markets in the United States,* by Gerald Engelman and Betty Sue Pence. Agricultural Marketing Service, Marketing Research Division. Marketing Research Report no. 223. March, 1958. Washington, 1958. 37 pp.

————. *Livestock Marketing Cooperatives in California,* by R. L. Fox. Farmer Cooperative Service. General Report 98. Aug., 1961. Washington, 1961. 64 pp.

————. *Resales at Maryland Tobacco Auctions,* by C. I. Hendrickson and F. H. Dahl. Agricultural Marketing Service. Marketing Research Report no. 148. Dec., 1956. Washington, 1956. 27 pp.

————. *Tobacco Market Review.* Washington: Consumer and Marketing Service, March, 1965. 54 pp.

————. *Ways To Improve Livestock Auctions in the Northeast,* by C. G.

Randell. Farmer Cooperative Service. FCS Circular 16. June, 1956. Washington, 1956. 10 pp.

MISCELLANEOUS MANUSCRIPTS AND REPORTS

American Tunaboat Association. Minutes. Transcript of Auction Proceedings, Jan. 4, 1965, through May 17, 1965.

Awad, Mohamed Hashim. "The Export Marketing of Sudan Cotton since the War." Unpublished M.S. thesis. University of London, 1964. 150 pp.

Cary, Harold F. "The Failure of the Present Auction System," *News Letter*, American Tunaboat Association, Issue 59-4 (May 19, 1959). 3 pp. Mimeographed.

Harvard University Graduate School of Business Administration. "The Copaco Case." *Ca.* 1962. 45 pp. Mimeographed.

Hasegawa, Akira, and Hirohiko Watanabe. "Distributive System and Cooperative Marketing of Fishery Products in Japan." Tokyo: Fisheries Research Institute, 1958. 15 pp. Mimeographed.

"The Hong Kong Fish and Vegetable Marketing Schemes." Hong Kong: Co-operative Development & Fisheries Department, Dec., 1962. 15 pp. Mimeographed.

"One Hundred Auctions," *News Letter*, American Tunaboat Association, Issue 58-14 (Oct. 31, 1958), pp. 48–50. Mimeographed.

Taylor, R. A. *A Report on the Economics of White Fish Distribution in Great Britain*. Hull: Hull University, Department of Economics and Commerce, 1958. 197 pp.

COURT CASES

American National Bank of Nashville v. *West*, 212 S.W.2d 683 (Tenn. Ct. App. 1948), cert. denied by Supreme Ct., July 17, 1948.

Becker v. *Crabb*, 223 Ky. 549, 4 S.W.2d 370 (1928).

Bethel v. *Sharp*, 25 Ill. 173, 76 Am. Dec. 790 (1860).

Biddles v. *Enright*, 239 N.Y. 354, 146 N.E. 625, 39 A.L.R. 766 (1925) affirming 203 N.Y.S. 920, 208 Ap. Div. 790 (1924).

Conover v. *Walling*, 15 N.J. Eq. 173 (1852).

Crespin v. *Puncheon*, 7 V.L.R. 203 (Australia 1881).

Daniel v. *Adams*, 27 Eng. Rep. (Amb.) 495 (1764).

Dennerlein v. *Dennerlein*, 46 Hun. 561 (1887), appeal dismissed, 111 N.Y. 518, 19 N.E. 85 (1888).

Foley v. *M'Keown*, 4 Leigh (31 Va.) 627 (1833).

Fulgham v. *Burnett*, 151 Miss. 111, 117 So. 514 (1928).

Furness v. *Anderson*, 1 Pa. L.J. Reps. 324 (1842).

Gordon v. *City of Indianapolis*, 204 Ind. 79, 183 N.E. 124 (1932).

Gray v. *Walton*, 52 N.Y. City Super. Ct. 534 (1885).

Heatley v. *Newton*, 19 Ch.D. 326, 45 L.T. 455, 51 L.J. Ch. 225 (1881).

Herndon v. *Gibson*, 20 L.R.A. 545 (1893).

Hirsch v. *City and County of San Francisco*, 143 Cal. App. 2d 313, 300 P.2d 177 (1956).

Holmes v. *Holmes*, 24 S.C. Eq. 61 (1850).

Kearney v. *Taylor*, 15 Howard (56 U.S.) 494, 14 L. Ed. 787 (1853).

The King v. *Chapman*, 3 Anst. 811 (1796–97).

Levy v. *Stone*, 97 Fla. 458, 121 So. 565 (1929).

McGrew v. *Forsythe*, 31 Iowa 179 (1870).

McMillan v. *Harris*, 110 Ga. 72, 35 S.E. 334 (1900).

Nash v. *Elizabeth City Hospital Co.*, 180 N.C. 59, 104 S.E. 33 (1920).

Peck v. *List*, 48 Am. R. 398, 23 W. Va. 338 (1883).

Rex v. *Taylor*, M'Cle. 362, 148 E.R. 151 (1824).

Rodgers v. *Rodgers*, 13 Grant's Ch. Rep. (Ont.) 143 (1867).

State v. *Miller*, 52 Mont. 562, 160 P. 513 (1916).

Territory v. *Toyota*, 19 Haw. 651 (1909).

United States v. *New England Fish Exchange*, 258 Fed. 732 (1919), modification of decree denied, 292 Fed. 511 (1923).

United States v. *San Pedro Fish Exchange*, consent decree, *CCH Trade Regulation Reports, Supp. 1941–43*, ¶ 52669 (1941).

United States v. *Seattle Fish Exchange, Inc.*, consent decree, *CCH Trade Regulation Reports, Supp. 1941–43*, ¶ 52887 (1942).

Village of Deposit v. *Pitts*, 18 Hun. (N.Y.) 475 (1879).

RECORDINGS

Missouri Auction School. *Auction School Highlights*. Kansas City, Mo.: Missouri Auction School.

————. *Training Record*. Kansas City, Mo.: Missouri Auction School.

————. *World Champion Livestock Market Auctioneer Contest*. Kansas City, Mo.: Missouri Auction School, 1966.

Wyrick, Kenneth. *Tobacco Auction: The System, The Sale*. Knoxville, Tenn.: Loran Baker Recording Service.

Index

Index